THE OPPORTUNITY EQUATION

THE
OPPORTUNITY
EQUATION

How Citizen Teachers Are
Combating the Achievement Gap
in America's Schools

ERIC SCHWARZ
FOUNDING CEO OF CITIZEN SCHOOLS

Beacon Press
Boston

Beacon Press
Boston, Massachusetts
www.beacon.org

Beacon Press books
are published under the auspices of
the Unitarian Universalist Association of Congregations.

17 16 15 14   8 7 6 5 4 3 2 1

This book is printed on acid-free paper that meets the uncoated paper
ANSI/NISO specifications for permanence as revised in 1992.

Text design and composition by Kim Arney

Library of Congress Cataloging-in-Publication Data

Schwarz, Eric
The opportunity equation : how citizen teachers are combating
the achievement gap in America's schools / Eric Schwarz.
pages   cm
Includes bibliographical references and index.
ISBN 978-0-8070-3372-2 (hardback)
ISBN 978-0-8070-3373-9 (ebook)
1. Community and school—United States.
2. Educational change—United States—Citizen participation.
3. Educational equalization—United States.
4. Community power—United States.
5. Social action—United States. I. Title.
LC221.S376 2014
370'973—dc23
2014009331

For Maureen, Ronan, and Orla,
with love and appreciation

CONTENTS

FOREWORD
*The Imperative of Equal Opportunity and the Importance
of Citizen Schools* —Lawrence H. Summers   *ix*

INTRODUCTION
The Opportunity Equation   *1*

SECTION ONE: Starting Citizen Schools

CHAPTER ONE
Building Blocks   *18*

CHAPTER TWO
Maureen   *34*

CHAPTER THREE
"It's My Turn!"   *40*

CHAPTER FOUR
Turning Point   *58*

CHAPTER FIVE
Organization Man   *66*

CHAPTER SIX
The Eddy Is Ready   *82*

CHAPTER SEVEN
*Scale, Spread, and the Pursuit
of Systemic Change*   *103*

SECTION TWO: How Citizen Power and an Expanded
Learning Day Can Narrow Achievement Gaps, Broaden
Opportunity, and Strengthen America

VOICES FROM CITIZEN SCHOOLS
Joyce King Thomas, volunteer **120**

CHAPTER EIGHT
Citizen Power and the Importance of Mentoring **124**

CHAPTER NINE
It's About Time **135**

CHAPTER TEN
*From a Nation of Consumers to a Nation
of Makers: Inspiring Creativity and Innovative
Thinking in Our Schools* **150**

CHAPTER ELEVEN
Social Networks and Social Skills **164**

CHAPTER TWELVE
Supporting Teachers, and Parents Too **176**

VOICES FROM CITIZEN SCHOOLS
Lindy Smalt, AmeriCorps Teaching Fellow **190**

SECTION THREE: Next Steps
for America and for You

CHAPTER THIRTEEN
A Civic Marshall Plan for Equal Opportunity **194**

VOICES FROM CITIZEN SCHOOLS
Agostinha DePina, student **201**

APPENDIX
*Expanded Learning Time Schedule
with Citizen Schools* **205**

ACKNOWLEDGMENTS **206**

NOTES **209**

INDEX **221**

THE IMPERATIVE OF EQUAL OPPORTUNITY AND THE IMPORTANCE OF CITIZEN SCHOOLS

Lawrence H. Summers is the president emeritus of and Charles W. Eliot University Professor at Harvard University and the former secretary of the treasury of the United States. In February 2014, Summers was elected chair of the Citizen Schools board of directors. His daughter Ruth, referenced below, served as an AmeriCorps Teaching Fellow at Citizen Schools from July 2012 to June 2014.

In an elitist age, the Duke of Wellington famously said that the Battle of Waterloo was won on the playing fields of Eton, attributing the leadership skills of the British military officers he commanded to lessons learned as students at England's top private school. I believe that the battle for America's future will be won or lost in our public schools— and today we are losing.

This was brought home to me when I was treasury secretary. I made it a practice every time I visited a city to go visit a public school. Once I was in Oakland meeting with a group of high school students and gave what I thought was a pretty good speech about the importance of education to national prosperity and individual opportunity.

After I finished, a young teacher—she was probably five years older than my daughter Ruth is now—came up to me and said,

"Secretary Summers, that was a terrific speech. But here's the problem:

"Why should the children believe that there's nothing more important to the future of this country than education when nobody has come in and painted this school in the last eleven years and the paint is chipping off the walls?

"Why should they believe you when you say science education is hugely important, but they get nauseous every time they do a chemistry lab because the ventilation system hasn't been fixed for a year?

"Why should they look around and believe you?"

I had no good answers, and I have been haunted by this question ever since.

America, if it has stood for anything, has stood for two hundred years for the idea of equality of opportunity. Everyone's income is not going to be equal in the United States. The way everyone lives is not going to be equal in the United States. We are going to try to make it fairer and better, but it is never going to be completely equal or fair. It cannot be in a free society.

What we can, and I believe must, aspire to as a nation is that everyone's children—all children—have the same chance to succeed. No child should be denied the opportunity to be educated, to follow their dreams, to create, to prosper, and to contribute because of the circumstances of their birth. Those with less money may live in smaller houses, take simpler vacations, and wear less expensive clothes. That is inevitable. But it should not be acceptable to anyone, liberal or conservative, that they be forced to have lesser dreams for their children.

This ideal of equal opportunity—that any child can grow up to be president, to be a billionaire, to win a Nobel Prize—is the American Dream. Yet, as Eric Schwarz's book powerfully illustrates, on the standard of equality of opportunity, our generation of Americans is failing. Of course, there are difficulties in statistics and measurement. But, as best as one can tell, for the first time in two hundred years, the gap in the life prospects of the children of the rich and the children of the poor is greater today than it was one or two generations ago. That should not be acceptable.

Nor should it be acceptable that the United States now trails most other major industrial nations in terms of equality of opportunity and social mobility. In Europe, it is easier for those from disadvantaged backgrounds to succeed than it is for their American counterparts. As a corollary, the successful are more entrenched in the United States than in the nations that are our biggest trading partners and competitors.

The Opportunity Equation offers stories and data that help us see inequality as not just a function of inequality in our schools but a function of the inequality of experiences offered by the broader society. The result is growing inequality in educational attainment, in income, and in family wealth. As just one example, the college completion rate for children of parents in the top quartile by family income has jumped from 40 percent to 73 percent since 1970, but for children of parents in the lowest quartile, it has only grown from 6 percent to 8 percent.[1] As an additional example, despite all that has been done to improve financial aid, the percentage of the students attending our elite universities who come from the upper half of the income distribution is greater than it was a generation ago. As a country, we are moving in the wrong direction with respect to equality of opportunity for lower-income children, and that is not acceptable.

It does not have to be this way. Determined national efforts can make a difference, as they have over the last half century with respect to racial equality. When I was a child, African Americans were massively underrepresented in higher education and the race-based achievement gap in our schools was sickeningly large. We still have a long way to go in fully addressing racism in our society. But whereas in the 1940s and '50s the reading and math skills of the typical white student were four to five grade levels ahead of the typical African American student, today more than half of that skills gap has been eliminated. In the nation as a whole, African Americans are still less likely than whites to attend elite colleges and universities and less likely to graduate, but an African American twenty-year-old is about as likely to be enrolled in college as a white twenty-year-old.[2] More needs to be done, but this is a huge national achievement. It is a national achievement of public policy. It is a national achievement of changed private attitudes. It is a national achievement of reform in almost every institution in our society. It is real progress.

As we have made great progress in combating racial inequality, so too can we overcome inequality of opportunity between the children of affluent and less-affluent parents. That is why I recently committed to chair the national board of directors of Citizen Schools, an organization committed to making such progress with respect to the class divide. I did this in part because I have seen the power of the program firsthand through my daughter Ruth, an AmeriCorps teaching fellow with Citizen Schools, and in part for three other reasons.

The first thing that attracted me to Citizen Schools was the program's commonsense approach of equalizing access to extra learning time in the afternoon and evenings, on weekends, and during the summer. For Boston students in grades six through twelve, the school day ends at 1:30, and across the country all children spend the great majority of their waking hours out of school. Children are three times as likely to be raised by a single parent as they were in 1960, and that parent, usually the mother, is more likely to be working.[3] Because low-income families lack money to purchase access to tutoring, camps, and after-school programs, the average lower-income child reaches age twelve having spent six thousand fewer hours engaged in formal and informal learning than the average upper-income child.[4] If that division stands we will never equalize opportunity.

A second compelling aspect of Citizen Schools is that it works with, but remains outside of, the public school system. I'm a Democrat. I'm a guy who believes in the government. I'm a guy who doesn't understand how you can love your country and hate its government. At the same time, I'm a guy with eyes, and I know that government cannot do it all. It is a long-standing truth that if we are going to succeed in solving problems, it cannot all just be the government saying what needs to be done, hiring people, and doing it. It needs to be a collective effort of the broader society and its citizens. Just as the children of England's elite learned to lead on the playing fields of Eton and Oxford and Cambridge, in America—in the twenty-first century—we need to provide children of all backgrounds with the experiences that will prepare them to lead and to compete.

The last reason why I was so drawn to Citizen Schools is that, despite my sometimes tearing up when I talk about my daughter Ruth and her powerful experience as a teacher in the program, I am really not touchy-feely when it comes to public policy. I believe in data. What impressed and inspired me about Citizen Schools is that they recognized that, as noble as all their intentions are, as good as their work made all of them feel, it really was not very important if, at the end of it all, children did not have better experiences and learn more. Before agreeing to become involved with Citizen Schools I spent time making sure that rigorous evaluation and external evaluations were a central part of the model. I learned that rigorous evaluation has not only been an important component of the model but that the evaluations completed so far have been highly encouraging about the efficacy of the program.

In the context of the vexed debate over strengthening education, it seems to me that Citizen Schools and the work described in this book represent a set of enormously promising and enormously powerful educational innovations. I salute Eric Schwarz, the founding CEO of Citizen Schools and the author of this fine book, for his vision and his dedication. He stands in a long tradition of American citizen-leaders who have moved this country forward.

W. E. B. Du Bois famously said that the problem of the twentieth century would be the problem of the color line. Though much progress has been made, the race-based achievement gap of my childhood has unfortunately morphed into an even starker class divide. Today, students from the top income quartile are four to five grade levels ahead of students from the bottom quartile—a gap that is twice as large as existed in the 1940s and 1950s. The question for the twenty-first century is how can we reduce this growing class divide and provide more opportunity for all children from all backgrounds.

This will be the task of America's parents: striving for the best for their children. It will be the task of all those on the frontlines in the schools: teachers and principals. It will be the task of those, like my daughter, who are not employed by the schools but work within them. But it is also the responsibility of citizens who care very deeply about the future of our cities and the future of our country. This book shows how ordinary people have made and can make a profound difference in lifting up opportunity for all children. And it demonstrates the importance of our doing all we can to help.

—LAWRENCE H. SUMMERS

THE OPPORTUNITY EQUATION

As Adam Barriga entered the Massachusetts State House, with its towering golden dome and rooms full of history, his sneakers squeaked lightly on the Italian-marble floors. Adam, age twelve, had been grumpy most of the day. But now, as he made his way to the capitol building's main lobby, walking past flags and portraits and a mural of the Revolutionary War Battle of Concord, he forgot entirely what had been bothering him. Once in the lobby, Adam joined hundreds of his classmates involved in all sorts of hands-on learning projects. The students were sixth and seventh graders attending public schools in Boston, and almost all of them qualified for a free or reduced-price lunch, meaning their family incomes were below or a little above the poverty line. About half of them had school-identified learning disabilities or spoke a language other than English at home or both. But soon all of them would be talking to an appreciative adult audience about robots they'd programmed, video games they'd designed, Android apps they'd invented, or, as in Adam's case, rocket ships they'd built.

The event was what we at Citizen Schools call a WOW!—a chance for students to showcase their learning and, hopefully, "wow" those in attendance. This particular evening the crowd included elected officials and executives from leading technology companies such as Google and Microsoft and Biogen Idec, one of the fastest-growing biotechnology firms in Massachusetts. I noticed how the politicians and executives moved through the State House effortlessly, smiling for pictures with families, asking questions of the students, and genuinely enjoying an event listed as a "stop-by" on their schedules. Cultivating support from guests at a WOW! was important, and I was pleased with the level of engagement. But what really stuck with me from that May evening in 2010 were the experiences of three others in the room.

First was Adam himself, then a sixth grader at the Clarence Edwards Middle School in Boston's Charlestown neighborhood. The Edwards, or Eddy, as it's known locally, had recently partnered with Citizen Schools to expand the learning day for all students from six to nine hours as part of a statewide Expanded Learning Time pilot program for struggling urban schools. Adam was demonstrating what he'd learned from one of his Citizen Schools apprenticeships, It *Is* Rocket Science!, and tentatively conversing with parents and politicians and anyone else who would listen. His confidence grew over the course of the evening as he talked about escape velocity, lunar windstorms, and solar flares, and as he described the final project he and his classmates had participated in: a simulated lunar landing performed by videoconference with real astronauts from NASA.

Second was David Mantus, the teacher of the It *Is* Rocket Science! apprenticeship and a repeat volunteer at Citizen Schools. David had grown up in the suburbs of Long Island, and he shared with me that his fondest childhood memories were of launching rockets in his backyard with his dad, a NASA engineer, and visiting science museums on the weekend with his grandfather. Later, Mantus earned a PhD in chemistry and eventually climbed the corporate ladder to become head of regulatory affairs for Cubist Pharmaceuticals. As Mantus moved further away from hands-on science in his own career (from mixing chemicals in the lab, to schmoozing regulators on the conference circuit), he had lost a little of himself. This increased his desire to inspire future scientists. At the State House, Mantus prompted his middle school apprentices to explain what they had learned, but then he invariably built upon their answers, adding scientific detail as he revealed more than a trace of boyhood excitement.

Adam and David each burst with pride, and in their unlikely relationship and shared enthusiasm for launching rockets, I saw great hope. But my greatest joy that night came from the smile of wonderment worn by Adam's grandfather, Eduardo Barriga. Barriga had emigrated from Peru thirty years previously. For almost his entire life in the United States, he had worked as a custodian at the State House. The marble floors where Adam held forth, and where CEOs and politicians gathered, were polished with his own hands. Now his grandson was standing on them with something important to say.

I started Citizen Schools because for students like Adam Barriga, opportunities like that night at the State House are far too rare. On the other hand, for upper-income Americans like David Mantus, and like me, the ascension from enriching childhood experiences to advanced education and successful careers has become too automatic, a ticket to success that upper-middle-class parents so reliably and consistently procure for our children that it stacks the deck against others who are less fortunate. I felt it was simply unfair that upper-income kids were the almost exclusive beneficiaries of an *opportunity equation* in which their abilities were multiplied by a dazzling array of extra learning opportunities.

My thinking on these topics was informed by my own childhood, every corner of which was piled high with the building blocks of opportunity. Like David, I too was surrounded by professionally successful adults—not rocket scientists in my case, but prominent lawyers and businesspeople and nonprofit leaders. I had extra time to learn and was given many chances to build the muscle memory of success. Further, as a descendant and namesake of the FAO Schwarz toy store family, I was connected to a powerful social network.

The opportunity divide is not new. Children like David and me have always had a leg up. But in recent decades, the story of opportunity in America has evolved in at least three important ways.

First, new research indicates the wealth-based opportunity gap is now a chasm. Access to the extra learning that families like mine take for granted is now so unequal that class-based achievement gaps in everything from elementary school reading to middle school math to college graduation have ballooned and are now substantially *larger* than when I grew up in the 1960s and '70s.[1] At that time, wealthier kids were a little more than two grade levels ahead of poor kids in reading and math. Now they are more than four grade levels ahead.[2] Gaps in harder-to-measure social skills—like the ability to ask for help and to network for a job—have also grown, and in turn contribute to ever-growing wealth and income gaps. For both the affluent and the impoverished, parental wealth now predicts adult success more than at any point in at least one hundred years.[3]

Second, children from lower- and moderate-income families are now at such an intense relative disadvantage in getting ready for productive adulthood that US economic competitiveness is being undermined. We simply can't afford to have so many workers not ready to perform in the modern economy. The blue-chip consulting firm, McKinsey, estimates our current income-based achievement gap imposes the equivalent of a 3–5 percent permanent national recession.[4] By failing to spread opportunity more broadly, we are slicing our economic pie unevenly, and we are also keeping the pie from growing.

Third, the *cause* of the growing opportunity and achievement divide is becoming clearer. In certain circles it has become fashionable to deride public schools as hopelessly inept, dragged down by incompetent teachers and stifling bureaucracies. For sure, many schools need to improve. But a close look at the data indicates that ever-widening achievement gaps are growing fastest *outside* of school. They are growing on suburban playing fields and at robotics competitions, at after-school math programs and specialized sleep-away camps, and elbow to elbow with parents around dining room tables all across America. The class-based education gap is accelerating *not* because teachers are lazy or because America's schools suddenly forgot how to churn out Horatio Alger success stories. And poor and working-class kids are not learning *less* than before, they are actually learning *more*.[5] Instead, the class-based education gap is accelerating because upper-middle-class children are accelerating faster, pulling away from their less privileged peers thanks to increasingly engaged parents and a cottage industry of coaches, counselors, tutors, and trainers.

So what to do about this opportunity chasm by which upper-middle-class families pass on success to their children, and children from lower-income families get left even further behind? Is it just about money, fixable only in a utopian, Lake Wobegon world where every family's income is "above average"? Or are there experiences and relationships routinely offered to upper-income children that our society, with modest investment, could make available to all children?

I recently asked Paul Reville, a professor of practice at Harvard's Graduate School of Education and formerly the highly regarded Massachusetts secretary of education, if he knew any system of education that routinely and at scale gets its students to high levels of educational achievement while preparing them for careers. "I know of one," Reville said: "The upper-middle-class family."

Reville's insight is startling. But what exactly *is* the opportunity equation that generally works for upper-income children? And can we make it work for all children?

In the summer of 1994 I was newly married and hoping to start a family. I had recently left a job with a leading national nonprofit organization and was reflecting on these questions of educational and economic opportunity. My questions led me to develop Citizen Schools, a startup program that began with just me and ten fifth graders.

What if we could harness the power of you and me—of millions of architects, engineers, lawyers, carpenters, journalists, and grandmothers who sew—to equalize opportunity and reduce the growing wealth-based achievement gap? What if we could create a new network of "citizen schools" to extend the traditional school day and provide time and space for all kinds of talented people to share their time and attention with lower-income students? I believed then, and believe even more deeply today, that if we offer all children more time with caring and accomplished adults, and more chances to build the muscle memory of success—by getting good at playing piano or building robots or writing poems—then, and only then, can we make American education what Horace Mann dreamed it could be: "the great equalizer of the conditions of men, the balance wheel of [our] social machinery."[6]

The very idea that I could create a new organization—particularly one dedicated to such fundamental change—was rooted in my own childhood experiences. My parents' weekend dinner parties provided an ongoing and indispensable apprenticeship in the profession of success. I remember being invited to join these dinners from the time I was ten years old and discoursing with editors from the *New York Times*, the New York police commissioner, nonprofit founders, Ivy League academics, leading civil rights lawyers, corporate executives, politicians, and more.

Deeper mentoring and hands-on learning and leadership opportunities came to me through specialized camps, workplace internships in my teenage years, and summer and vacation jobs arranged by my parents. For my senior project in high school I worked for a prominent New York planning firm and studied the walking patterns of visitors to the nine principal museums located between the Museum of the City of New York on 105th Street and Fifth Avenue and the Metropolitan Museum of Art on 82nd Street. I wrote a report that helped make the case for designating that sparkling stretch of Fifth Avenue as Museum Mile.

These connection points with talented professionals were critical to my upbringing. But it's one thing for successful adults to indulge in conversation with the son of a friend at a party—or even to take him in as an intern. My idea for Citizen Schools was different. I wanted adults to turn their life skills into deliberate hands-on apprenticeships and to share these lessons with their own children and neighbors but also with children they don't know, and to show up consistently for kids from a different side of town, carrying a different outlook on the world, and maybe speaking a different language at home. Would busy professionals do that? And would kids give up their afternoons or weekends to spend time with professionals who knew little about teaching, and, in many cases, even less about the neighborhoods where the kids were growing up? Finally, even if the kids and adults came together and liked it, would it make a difference in their lives? Would it change the equation? Or would it provide only a fleeting feel-good experience; or worse, a mirage—enticing children and adults alike to chase after a more be-loved future, but ultimately leaving them parched and unsatisfied?

In September 1994 I volunteered in Margie Tkacik's fifth-grade classroom at the Dever Elementary School, located a quick walk from Boston Harbor and across the street from the massive Harbor Point mixed-income residential community. With the help of almost $200 million in federal financing and subsidies, Harbor Point had risen to replace the notorious Columbia Point housing development, where in the 1970s and early '80s drug dealers reigned, two-thirds of apartments were vacant, and ambulances on several occasions refused to offer ser-vices because of assaults on their staff. By any measure, Dever was still a struggling urban school. Test scores were low, and many students suf-fered from the grinding poverty reminiscent of Columbia Point. But Dever also included a growing number of working-class families, and Principal Nydia Mendez, then in her third year at the helm, imbued the school with moxie and a measure of optimism. Nydia offered me the chance to test the Citizen Schools concept and to serve as my own guinea pig—our first volunteer "citizen teacher."

Margie Tkacik presided over Room 202 with boundless energy: part loving aunt filled with empathy and compassion for the children, and part mad scientist full of wonder and provocative questions. She was a veteran teacher and a former Golden Apple award winner (an award given to the district's top teachers). She lived in nearby South Boston, and her husband ran the bar across the street from the teachers' union office where she and colleagues would gather for a few drinks on Fridays after a long week of work. On my first day in Margie's class, I marveled as she circled the classroom like an observant shepherd, sharing a word of encouragement here, a new assignment there, and, as needed, a nip of discipline. After college I had worked as a journalist, and Margie and I agreed that for two hours a week I would work with ten of her students to publish a newspaper. This would give me a chance to pilot Citizen Schools, and Margie a few hours a week to work more intensively with the remainder of her class.

I remember nervously making last-minute adjustments to my lesson plans as I walked to my first class from the train station, the imposing

Boston Globe newsroom behind me and the Dever fifth graders ahead. When I entered the classroom I handed each student a narrow, spiral-bound reporter's notebook and held a "press conference" in which the students asked me questions to learn the design of the class. That part of the session worked well. Then I tried a brief lecture on the Five Ws of journalism (What, When, Who, Where, and Why), and found the students slumping in their chairs, disengaged despite my best efforts to interest them. A flop! By week three, I recruited a young co-teacher from City Year, the national service program I had previously worked for, and the class settled into a productive routine that maximized learning by doing and minimized teacher talking. We started each class with students conducting phone or in-person interviews—of the principal, local civic leaders, teachers, and even fellow students. Then each student had some writing time, during which my co-teacher and I would circulate and make suggestions. I would then offer a five-minute group lesson on a writing-related topic and, to close, we would pair up for twenty minutes of peer editing. I wasn't a great teacher, but the kids loved the class. I was a real editor, and they became real journalists.

The kids weren't my students; they were my apprentices, learning the tricks of a real trade by doing it. Every child in the apprenticeship wrote at least two articles for our paper, which we called the *Dever Community News*. They edited one another's work and were edited by me too. Our paper included comics, a crossword puzzle, a horoscope, and dozens of news and feature articles—including a front-page feature by eleven-year-old Nick Earner about life growing up in South Boston's Old Colony public housing development.

"One day I witnessed a man on the roof of my house with a gun," wrote Nick. "He almost took his life because he had his children taken away by DSS [the Massachusetts Department of Social Services]." Nick continued with a startling and eminently publishable piece of citizen journalism, ending with a description of his motivation for sharing the story. "What made me write this article," Nick shared, "was about three weeks ago two African American men were almost beaten to death for no good reason by five teenagers. This upset me because I never thought that was supposed to happen in this world."

Nick's article described a world unfamiliar to most eleven-year-olds, and familiar to most adults only through books or TV shows, or not at all. I worried for him. But I also appreciated Nick's moral compass and desire to tell his story, and as he and I worked through successive drafts of his writing, we developed a close bond.

To pay for printing the paper, the students sold $400 worth of advertisements to local businesses. Then one day in our last week together we all piled into a rented van and drove to a printer in Chelsea, a small city across the Mystic River from Boston. We watched in awe as our creation flew off a huge old printing press that folded the papers, stacked them in bunches of five hundred, and wrapped them tightly in plastic twine. When we got back to Dever, the kids walked a little taller as they distributed their newspapers to classmates and teachers. I like to think that their writing improved too—not just for this project but for all their classes.

As for me, I was hooked. And Citizen Schools was born.

In the almost two decades since we published the *Dever Community News*, Citizen Schools has blossomed into a national movement serving more than six thousand students annually from coast to coast and providing exuberant, college-bound proof that low-income kids can learn at high levels. We've shown that some of the nation's lowest-performing schools—schools in places like East Harlem and East Oakland—can, with help and partnership, provide their students with the same experiences as suburban kids and thereby deliver suburb-worthy results.[7] We've been honored by the White House for our work eliminating achievement gaps in academic performance, high school graduation rates, and college enrollment; we've been profiled on the evening news; and we've begun to lead a movement to expand the learning day and to eventually bring millions of caring, talented adults together with children to improve education in America. Of course, we've made our share of mistakes too, and learned some humbling lessons along the way. Tragically, even as Citizen Schools and dozens of other strong educational interventions have grown, so has the achievement gap between rich and poor. Today we are helping thousands of children beat the odds. But we aren't changing the odds—at least not yet.

Citizen Schools illuminates a story of opportunity, of accomplishment, and of citizen power in America. At a time when many educational leaders are looking for new, silver-bullet shortcuts to educational excellence—things like software-driven learning, vouchers, merit pay for effective teachers, and more—I believe the best solution is human-centered, rooted in American tradition, and, as I hope to show in this book, achievable. To be fair, to build our economy, and to recommit to the American ideal of equal opportunity, we need to provide lower- and moderate-income children with the following five building blocks of opportunity:

1. More mentorship by caring and professionally successful adults
2. A longer learning day, allowing more time to master the academic basics and chances to participate in sports, art, and music as part of a well-rounded education
3. More chances to practice creativity and innovation—critical skills in the modern economy
4. More chances to build the social networks and social skills that help drive professional and life success
5. Better support of full-time teachers and parents, the primary caregivers for lower- and moderate-income children

We need people like Deb Daccord, a lawyer who for eight years in the prime of her career helped prepare middle school students, dressed in their Sunday best, to argue mock trials in front of federal judges; people like David Mantus, the son of a rocket scientist, who seven times has taught Boston sixth graders like Adam Barriga how to launch rockets and do simulated lunar landings, working with real astronauts from NASA; and people like Alan Su, a Google engineer who for the last four autumns has taught sixth graders how to create new Android apps with a community purpose.

Daccord, Mantus, and Su have advanced degrees and prominent careers, and we need people like them if we want to equalize opportunity. We also need talented artists and tradesmen, like Joel Bennett, a carpenter, who taught Citizen Schools apprentices important lessons about math, and about life; and we need grandmothers like Earline Shearer, who was sad she hadn't passed on her love of sewing to her own children and grandchildren but through Citizen Schools found a way to teach her craft to other people's children. The stories of Earline Shearer and Joel Bennett and Alan Su are inspiring stories of noble intentions. But these volunteers are not just do-gooders. They are do-gooders with grit who are achieving measurable results in the lives of real children and showing a pathway to strengthen America.

The narrative thread for this book is Citizen Schools, and my own journey as its cofounder and leader, trying to reimagine the who, when, what, where, and how of education. In the coming pages I will first tell my childhood story and that of my wife (who grew up with a very different background and much less privilege). My goal in these opening chapters is to unpack and better understand the building blocks of professional success that have elevated generations of Americans. When we say a child is privileged, what mix of experiences, connections, and extra supports are we talking about? And how have millions of poor and working-class kids gained access to similar building blocks in the past? The heart of the book is the story of Citizen Schools, and the stories of children we serve, who were born with little money and few connections but by virtue of repeated positive experiences with professionally successful adults are now catapulting their way into good colleges and good careers.

These questions are explored against the backdrop of an increasingly contentious and urgent national debate about how to deliver the education our children need.

In just one generation, the United States has dropped from first in the world in college graduates to sixteenth.[8] In science and math proficiency—subjects required for the fastest-growing occupations—we rank twenty-first and twenty-sixth, respectively, among the world's industrialized nations.[9] For every future engineer graduating from a US college, ten graduate in China.[10] These gaps threaten our economy, because we live in a "flat world" in which many of the best knowledge-based jobs are mobile and will increasingly go to places with the most educated workers.

This is bad news. But the really bad news is the growing class-based achievement gap within America. While the achievement gap between whites and blacks has narrowed over the last two generations, an important step on an incomplete journey, achievement gaps based on parental income levels have doubled since World War II and continue to widen, as is powerfully documented in *Whither Opportunity?*, a compendium of recent scholarship pulled together by educational economists Greg Duncan and Richard Murnane.[11] Forty years ago, 40 percent of upper-income Americans earned a four-year college degree by their mid-twenties, while 6 percent of lower-income Americans did. Now it's 8 percent for low-income students and a fast-growing 73 percent for their upper-income peers.[12] Upper-income students who are academically low-performing (on the SAT and in their course grades) are as likely to earn a college degree as lower-income but academically high-performing students.[13]

American capitalism and our democracy rest on the idea that differential results for individuals are one part luck and two parts effort and ingenuity. If that equation flips and career success becomes only a little about differential effort and talent and mostly about what zip code you were lucky enough to be born into, then we've lost the American identity.

So what's causing these growing gaps? As mentioned, it's not that the academic skills of poor children are slipping. Actually, they are growing modestly. The class-based education gap is accelerating because children from upper-middle-class families are accelerating rapidly, benefiting from an awesome web of support and growth opportunities, including many I received. This is the opportunity equation. In the 1970s, low-income families spent $835 per year on out-of-school enrichment for their children—things like music lessons, tutoring, summer camp, and participation on travel sports teams—while upper-middle-class families spent $3,536. By 2006, these investments, adjusted for inflation, had grown to $1,315 for lower-income families and $8,872 for upper-income families, nearly a tripling of the investment gap![14]

Upper-income children are also bathed in the most precious resource of all: their parents' time. A generation ago, lower-income children spent more time with their parents than upper-income kids did. Now it has flipped, and wealthier parents are spending four hours more per week with their children: reading to them, talking at the dinner table, driving them to sporting events and music lessons, and thereby packing their suitcases for a lifetime of success.[15]

Class-based achievement gaps are growing at a time when education drives access to career success more than ever before, meaning the gaps are more consequential. Forty years ago, college graduates earned only about 20 percent more than high school graduates over the course of their lifetimes.[16] Good jobs requiring little education were plentiful, and those with a modest education could work their way up. But most of those low-skilled and high-wage jobs have gone away, because they consisted of tasks that were easy to computerize, since they involved following simple rules, or to outsource. Now high-wage jobs require workers to use higher-level thinking skills, to communicate well, to work well on diverse teams, and to solve problems where no clear rules apply. These are the skills college grads generally have, and this explains why they now earn almost twice as much as their less-educated peers, a quadrupling of the college–high school wage gap.[17]

It's a vicious cycle: Children of parents with money race further ahead, buoyed by tutoring, paid enrichment, lessons, and formal and informal mentoring. And the resulting educational gains reap bigger economic gains. On the surface it looks like we live in a more meritocratic world—one in which what you learn is what you earn. Upper-income families have figured this out and invest accordingly. Lower-income families are working longer hours but lack the money and time and social networks to provide the enrichment and extra learning that is taken for granted by the children of their wealthier peers. The result is a world that is actually less meritocratic and in which our society loses out on the rich cultural and economic benefits that would flow to all of us if more children had a chance to fully develop and nurture their talents.

There is a raging debate among education reformers in which, to simplify, one side says the achievement gap is caused by poverty and can't be fixed by schools without fixing poverty, and the other side says poverty is no excuse and that bad schools and bad teachers cause most of the growing gaps between rich and poor students. This is an unproductive debate in part because it confuses causes and solutions. Based on my own experience and the available research, the cause of America's class-based achievement gap is about one part school—and three parts out-of-school factors. The part that is school is a difference between teacher quality and expectations in upper- and lower-income public schools. Schools serving upper-income children have higher expectations and more "highly qualified" teachers, in large part because teachers in those schools have more support. We need to change this, as various current reform efforts are endeavoring to do. But exhaustive studies by educational researchers Joseph Altonji and Richard Mansfield and others indicate that only 20 to 30 percent of the achievement gap is driven by these school-related factors. As an example, they find that moving low-income students from a school and associated community at the tenth percentile of quality (as measured by test scores and graduation rates) to a school at the ninetieth percentile increases the likelihood students will graduate high school on time by only eight to ten percentage points, leaving in place a thirty-percentage-point gap.[18]

The really big difference for kids is that upper-income families spend seven times more money supporting student learning *out of school.* And because upper-income families live in communities populated by professionally successful people, upper-income children are naturally exposed to more successful adults, starting with their parents. Success is modeled for them from birth through high school, college, and beyond. That's what drives the achievement gap.

My own community of Brookline, Massachusetts, illustrates the point. Like hundreds of families before us, we moved to our neighborhood because of the William H. Lincoln elementary school. In the

1960s and '70s the Lincoln had been dubbed "Stinkin' Lincoln" due to its older, dilapidated classrooms and because its catchment area, while dominated by gracious homes and tree-lined streets, includes Whiskey Point, Brookline's lowest-income section and home to modest triple-deckers and hundreds of units of public housing. But in the 1980s, in an effort to upgrade the Lincoln for all its students and also to retain more wealthy families (many had left for private schools), Brookline built a new Lincoln school, supported by increased taxes and a special private fund-raising campaign, and designed by acclaimed architect Graham Gund. An energetic principal, Barbara Shea, helped make it one of the highest-performing schools in the state despite the challenges faced by some of its students.

Today the Lincoln serves 570 students, hailing from thirty-one countries, in kindergarten through eighth grade. Half of Lincoln's students are nonwhite, and a full 25 percent of the Lincoln students are low-income and eligible for free or reduced-price lunch, but the school community also includes hedge fund managers, architects, and academics. My wife, Maureen, and I have gotten deeply engaged in the school community, coaching teams, supporting field trips, raising money for after-school programs, serving on the school advisory council, and more. We love the school. But, like our upper-income neighbors, we've also signed up our kids for private tutoring and music and sports lessons, and we provide hundreds of hours of extra academic coaching at home. The investments pay a large return, and as our kids enter Brookline High School they are moving ahead of most of their lower-income classmates—even though they attend the same excellent public schools and live in the same neighborhood.

If upper-middle-class families want to know who is causing the achievement gap, we should look in the mirror. It is us. We go to the ends of the earth to help our kids succeed. Our kids deserve it. But so do all kids.

SECTION ONE

STARTING CITIZEN SCHOOLS

CHAPTER ONE

BUILDING BLOCKS

Family lore has it that my first words were *nani, nani* ("more, more"), spoken in a northern Nigerian dialect used by just sixty thousand people in the region of Kaduna. My parents had brought me to Africa in 1961 at the age of nine months. My father, scion of the FAO Schwarz toy store family, was fresh out of Harvard Law School. He was serving through the MIT Fellows in Africa program as Assistant Commissioner for Law Revision for the Northern Region of the newly independent Nigerian republic. My mother, a recent graduate of Radcliffe College and a member of a large Boston Brahmin family, had signed up to teach a high school course in African history. I was along for the adventure.

I have no clear memories of my year in Africa. But from the photographs I grew up with and the stories I have heard, the trip foreshadowed my childhood with its sense of adventure and its extraordinary exposure to stimulating people and places.

After living and working in Africa for fourteen months, my family settled on the rapidly gentrifying Upper West Side of Manhattan. My father joined a large law firm, Cravath, Swaine & Moore, and stayed active in civic causes. My mother had a second and then a third child (my sisters, Adair and Eliza) and began postgraduate studies at Columbia University, eventually earning a PhD in linguistics.

Our turf on the Upper West Side stretched from Broadway to Riverside Park and from 100th to 106th Streets. It featured turn-of-the-century brownstones, rent-controlled apartment buildings, and subsidized housing—a chock-a-block mix that supported a diverse population of professionals, artisans, blue-collar workers, small-business owners, and families on welfare. This was before the crack epidemic and resultant crime spree of the early 1980s, and my parents, and therefore I, had virtually no fear of crime. Starting at age six, I had permission to play handball in front of our building, to walk unescorted to Riverside Park for games of baseball and kick the can, or to head over to Broadway, where for a single quarter my friends and I could pick up a slice of pizza. A nearby bodega often had chickens running around the back part of the shop and was run by a friendly family from Puerto Rico.

As I approached nursery-school age, my parents and our Upper West Side clan of cousins and friends decided the educational options available to us weren't good enough. So they started their own school— the West Side Montessori School, patterned after the hands-on, self-directed learning approach developed by famed Italian educator Maria Montessori. It was the first school in the city to include both low-income students with public subsidies and full-paying families like ours. In 1966, at age five, I was one of nine children in the school's first graduating class. I still remember one assignment—a number line in which I counted from 1 to 4,387, running the numbers down successive strips of yellow paper that I would tape together. I am not sure this deeply improved my math skills. But when I was done with the assignment I had a number line that stretched all the way around our living room two times. I was proud and felt I had earned a badge of success.

The following fall I headed as a first grader to the Collegiate School, which was founded by the Dutch East India Company in 1628 and has offered a rigorous—and increasingly prestigious—all-boys education ever since. Two years later, on the first day of third grade, our teachers pulled us together to let us know that we would be joined by a new classmate, John Kennedy, son of the late president. John added unmistakable star power and a Secret Service detail to our already well-heeled class. His mother, Jackie O, was a fixture on the sidelines of our soccer games and, years later, sponsored a memorable eighth-grade class trip to Boston.

Up to the end of third grade my childhood progressed smoothly. I made friends easily enough; showed athletic promise in several sports, including basketball, which was my favorite; and demonstrated aptitude in school even if it was sometimes wrapped in a daydreamy fog.

In fourth grade, however, things took a turn for the worse. The best I can recall is that the trigger was a bad match with my homeroom teacher, Ms. Goldberg, though clearly more was going on. My teachers to that point had been warm, maternal figures who softened the authoritarian feel of Collegiate, with its giant stained-glass windows and its centuries of tradition and coat-and-tie uniforms. But Ms. Goldberg was stern and British, and didn't take kindly to my daydreamy ways. We got off to a bad start when she said I was spelling my name wrong (actually *she* was, as our "Schwarz" contains no *t*), and things spiraled downhill from there. School started feeling like a hostile environment, and I started feeling unsuccessful. I stopped doing my homework, earned mediocre to poor grades, and began an academic slide that continued for many years. When the final bell rang on the last day of fourth grade and we were dismissed, I jumped up and literally danced a jig as I raced out of the school.

I have faint memories of school in the ensuing middle-grade years. But I remember my out-of-school time in full, living color. I typically left Collegiate at four or four thirty in the afternoon (after an eight-plus-hour day) and walked a few blocks down Broadway to H&H Bagels, with its large bins of freshly cooked sesame, salt, poppy, onion, and "everything" bagels. I would buy two of whatever was warmest and then eat the bagels plain as I headed home on the Broadway 24 bus. When I got home, I would be greeted by a live-in au pair and, usually, my two younger sisters. I'd inhale two bowls of cereal or a couple of grapefruits, and then play basketball in my room or at a park that was three blocks away. Mom would get home in time to make dinner, and Dad would usually arrive a little later in the evening.

Oddly missing from these evenings was structured homework time—a staple, I am sure, for most of my classmates then and for my children and their peers today. I think my parents just assumed homework was something that kids did on their own.

In middle school my challenges worsened and occasioned lots of special meetings with my teachers and parents. I hated these "Eric is struggling" conferences, but they continued to be held at least two or three times a year. My mother would make a special trip into school and we would meet with one or a few teachers. Sometimes a guidance counselor or the principal would join us as well. I would hear about all of the assignments I hadn't completed and the potential I wasn't fulfilling. Then I would make a halfhearted promise to improve, and the meeting would be over. Sometimes I would study harder for a few weeks. My parents might do a homework assignment with me elbow to elbow. But I had negative momentum. I was unengaged in school, disorganized, and ashamed. And the meetings continued. I remember that after one particularly difficult conference in sixth grade, my French teacher looked sadly at me and said, simply, "Your poor mother."

Compounding my academic disengagement in these middle-grade years, I also pulled back socially, maintaining a few close friendships but living far from the center of my school's social scene. Once in high school, with a deepening feeling of alienation, I started smoking marijuana daily, drinking heavily on weekends, and experimenting with other drugs. I attended three private high schools in three states, never getting officially expelled but earning multiple suspensions and mostly poor grades. It wasn't a pretty picture.

Amazingly, throughout these difficult years I continued to have positive learning experiences. I was an obsessive fan of my hometown sports teams, in particular the Yankees in baseball and Knicks in basketball, and I digested the statistics of my favorite players so thoroughly that I developed an advanced number sense and statistical acumen far out of proportion to my academic standing or hours of formal study. I attended top-flight private schools. And while I certainly didn't maximize my opportunities, the schools offered rigorous academics and a rich sampling of creative arts, sports, and various extracurricular clubs. Some of that learning did stick.

I attended several sleep-away summer camps as well, which provided important learning experiences. At Tamarack Tennis Camp in the White Mountains of New Hampshire, the mosquitoes were so large they gave me cauliflower ear—no doubt from a combination of numerous bites and the cuffs I administered to my ears in a futile effort to squash the maddening bugs; but the camp's counselors were fun-loving and full of praise. And camp proprietor Jack Kenney—the grandfather of skiing legend Bode Miller, who was homeschooled on the Tamarack grounds—was an innovator in tennis instruction. Kenney used state-of-the-art photography to give campers an eight-photo depiction of their serving motion. And he used low-tech teaching tools too, like an adjustable upside-down bucket that hung high above the courts and allowed campers to practice the perfect toss for a first or second serve. Kenney and his team built up my skills in tennis, helping me at age thirteen develop the muscle memory for solid ground strokes and a powerful serve, which on a good day I can still call up four decades later. Even more important, at Tamarack I developed the confidence that comes with getting good at something—anything. That summer I won awards for proficiency and improvement, as well as the coveted camp-wide award for sportsmanship. As I collected the last of these at the camp's closing ceremony, camp owner Kenney cracked that with all of the trophies I'd won I could open a hardware store. My heart was jumping out of my chest with joy.

Two summers later I transitioned from attending camp to helping run a camp. I was fifteen, and I got support from my parents to run a small day camp for younger cousins and neighbors at our country home, one hour from New York City. My sister Adair and I were two of the three counselors, and for two weeks we offered a rotation of tennis, swimming, and horseback riding to nine young neighbors and relatives. The camp was a success, perhaps even an opening to my later career at Citizen Schools. But there is no way I would have had the experience of "running" that camp without tremendous support from my parents.

It wasn't just that they provided the tennis court, the pool, and two horses—critical ingredients, to be sure. They also recruited the campers! It was left to us to design and lead four hours of daily activities, to prepare a daily snack, and to communicate with the campers and their parents once the camp opened.

Education scholars such as University of Pittsburgh professor Lauren Resnick would call the experience I had that summer an apprenticeship, or—to update the image from that of a young boy in a blacksmith's or printer's shop—a "cognitive apprenticeship."[1] What my parents provided is called scaffolding, and it is a part of a sequential four-stage learning process as old as humankind—though sadly missing from many schools and childhoods today. Apprenticeships start with the expert (this can be a parent, a more experienced colleague, or a master craftsman) *modeling* success; then comes *scaffolding* (support to the apprentice—like the ladder that helps a painter reach the second floor, or the initial recruiting that helped get our camp off the ground); then *coaching* as the apprentice begins to perform the tasks; and, finally, *fading* as the apprentice begins to lead.

Whether it is Ben Franklin apprenticing to a Boston printer, a young lawyer beginning her career by clerking with a senior judge, or a medical resident on rotation with an experienced surgeon, not-yet-successful people learn through apprenticeships with already successful people. For me, I had lots of these chances. Before I turned twenty, I completed the summer-camp apprenticeship and then additional unpaid internships—or apprenticeships—with prominent lawyers, city planners, and a US senator.

Despite these burgeoning opportunities, my teenage years continued to be difficult. I made lots of mistakes. But when I made them, I got help. For instance, when I drank too much on an early-spring night in 1978 (I was seventeen) and was chased by police officers in a paddy wagon through the Boston Common, arrested, and taken to jail, I was bailed out a few hours later by family friend Gil Burke. Like my father, Gil was a Harvard-trained lawyer. In retrospect, that one drunken night could have changed the trajectory of my life. Lesser mistakes have ruined the lives of other children. It could easily have been three days in jail, not three hours. It could have been a permanent arrest record, not a quick release. It could have been a source of deep family hardship, not a bachelor-party story, as it became for me.

The great psychologist Erik Erikson wrote that all adolescents should have the chance for a period of *Wandenchaft*, or wanderlust, in their later teen years, when they are free to experience the world and to make mistakes as they find their footing and discover new truths about their souls. I had this time, and for me it was one of life's greatest gifts. I wasn't a bad kid as an adolescent. I was just lost and trying to figure things out.

Instead of my three-hour visit with the Boston Police Department, it was my 1980 internship with US senator Gary Hart of Colorado that became the turning point in my life. The opportunity arose for two reasons: my dad knew Gary Hart, and I was dating a girl in Colorado.

In early June I arrived in Denver in my beat-up Chevy Chevette and made my way to campaign headquarters, which was stuffed into a three-story Victorian on High Street in one of Denver's nicer residential neighborhoods. I tucked in my shirt, rang the doorbell, and was greeted by Mary Cromer, the plainspoken office manager whom I had been speaking with by phone as I drove across the country and who had lined up a basement room for me to sleep in. After getting acquainted for a few minutes, Mary gave me my first campaign assignment: "There's a lawn mower in the garage out back and the lawn needs to be mowed," she said. "Okay," I said, and I headed out back, suddenly a little unsure what I was getting myself into. When the lawn was done I spent four long days counting pennies, nickels, dimes, and quarters collected at a recent state convention in coffee cans covered in HART FOR SENATE bumper stickers. I settled into an almost Zen meditative state as I counted out piles of coins and stuffed them fifty or twenty-five at a time into rust-colored paper rolls and then crimped the ends and stacked the rolls in small cardboard boxes. I didn't complain about the menial work, but I had been taught to ask for more responsibility, so I did. In my second week, the campaign manager said I could work as a ghostwriter, crafting letters to the editor for in-state campaign volunteers to sign and submit. Then, with an endorsement from Cromer, I graduated to position papers and was assigned to draft a campaign brochure on small business.

Later that summer, I helped organize benefit rock concerts performed by Linda Ronstadt, Jimmy Buffett, and Stephen Stills—all of them recruited to the cause by Hart's good friend Warren Beatty. I was just nineteen, and the concerts were an incredible thrill for me, and lucrative for the campaign. In retrospect, they were an uncannily perfect bridge between a teenage desire to attend as many pot-infused rock concerts as possible and a young-adult opportunity to manage a six-figure enterprise for the reelection campaign of a United States senator. The entire campaign experience, as well as the mentors I got to work with, was incredible. I had grown up *around* power, but now, as through transference, I was working *with* power. I called my parents and my college, the University of Vermont, and asked to withdraw from the fall semester of my sophomore year so I could continue working through Election Day in November.

That fall I organized college students across Colorado and discovered I had a talent for mobilizing people behind a cause. On Election Day I led a statewide network of hundreds of student volunteers from a borrowed Boulder dorm room. We stationed volunteers at college polling places across the state with lists in triplicate of all the registered Democrats in those precincts. At midmorning, midafternoon, and dinnertime, we checked to see who had voted and then dispatched students to dorms, libraries, and cafeterias to search for other students who still needed to exercise their franchise. Of the fifteen-hundred-some students living on campus at the University of Colorado at Boulder and registered to vote as Democrats, all but three turned out to vote that day. Students also came out strong in Colorado Springs, Fort Collins, Greeley, and in small college towns across the western slope of the Rockies. Senator Hart won by fewer than twenty thousand votes, withstanding Ronald Reagan's landslide victory over President Jimmy Carter and positioning himself for a presidential run of his own in 1984.

I came back to the East Coast with a new sense of purpose and pride. I had done real work with real responsibility and had a chance to work with numerous caring and experienced professionals who invested their time in my development. By January of 1983, as I began my last semester of college, I was working full-time for Senator Hart's presidential campaign. I served as his national student director and worked closely with the youthful codirectors of his campaign, Bill Shore and Kathy Bushkin, and with the savvy Jeanne Shaheen (now a US senator), who ran our campaign in New Hampshire. I helped to lead our efforts in Vermont and mobilized thousands of students to volunteer in the crucial early caucus and primary states of Iowa and New Hampshire.

In the winter of 1983, with our campaign in last place in most polls and almost out of money, I organized 104 simultaneous press conferences announcing "Students for Hart" chapters on major college campuses across the country. My method was straightforward. Working from a short list of students who had contacted the campaign, and from a longer list of College Democrats chapter heads, I called people and asked if they would gather a few friends and hold a simple press conference for their college and local papers, announcing the formation of a Students for Hart chapter. If those I spoke with showed any interest, I would immediately send them an information packet and ask who they knew on other campuses that might be a prospect to join the effort. I would follow up with a call every few days. I began my phone calls after dinner at six or seven o'clock and often ended for the night when I started waking people on the West Coast—at two or three in the morning, my time. The hard work paid off, and the Students for Hart event was a success, earning a positive article in *Newsweek* magazine, building momentum that helped establish Hart as the youth candidate and earning me a reputation as a skilled campaign organizer. A year later, young people helped drive Hart's surprise second-place finish in Iowa and his upset victory over front-runner Walter Mondale in the 1984 New Hampshire primary.[2]

My experience as Hart's national student director in 1983 and 1984 was my first job out of college. It taught me I could be successful on an adult stage, and it remains an early source of my conviction that citizen power, properly mobilized, can change the world.

■ ■ ■

My parents provided the initial connection to Gary Hart. And I was ready, finally, to take advantage of the opportunity because of the caring, the connections, and the powerful example they had provided much earlier. They were weak on supervising homework and in a few other areas, but overall both my parents were an inspiration. I love them deeply.

At six feet, one inch tall, my mother, Marian Lapsley Cross (she is now remarried), is an imposing presence. Often my friends and those of my two younger sisters found her intimidating. Mom was descended from Quaker activists and New England businessmen and, like my father, was big on long walks, conversations about social policy, and Yankee asceticism. We made do with beat-up old cars, leaky toilets and faucets, moth-rampaged blankets, and rumpled clothing. My dad, Fritz Schwarz, was a successful corporate trial lawyer whose career included defending IBM from monopoly charges, representing Polaroid founder Edwin Land, and winning access to Major League Baseball locker rooms for Melissa Ludtke, a female reporter for *Sports Illustrated*. We had plenty of money, attended private schools, owned a country house, and enjoyed long vacations in Europe, Africa, and the American West. But we also cut our own lawn, often wore clothes until they were threadbare, and usually skipped dessert. If Dad really wanted to mark a milestone, like a new tooth or an athletic or academic award (I didn't have many of those), there was no fancy dinner out or trip to the movies. Instead, he would offer, in his words, "a really big prize—a home-cooked spaghetti dinner."

In retrospect, our selective frugality was a little eccentric, given that Dad's salary put us in the upper echelon of the top 1 percent of earners in the nation. But my parents' work ethic and grit and populist outlook made a mark on me for which I will always be grateful. Dad had a hard time showing affection or emotion, but he saw the best in me and other people and looked to draw that out. In addition to his positive outlook, Dad's ferocious competitive spirit left a deep imprint on me. One night Dad took me to an office softball game played under the lights in lower Manhattan. He was in right field, one of only two lawyers on a team of younger, burlier moving men, messengers, and clerks from the firm. Late in the game a towering fly ball was hit near him. Initially he misjudged it, racing in and toward the foul line when the ball was actually hit deep in the right-center-field gap. Then he reversed course at a sprint and launched himself with a full dive, catching the ball back-handed as he skidded along the patchy grass and then jogged in toward the dugout with a broad grin that was both sheepish and proud. On another night—a Sunday night in the dead of winter—Dad excused himself after dinner and went outside in his winter coat. I went to look for him thirty minutes later and found him a hundred feet from the house in the bitter cold, practicing a speech that he needed to give the next day to a few hundred lawyers working with him on a big case.

Years later, Dad's Harvard college friend, Dan Morgan, summed up to me why he loved Harvard by saying that it exposed him to people like my father. "Your father had little athletic talent," Dan told me, "yet he managed to become stroke of the Harvard crew just through sheer effort and determination, and he has applied that determination and drive to his entire life. As a kid who grew up on a farm in upstate New York, being around people like that was an incredible education."

While I have come to deeply appreciate the drive my father passed on to me, I suspect his competitive intensity and his towering professional success intimidated me as a child. I was the oldest and only son and the oldest grandchild on both sides of the family. Expectations were high. It felt as if, as a ten-year-old, I had been placed on a powerful stallion of ambition that I lacked the skill and interest to ride.

Mom was my partner on all kinds of cool projects, from baking bread, to building a dollhouse for my sister, to raising and killing chickens, to learning macramé. But I also knew her as a ninth-grade English teacher at Benjamin Franklin High School, on 116th Street overlooking the East River in East Harlem. My private school had a different vacation schedule than Mom's public school, so I often had a chance to visit her classroom. Her students were only a few years older than me, and I was inspired by her ability to engage them. Once on the first day of school she assigned them to paint their dingy classroom bright yellow, handing out painter's tape and rollers to her shocked students. The students called Mom "Slim" and seemed to have a deep affection for her as a teacher who was curious about their lives and concerned about their futures. One day I walked across East Harlem with the whole class as they started to put together an end-of-year musical slide show that documented the school's environs. We must have made an unusual sight—a tall white lady walking at the front and a few dozen African American and Puerto Rican fourteen- and fifteen-year-olds, many holding cameras, along with one long-haired blond boy trailing behind. To me it didn't feel odd at all. Instead it felt like a big, happy family adventure.

A larger-than-life figure in my childhood was my paternal grandfather, Fritz Schwarz, who we called Grampy. Grampy was the managing partner of the white-shoe Wall Street law firm Davis, Polk & Wardwell and for many years the chairman of FAO Schwarz, the iconic toy store founded by his grandfather—my great-great-grandfather—in 1862.

The original Frederick August Otto Schwarz came to America in 1856 with his three brothers, Gustav, Richard, and Henry, after fleeing the Westphalia region of Germany because of political instability. The brothers settled in Baltimore and Frederick got a job as a clerk at a local stationery shop. In time he won the confidence of the storeowner and asked if during the Christmas season he could display and sell toys made by friends and family members from Germany and Austria. The storeowner agreed, the toys were a hit, and soon thereafter Frederick and his brothers struck out on their own and opened the Schwarz Toy Bazaar. The store grew modestly in Baltimore and then, after a devastating fire in 1868, relocated to New York City as FAO Schwarz: Purveyor of Fine Toys.

By the time of my grandfather's birth in 1902, FAO Schwarz had become, according to catalogs of the day, the largest and best-known toy store in the world, with branches in several other prominent cities, including Boston, Philadelphia, and San Francisco. It was known then (and still) for its larger-than-life stuffed animals and one-of-a-kind dolls and toys. Many of the toys, like the legendary Steiff teddy bears, were imported exclusively from small toy makers in Europe.

In the early 1900s Henry Schwarz, the son of the founder (and my great-grandfather), took over management of the store. He had just a high school education, but Henry grew the store's catalog business and relocated the flagship store uptown to Fifth Avenue near its current location on Fifty-Eighth Street. The family lived in Greenwich, Connecticut, on a large estate that is now home to the Greenwich Country Day School. According to family lore, at the outset of World War I the family purchased an iron canon to ward off any neighbors who might resent their German heritage.

My grandfather, who like my father went by the nickname Fritz, was educated at the Hill School in Pennsylvania and at Harvard College, where he was president of the student newspaper, the *Crimson*. After his graduation in 1924 he enrolled directly in Harvard Law School and earned a spot on the law review. During my grandfather's third and final year of law school, his father fell ill and died suddenly. Not yet twenty-five, Grampy assumed oversight of the family business and commuted to New York regularly to support his mother and manage the toy business. He declined a prestigious clerkship with Supreme Court justice Oliver Wendell Holmes and ran the store through the early years of the Great Depression before assuming the role of chairman and beginning a career as a corporate lawyer.

In 1962, just as my parents and I were returning from Africa, and one hundred years after the store's founding, Grampy decided to sell the business. None of his children were interested in taking it over, and he wisely wanted to avoid the family disputes that afflict many next-generation family businesses. In the ensuing years, FAO Schwarz has been sold at least a half dozen times, most recently to Toys "R" Us, and has declared bankruptcy twice. The toy store remains a source of family pride, however, and I now chair a small family foundation that uses proceeds from the business to support fellowships at high-quality child-serving organizations.

Sociologist Bruce Feiler, in the 2013 book *The Secrets of Happy Families*, writes that children who know a lot about their families tend to do better when they face challenges. Children with the highest self-confidence, he said, have an "intergenerational self," meaning that they know they belong to something bigger than themselves.[3]

I grew up with an extra dose of intergenerational self, as well as turbocharged mentoring from my extended family and their personal and professional networks. I also grew up with a deep subconscious fear that I would fail to live up to my forebears. Metaphorically, I had been drafted by the Yankees and was about to take my turn at the plate, just after Babe Ruth, Joe DiMaggio, and Mickey Mantle had belted home runs. That fear caused anxiety that likely contributed to my adolescent struggles. But on the other hand, I was a Yankee! I was surrounded by success and could learn from the best. Much as I floundered at times, I, like my privileged peers, had a glide path to the future.

As I reflect on my childhood and early adult life, I am immensely grateful. My life was far from perfect; my parents, like me, have plenty of flaws, and I stumbled many times as I made my way forward. But every time I stumbled, I had a helping hand and a new chance. I learned the language of professional success through trial and error and through dozens of in-depth experiences with accomplished adults who took an interest in my development and helped me open doors.

What's different for the young people I have come to know through Citizen Schools? Most also have hardworking parents who love them deeply. Many have received important support from mentors in or out of their family. But I have come to believe that the mentoring, the coaching, the networking, the experiences with success, the academic support, and the modeling of workforce opportunity available to them are rarely as deep or persistent as they need to be.

Poverty creates a gravitational pull that holds people down. By contrast, wealth underwrites opportunity in obvious ways (better schools, camps, lessons, etc.) and in less obvious ways, like giving young people stories of accomplishment to internalize and the confidence and safety net to take productive risks, such as leaving jobs and creating new ones.

Leaving poverty is harder today than it used to be. When my Schwarz ancestors came to America in 1856, a recent immigrant from

Germany with no formal higher education could start a small business
and put his son on a path to own a country estate and his grandson to
graduate from Harvard Law School with an offer to clerk for a Supreme
Court justice. Today in America, a smaller share of lower-income people become upper-income earners—compared to previous generations
in America and compared to other industrialized nations today. A 2010
report from the Organisation for Economic Co-Operation and Development (OECD) found that with respect to social mobility across generations, the United States now ranks well below many other developed
nations, including France, Germany, Spain, and Canada.[4] In my home
of Boston, a child who starts life in the bottom fifth of all Americans
in family income has just a 10 percent chance of reaching the top fifth.
And Boston has more social mobility than most US cities. A poor child
raised in Atlanta or Indianapolis, for instance, has less than a 5 percent
chance of reaching the upper middle class.[5]

Leaving poverty in the United States today requires escape velocity.
Just as a rocket ship needs extraordinary fuel and thrust to escape the
gravitational pull of the earth, escape velocity for a kid leaving poverty
requires high expectations, persistent coaching and mentoring, and lots
and lots of learning experiences with successful professionals throughout childhood.

The reason that few poor children achieve escape velocity—and
therefore remain poor—is not rocket science. It's due to basic things.
Things like no adult being able to help with homework, either because
the parents are working two to three jobs and aren't available, or because
they are available but—owing to their own bad experiences in school or
their limited English proficiency—don't know how to teach long division or the Pythagorean theorem. And when Citizen Schools' parents
can't help because they lack the time or skill, they generally don't have
the means to hire live-in babysitters or specialized tutors to fill in. Students from low-income families generally don't attend sleep-away camp,
play in sports leagues, take private music lessons, or have many chances
to develop the muscle memory of success. They don't get many chances
to win trophies. If it weren't for Citizen Schools, the students I have
come to know wouldn't have internships with politicians or lawyers, or

apprenticeships with scientists and engineers, even though these fields are growing fast and need more talent. How likely is it that a child will grow up to become an engineer if she has never met one? Their mistakes, when they make them—and growing up by definition includes making mistakes—will likely have far more serious consequences than mine did. Further, they face an added burden of unknown weight: many of them have known hunger, homelessness, a relative who has been jailed or killed, violence against their bodies, or several of these things.

Backgrounds like mine don't guarantee success. Despite initial advantages, a small number of my close friends from childhood and members of my family have encountered great hardship, including homelessness, joblessness, wrenching addiction, deep sadness, and even poverty. But the odds are overwhelmingly stacked in our favor. Similarly, it is still true in America that many exceptional young people grow up in the most difficult of circumstances and yet lay claim to the American Dream of a good education followed by good jobs, a stable family life, home ownership, and more. These children beat the odds through some combination of hard work, force of personality, happenstance, and, usually, great mentoring by determined parents, skilled teachers, and loving community members. But sadly, the rags-to-riches American Dream stories occur less often today. America's current opportunity equation dictates a tough life for most poor and working-class children—the children I have come to know through Citizen Schools. It does not need to be this way. In the chapters that follow, I hope to show how we can become a better nation and properly honor America's founding legacy of opportunity by changing this equation.

CHAPTER TWO

MAUREEN

My friend Amie's Cape Cod home, built by her Ohio industrialist great-grandparents, was large and rambling and featured a sweeping view toward the Elizabeth Islands. The dining room table comfortably sat twenty-four, and the unmodernized kitchen was designed for operation by a household staff of six. One weekend I arrived late for a party Amie was hosting, and while carloads of visitors were being dispatched to secure provisions, I was put to work preparing food. Soon another guest entered the kitchen, just back from an end-of-day bike ride. Her name was Maureen and she had a smile that was at once warm, powerful, and mischievous. I was instantly drawn to her. We spoke for just a minute and then were separated as we searched endless cupboards to find twenty-four beautiful but mismatched bowls for our first course, a bountiful fish stew. When dinner was served, Maureen and I found ourselves seated at opposite ends of the endless table, though I was pleased we occasionally shared smiles across the distance.

After the dinner plates were cleared, people took different places around the table and Maureen and I sat together for dessert. I learned she was an artist and was pursuing a college degree at Tufts University and the School of the Museum of Fine Arts. Her parents were Irish immigrants with limited formal education, and as the fifth of eight children, her upbringing, at least materially, was as different from mine as night from day. Maureen, who was then twenty-five, described leaving home when she was seventeen and making a living on her own ever since. She had attended the local vocational and technical arts high school because her junior high guidance counselor told her that based on her family background she was not college material and should learn a trade. Haircutting became her trade, and in her late teens and early twenties she made a good living working at various salons west of Boston and eventually on fashionable Newbury Street in Boston's Back Bay. Now she was attending Tufts full-time but still cutting hair to pay her rent and cover tuition and bare-bones expenses.

Maureen's whole persona was as foreign to me as it was attractive, and by the end of dessert, and after several glasses of wine, we discovered that we were the only ones left in the room. Above the table we were engaged in a deep conversation about childhood, while below it our feet were engaged in a wonderful game of footsie. We took a moonlit swim together and stayed up the entire night talking until I had to leave early the next morning.

Maureen and I drifted away from each other for almost a year, but throughout that time she persistently reentered my consciousness, and she always made me smile. When I would get into deep conversations with friends, or with a therapist I was seeing at the time, the conversation would turn to soul mates and I would invariably think of Maureen, the Irish woman with substance and sparkle. Almost a year after our first meeting, we had a warm reconnection at a mutual friend's birthday celebration. Then weeks later, Amie held an anniversary sequel to her Cape Cod weekend party. By the end of the weekend Maureen and I were again together. This time it stuck, and just weeks later Maureen and I went on a vacation together in Maine. I was head-over-heels in love. We moved in together that fall and were engaged to be married the following spring.

As I got to know Maureen I came to better understand her road from a subsidized-school-lunch kid and first-generation immigrant in small-town Hudson, Massachusetts, to an honors-level graduate from one of the nation's most prestigious colleges. It's in many ways a prototypical American Dream journey, but also, as discussed in the previous chapter, a road less traveled today. I wondered how it worked for Maureen.

Maureen's mother, Mary, was the oldest of nine girls raised on a small dairy farm outside Galway, Ireland—the daughter of a tall and tough man, John Gilmore, who worked hard and was spare in his sharing of affection. Mary's mother, Margaret, lived to ninety-nine years of age and held the family together with the help of rituals and habits common to the place and time, including daily prayers together in the kitchen and weekly mass at the local Catholic church. I met Grandma Gilmore shortly after Maureen and I got engaged and was amazed to learn that her sons-in-law visited her every afternoon for a glass of buttermilk or cup of tea and a slice of her fresh-baked brown bread or raisin scones. Their social network was strong.

Maureen's father, Joe, grew up just a few miles away in the Salthill area of Galway. When Joe was six months old, on the night before Christmas, his dad was killed by a speeding motorist while fixing his car on the side of the road. Joe's mother took to her bed with grief and didn't get out much until she herself died almost four years later. After Joe's mother died, he was raised by relatives in a household he described as devoid of affection for him and with few material comforts. For those familiar with Frank McCourt's prize-winning memoir *Angela's Ashes*, Joe's story would strike a similar chord.

In his later teens Joe became a carpenter. He met and married Mary Gilmore, and in 1957 the young couple moved to America, settling with Joe's aunt in an apartment in Waltham, just west of Boston. Joe's first job was as a baker's assistant working for ninety-nine cents an hour. Joe and Mary didn't have a car, so he walked six miles to and from work every day. A year later Joe joined the carpenters' union, and in good times he would have steady pay, though at other times, particularly in the winter, he could go for months and months without work. In 1962 Joe and Mary bought the home they have lived in ever since—a split-level ranch in Hudson, a small mill town forty miles west of Boston.

As Maureen looks back at her childhood, she recognizes a variety of forces that helped push her forward. There was a strong sense of identity that came from belonging to an immigrant clan—a family of ten and a big team of cousins and friends that got together often for Irish ceilis, social gatherings filled with singing and dancing and storytelling. Maureen would banter and dance with the older men and women and feel part of an important tribe within the larger American family.

There were also teachers who saw promise in Maureen and made her feel recognized. A fifth-grade art teacher told Maureen she had talent and asked her to stay after school for a special art club. A seventh-grade science teacher beloved by students for her countercultural views invited Maureen to her house, where there was a door made of beads and a living room rug made from colorful squares of recycled carpet swatches. It was different and mind opening. A high school English teacher at the vocational technical school told Maureen it was okay to pursue a liberal arts education and talked with her for hours outside of class about literature.

"When a teacher is in front of the class, they may be a great teacher but you know they are paid to do what they are doing," Maureen observed. "They *have* to be there, so it's harder to feel there is anything special about the relationship. But when they reach out on their own time and they see something positive in you and talk with you, it's a whole different level of recognition and a feeling of really being noticed and having something specific about who you are reflected back on you."

Important to Maureen's childhood were a series of work experiences that broadened her horizons and lifted her confidence. Maureen started working at age ten because, she recalled, "If I wanted to buy a slice of pizza on Saturday with my girlfriends, or buy a pair of Levi jeans because that's what everyone was wearing, I needed to have my own money." Her first jobs were as a babysitter, and while some of the families she worked for were familiar and similar to her parents, the husband and wife in one family Maureen worked for had both completed college and were working as professionals. The experience was eye opening.

"The family environment was just different," Maureen recalled. "Everything from their wardrobes to the things they talked about and asked about was different from what I experienced in my own family. What really made an impression on me was that this family that had been away to college recognized my work ethic and my value and hired me weekly for a long time. They made me think differently of myself. It's not that I had low self-esteem but still they helped me to see myself in a new way. I had a positive response reflected back on me because of my work ethic, skills, and gumption."

When Maureen was twelve she took over her brother's daily newspaper route and was pleased by the generous tips and friendly comments she received from many of her nearly one hundred customers. Later, Maureen lied about her age to get a job at the local pharmacy. She forged a bond with the pharmacist, whom she remembers as a Renaissance man who could play the guitar and carved decoys with a penknife during slow points in the day.

The world of work was a proving ground and an opening to new people and new views, and this became especially true as Maureen started cutting and styling hair full-time right after graduating from Assabet Valley Technical High School. She started at a salon on Main Street in Hudson doing hair for her friends and for older women getting roller sets. In a year her gregarious personality and strong work ethic led Maureen's boss to promote her to manager. Later she moved to a different salon in upscale Wayland, where her customers included staff and faculty from Wellesley College, a bank executive, and a nice older woman who became Maureen's "Jewish mother."

"It's a very intimate relationship when you are cutting people's hair," Maureen recalled. "People ask for advice and may be vulnerable with you in a way that is unusual for them, and they would also give advice. About the time that I was working at the salon in Wayland I was starting to think of finally going to college and I was looking at studying textile design, because it was a career I could envision. My Jewish mother at the salon said, 'Maureen, you seem like a Wellesley girl to me. You need to go to Wellesley and then you can do whatever you want.'"

When I met Maureen she was a year away from earning her degree from Tufts University through its partnership with the School of the Museum of Fine Arts and was cutting hair privately for about ten clients a week while also painting and finishing her studies. She and I had traveled on very different journeys, but for both of us our early work experiences had been critical to an adolescent and early-adult transformation. A lifeline for me was attending and then working at summer camps, helping organize campaigns in Colorado and across the country, serving as editor in chief of my college newspaper, and getting to know the world as a young journalist. These work experiences lifted me through a dark adolescent fog and helped me make the most of the bountiful opportunities I had been given. Maureen used after-school clubs and intensive and financially necessary work experiences to open new doors and to build confidence, skills, and a network. For sure Maureen had a few great teacher-mentors in school, but it was her out-of-school experiences, particularly her real-world work experiences, that allowed her to close opportunity and achievement gaps with her wealthier peers.

Sadly, for low-income children today, work experiences are drying up and blowing away. Newspapers, to the extent they are even read in traditional paper form these days, are now delivered by adults, usually underemployed men, not by teenagers breaking into the world of work. The proportion of older teens (sixteen to nineteen) who work in the summer has declined from two-thirds a generation ago to just one-third today. And in just the last decade, the percentage of sixteen- to nineteen-year-olds working part- or full-time during the school year has declined from 46 percent to 27 percent.[1] We are raising a generation that will have a much harder time navigating the work world and that, in the case of lower-income children, will lack the steppingstones teenage work provides to a brighter future. Wealthier teens will suffer too, but in many cases they will get unpaid internships and apprenticeships, funded by their parents, to provide some of the same workforce skills that teen jobs provide. Lower-income teens will suffer more, with the lines that isolate them from the world of success and of enterprise drawn more boldly than ever before.

CHAPTER THREE

"IT'S MY TURN!"

It was 98 degrees and just past noon when Maureen and I finally began to pedal. "Off at the crack of noon," I joked, and we turned in our hard leather bicycle seats to share knowing smiles. After an exhausting year I had wrapped up my work with the national nonprofit City Year, and Maureen was on vacation from her position as director of student life at the Museum School. Maureen and I were both excited for a restorative late-June bike trip on the back roads of New England—a trip that ended up serving as the bridge to the launch of Citizen Schools. We decided to plan our routes and destinations just a day in advance and to meander, clockwise, from Boston to Vermont, then back through New Hampshire to coastal Maine, and then home.

We packed just the essentials: necessary clothes and two books, a guide to New England bed and breakfasts and—in what became a joke between us for years to come—a five-pound cinderblock of a book, *Women Who Run with the Wolves*, that Maureen insisted on bringing along (and in my panniers, no less!) but never read. We headed west, rolling over the potholed side streets of South Boston and through the skyscraper canyons of downtown Boston. We bisected the MIT and Harvard campuses on Massachusetts Avenue, and soon we were cycling through historic Concord and bucolic country towns, feeling free and soaked in perspiration. In Groton we pulled over and guzzled a half gallon of Gatorade, and then took turns pouring a gallon of cold water over each other's heads. Our longest training ride had been about thirty-five miles, and yet for day one of our trip we'd planned twice that distance and hadn't counted on the heat wave. As we finally wheeled our rusty twelve-speeds into the Cathedral of the Pines Bed and Breakfast in Jaffrey, New Hampshire, it was dusk and we were bone-tired.

We rode across New England for a week, and by the time we left for Boston on our final day of cycling, my creative spirit felt rested and all kinds of ideas for a new venture were percolating in my mind. I had known since my April 1994 decision to leave City Year that I wanted to create a new organization that rallied citizens to improve education. But the precise vision had not yet crystallized. The more I daydreamed and planned that summer, the more I zeroed in on the middle grades, which had been so difficult for me.

The image that settled in my mind was of a thirteen-year-old me, alone in my room on a hot summer day, dreading the start of school a few days later. A letter had come in that day's mail from Henry Singer, my lead counselor that summer at Tamarack Tennis Camp. "Your serve is wicked good," it read, "one of the best in camp." The handwritten letter went on for three pages, detailing things I did well and could build from, while also raising critiques and making suggestions. I had spent just a few hundred hours with Henry Singer, but he had pushed me, and supported me, and come to know me. I read through the letter many times that day and in the weeks and even years to come, and it made me feel good every time.

The idea for Citizen Schools initially emerged more from my heart than my head. I was searching for ways to help kids feel more successful during that adolescent period of vulnerability that had been so painful for me. I wanted to offer other children more relationships with mentors like Henry Singer, and more chances to feel successful, as I had begun to do at Tamarack.

I began to think through the political and programmatic implications of the experiences I had at Tamarack and of the informal apprenticeships

I had with our family summer camp when I was fifteen, with city planners and lawyers in high school, and with Gary Hart in college. In July, I came across an *Atlantic* magazine article by Massachusetts state senator Michael Barrett that described how many European and Asian countries were implementing a significantly longer learning year and were starting to achieve better educational results than the United States.

I had never thought much about the length of the school day, or year. But I did the math. Since the early twentieth century, the typical American school has operated for about 180 days per year and a little more than six hours per day. As someone who hadn't liked school very much, these thousand or so hours in school seemed like plenty. But when I calculated how many hours the typical student is *awake* over the course of an entire year, I realized it was more than five thousand hours. The math was elementary, but for me it was a light bulb moment. I realized American kids were out of school for almost 80 percent of their waking hours! As a country, we were banging our heads against a wall trying, with little success, to change the 20 percent of time when kids were in school. But we were doing little to expand that time or to transform the educational opportunities offered when children aren't in school. I developed a nifty pie chart showing how little of a kid's waking hours were spent in school, and I started talking to anyone who would listen about the opportunity of out-of-school learning. *Carpe the afternoon!* became my informal rallying cry.

As the summer went on, ideas kept percolating. A friend sent me a delightful article, "Chekhov for Children," which detailed the efforts of a Manhattan drama teacher to utilize after-school time to introduce the play *Uncle Vanya* to a group of fifth and sixth graders. I heard about a science camp in which kids built robots and about a Saturday program at one of my alma maters, Milton Academy, where kids chose courses in everything from carpentry to ceramics to filmmaking. Out of this stew of ideas came my own personal commitment to publish a newspaper with students—whom I called apprentices—and the first draft of my concept paper calling for a new network of "Citizen Schools."

"There is a sleeping giant of education reform," the argument began, "and it is us: average citizens from all walks of life. More than any new curriculum, new funding source, or new management plan, what students need is more attention, love, teaching, and guidance from more adults. In our search for better outcomes for kids, we need to stop bashing schools. The rest of us need to pitch in."

The concept paper went on to detail a summer and after-school curriculum built around apprenticeships taught by successful professionals and artisans. Kids in Citizen Schools would also learn through field trips to colleges and museums, through reading circles, and through targeted homework help, all provided by teaching fellows, who in the early years would work part-time while attending college or graduate school. But the special sauce of the program was apprenticeships taught by volunteer "citizen teachers." My vision was to give kids from some of Boston's poorest neighborhoods and lowest-performing schools the chance to work with leading professionals, to learn from the model of their success, and to create products and performances that made their peers, their parents, and other adults say: "Wow! I can't believe kids did that."

Fortunately, the apprenticeship idea resonated with Dever school principal Nydia Mendez, who invited me for a long walk along Boston Harbor when I asked about trying out the Citizen Schools idea with her students. As we walked along the South Boston beachfront on a beautiful late-summer day, I shared my vision for Citizen Schools, focusing on how it could turn schools into places where students not just consumed but created knowledge, and where they discovered connections between school and future careers. Nydia shared her experience growing up as the daughter of an educator in Puerto Rico. "My father always said that education was about the head, the heart, and the hand," she told me. "But now in our schools, too often it's just about the head." I told her about my idea of creating a newspaper as an initial pilot, and she welcomed me into the Dever family, connecting me in September 1994 with the fifth-grade students in Margie Tkacik's classroom.

As described in the introduction, that first journalism class was full of learning (for me, at least), with ten eager students pitching in to write and edit an eight-page newspaper that we had professionally printed and then distributed all over the school and surrounding neighborhood. There was Freddy, who had a bright smile and moody, deep-set eyes. He had spent all of the previous summer cooped up alone in a hot Dorchester apartment because his mother was working as a nurse's aide and thought it was too dangerous for him to go outside and play. And there was Candace, a diligent fifth-grade journalist who would later defy the odds and graduate from St. John's University in New York, where she ran the college's cable-television news station. Kaitlyn was another of my students. Soft-spoken and in the middle of the pack academically, Kaitlyn drew no particular notice. But one day as I circulated among the students to edit their stories, Kaitlyn seized my attention. "It's my turn!" she exclaimed firmly, slamming her hand down on the table and punching out the words with fierce urgency and only a trace of her customary smile. I had not been sure Kaitlyn was getting much out of the class. But now I had a flash of recognition that Kaitlyn, like most people, learned primarily from relationships and experiences. Foreign as I may have seemed, I was providing Kaitlyn with a successful experience and a caring relationship. And she wanted more of both.

It *was* Kaitlyn's turn. And it was my turn too—my turn to try my hand as a social entrepreneur, to test and develop the Citizen Schools idea and try to bring it to classrooms across the country.

It's often attributed to the philosopher Ralph Waldo Emerson that "if you build a better mousetrap, the world will beat a path to your door." That's probably true in the mousetrap business. But it's not always true in education or social services. Too often resources are spread around like peanut butter rather than being targeted to organizations with the best results. Or they flow to established nonprofits with good lobbyists and marketers to the detriment of able but newer or more humble practitioners. Although there has been some recent movement in philanthropy and government toward investing in organizations that have measurable evidence of success, change has been slow. As a result, while it's relatively easy to start a nonprofit, it's hard to grow one. According to the IRS, of the 1.6 million nonprofits that have qualified for tax-exempt status, only 17 percent of them have grown to annual budgets of $1 million or greater.[1] Bridgespan, the nonprofit consultancy, estimates that outside of hospitals and universities, only 0.1 percent of all nonprofits formed since 1975 have grown to a size of $50 million or greater.[2]

The odds of growing Citizen Schools were daunting. I could become a modern-day Don Quixote tilting at the windmills of my time—or a monomaniacal Captain Ahab chasing Moby Dick. But with a fifteen-page concept paper and pilot journalism apprenticeship under my belt, I set out to build Citizen Schools as an impact player in the education arena. I was determined to try.

When I had left City Year, my going-away presents were a laptop computer and help securing two important fellowships. One was a one-year public service fellowship at Harvard's John F. Kennedy School of Government, which consisted of free access to a photocopier and meeting rooms, the chance to sit in on classes and seminars, and a sixty-four-square-foot cubicle. The neighboring cubicles belonged to twenty retired military leaders from the former Soviet Union. I imagined them feeling obsolete in this post–cold war era of glasnost, and they spoke in hushed tones during their short days at the office.

Ed Cohen, a member of the City Year board, provided the second fellowship—and a valuable head start. Ed at that point was running the Echoing Green foundation but had previously been a Wall Street lawyer, a McKinsey business consultant, and the managing partner of General Atlantic, a leading private equity firm. Echoing Green had given the first $100,000 grant to City Year and had been an early funder of other leading social entrepreneurs, including Wendy Kopp at Teach For America, Vanessa Kirsch at Public Allies, and Aaron Lieberman at Jumpstart for Young Children. Ed made me an Echoing Green education fellow, an honor that came with a two-year $50,000 grant and a support system to help Citizen Schools get off the ground.

Buoyed by the initial grant and the landing pad at the Kennedy School, I labored away amid the Soviet generals. Day after day I banged away on my laptop, typing the way I had learned as a newspaper reporter, with two fingers and at speeds up to fifty words per minute, trying to conceptualize and launch Citizen Schools. I built working committees to help us develop our curriculum, our training program, and even our organizational values.

Most of my time was devoted to meeting with people to get advice on Citizen Schools, doing consulting gigs with other nonprofits to earn money (the public service fellowship was unpaid and I wasn't yet drawing a salary from Citizen Schools), and revising the concept paper. I met with police officers, lawyers, architects, zoologists, and more in search of future volunteers. One afternoon I took the subway, called the T in Boston, all around the city so I could meet with street musicians and ask them what they thought of the Citizen Schools idea and whether they would like to teach. I remember the response of one talented young guitarist in particular. "I've always wanted to teach music," she told me. "But no one ever asked me to." I hoped Citizen Schools could change that.

I doggedly pursued the building blocks of a nonprofit organization—a strategic plan and budget, tax-exempt status from the IRS, a team of volunteers and paid staff, schools to partner with, an office, and money to pay for everything. I asked my college friend and roommate, Ned Rimer, already an experienced nonprofit leader, to join me as a co-founder; and in the winter and spring of 1995, Ned, who in college had run the University of Vermont Rescue Squad, taught a first-aid apprenticeship at the Dever School in which a team of students became "first responders" for students who suffered skinned knees and other mishaps on the playground. By May of 1995 Ned was aboard almost full-time. I signed up interns from City Year and the Harvard Graduate School of Education. I met two extraordinary young educators, John Werner and Anita Price, and asked them to lead a planning process for our first summer program and then to run it together. I secured pro bono legal help from one of the top firms in the city, Hale and Dorr (now Wilmer-Hale), and on January 18, 1995, we incorporated as a nonprofit with me as chair, Ned as vice chair, and my wife, Maureen, as secretary.

For year one, our budget was $130,000. That was enough to pay Ned and me a modest salary for part of the year, to hire eight staff to lead a six-week summer pilot for sixty students at the Dever, and then to operate a small after-school program just two days per week in the fall. We imagined ramping up to three summer and after-school programs in 1996.

To receive mail that first spring, we opened a post office box in Cambridge, two blocks from my Kennedy School cubicle. Every day, I walked to the little metal box, clutching the key that connected Citizen Schools to the outside world. Some days the box would be empty and I would return to my cubicle feeling lonely. I'd resolve to send more proposals, distribute more applications, and once again phone the people in my doublewide Rolodex. On other days there would be applications from potential staff, or volunteers, or students. Navigating Harvard Square traffic as I walked back to my office, I would rip open the envelopes to read the letters and applications, feeling elated at the growing interest.

By late June we had accepted—miracle of miracles—sixty-three pioneering students, recruited and trained sixty volunteer citizen teachers, and hired six team leaders and two interns to run the five-days-a-week summer program under John Werner and Anita Price's energetic direction.

The staff was an interesting lot. Sarah Light, one of the first hired, was the brilliant daughter of a professor and had just graduated from Harvard. She took over my journalism class and, while she struggled, as I had, with classroom management, she willed her way to build writing skills and justifiable pride among her students. Keith Mascoll was an actor and, at twenty-seven, a relatively experienced educator from Cambridge. Keith served as a role model for our kids and, along with Brendan Hughes—another skilled theater person—as the hilarious leader of our opening and closing circles. Keith and Brendan introduced all sorts of ideas through skits. If we wanted to encourage student curiosity, for instance, they would recruit student actors and act out behaviors to avoid—the too-cool-for-school preteen rolling his or her eyes—and behaviors to emulate—the eager-beaver learner firing their own and their peers' imaginations with wide-eyed questions. Students and staff enjoyed the skits and they seemed to be effective in communicating key messages. The last hired was Biz Pinsky, just eighteen and headed to Columbia University and then a career in medicine. Her father was United States Poet Laureate Robert Pinsky, and Biz brought a love of Dr. Seuss and a strong creative spirit to the children on her team. The best teacher in the group was Tim Proskauer, a recent graduate of Wesleyan University who was already married and committed to a career in education. Years later Tim would move with his family to Puerto Rico and be named Teacher of the Year for the Department of Defense school system, which serves students on military bases across the United States and in Puerto Rico and Guam.

To sign up for a totally new program—one with no track record and uncertain financing—staff members and volunteers needed to be idealists and open to adventure. In many ways, they were all inventors. I learned a lot from each of them. One of our volunteer citizen teachers was named Kikuko. She was a seventy-two-year-old shiatsu massage master from Japan who taught the basics of shiatsu, and I learned from her that even the most hyperactive eleven-year-old boy can be serene when given clear, calm instructions and shown the power in his hands. Another volunteer was Jake Tucker, a legally blind chef at a swank Beacon Hill restaurant. As he and his charges prepared for a banquet on their final session, I learned how eager parents are to see their kids be successful and how everyone feels special when they are treated to a white-linen dinner party—particularly when the chefs are preteens. Denis Rorie was a Boston cop—a so-called "community police officer," and another of our citizen teachers. Dennis and his colleagues taught a community policing class in which students developed a brochure with crime-fighting tips. "Leave it to the rest of the police force to catch the bad guys," Denis would tell us. "My job—and your job at Citizen Schools—is to catch kids doing things right." Denis was an inspiration for us, and his advice about "catching kids doing things right" became a hallmark of our educational philosophy. I treasure a picture of him in his standard police blues, with a big, wide smile, jumping high on a pogo stick in front of Dever School.

That first summer was brutally hot. The school had no air conditioning, and each classroom was outfitted with just one plastic fan that Ned had bought at the nearby OfficeMax for $14.99. Despite the heat, as the summer wore on we had some reason to believe that things were going well. For one, the kids kept showing up, waking up early and getting dropped off by their parents at eight, or riding public transportation to the nearby subway stop where we would post a staff member to escort students to the school. Every week students had two two-hour sessions for each of three apprenticeships they had chosen, plus they had daily reading circles, twice-weekly field trips to museums or scavenger hunts in different neighborhoods, and additional time for physical recreation, games, team discussions, and our daily opening and closing circles with all sixty-three students. Every day we witnessed learning breakthroughs—such as when Sydney jumped for joy after she finished creating her children's book. (Later, as part of the Boston Public Library's 150th birthday celebration, Sydney's book was added to the collection and placed in the stacks of the main branch, Dewey decimal number and all.) We also took pride in simple gestures of kindness, like a kid writing a nice note to another kid through a system of appreciation mailboxes we had created, or a new student volunteering to speak at closing circle. We were particularly excited when we received an upbeat report from Kikuko, Denis, Jake, or any of the sixty volunteers who teamed up to teach twenty-two apprenticeship courses that summer.

But there were other days when we felt lucky to escape with no one getting hurt, or when we wondered if we were ready for the responsibility we had taken on. There were a couple of fistfights. There was the day that Dorzell, just ten years old, learned his father's jail sentence would be extended. He ran through the halls screaming, finally punching a wall and almost breaking his hand. And there were days where kids just didn't seem to want to learn and staff wilted in the heat, doubting their effectiveness.

I am eternally hopeful. A friend once told me, "You're not just a pie-in-the-sky optimist, but a whole-bakery-in-the-sky optimist." Generally I took the challenges in stride. But it was painful to see our staff struggle and heart-rending to see the daily challenges that confronted Dorzell and so many of his peers.

Week four of the five-and-a-half-week summer session was the toughest. The initial honeymoon period was over. It was steaming hot. And the adults were anxious about the upcoming WOW! event, at which students from each apprenticeship would showcase their learning. Some of the kids, perhaps sensing our fatigue, were stepping up their misbehavior.

At the end of the week I left the school for a meeting I had scheduled with ten parents. We all felt relieved to meet in an air-conditioned conference room at the Harbor Point housing development across the street from the Dever School. The purpose of the meeting was for me to ask them about Citizen Schools and to get their advice on a fall after-school session we were planning. But I was nervous. After four weeks of Citizen Schools, what did they think? What were their children saying? Were they learning? Growing? Would the parents want to enroll their children in our planned after-school program, or in future summer sessions?

Around the table were ten moms—one white, three Latina, and six African American. All of them had paying jobs: there was a nurse, a nurse's aide, and several entry-level hospital workers; a cleaning lady; a filing clerk; and a few who stocked shelves or staffed registers in pharmacies or convenience stores. Most of the women earned just above minimum wage—or about $13,000 per year, putting them below or just above the federally defined poverty level. A majority served as the only breadwinners in their families, typically supporting three children or more.

As we introduced ourselves and started sharing impressions of the summer, the first thing I noticed is that the mothers were very solicitous of each other. Several of the moms exchanged numbers and made plans to talk more or to get together. They would nod familiarly as they heard stories about challenges another child was having. Fear about neighborhood crime and gang initiations ran high, particularly among the mothers of young boys. I also heard about typical adolescent challenges such as growing disinterest in school, a new willingness to talk back to parents and challenge their authority, and social exclusion at school and in their neighborhoods for being too heavy or too quiet or too something else by the standards of the cool clique.

The second thing I noticed was a powerful sentiment of gratitude. These moms were being pushed away by their children, because that's what happens when your kid turns twelve or thirteen. They were trying to raise kids under trying circumstances and in difficult neighborhoods. After a decade of being the earth to their son's or daughter's moon, they sensed their gravitational pull was waning. But Citizen Schools seemed to mitigate the growing sense of distance or loss. The moms talked about how relieved and delighted they were to see new role models step into their kids' lives. They kept saying how their children loved the volunteers at Citizen Schools, and loved the hands-on projects, and loved the special trips to museums and to the Boston Harbor Islands. Keith, the one African American man on our staff, got many shout-outs as a great role model to the African American boys in the program. I also heard from the parents about Brendan's funny stories, and Biz's positive reinforcement, and Tim's patience, and John's incredible creativity and energy, and Anita's warm but authoritative presence. Apparently, *this* is what the kids had been talking about at home.

Immediately after the meeting, I drove to Lambert's, a local vegetable and flower market, and bought twelve of the biggest sunflowers I could find—enough for every staff person and intern we had. As we gathered for our closing circle that day, after the last child had gone home, I shared a flower with each person and a story of appreciation from the parents. Soon thereafter, in one of the hokiest decisions in organizational history, we named the sunflower the official flower of Citizen Schools.

A week later we held our culminating WOW! festival—a three-tent extravaganza that allowed our students to showcase their skills. We encouraged parents and community leaders from across the city to join in celebrating our young people. Kikuko and her team of novice shiatsu aficionados offered free massages. A group of students who worked with engineers from Bolt, Beranek, and Newman—the Cambridge firm that helped develop the Internet—gave surfing lessons on the still-novel World Wide Web to a rapt circle of adult pupils, including then Boston mayor Tom Menino. Theater and dance groups performed on a main stage. Sarah's journalists handed out their newspapers. And Jake's young chefs—augmented by moms and some dads who brought their favorite dishes—provided most of the food. We even had a group of young bike-repair apprentices offering free bike tune-ups to neighborhood kids. It was amazing. And it all took place under sunny skies, on the well-tended lawns at Harbor Point, the mixed-income community rising from the shores of Boston Harbor across the street from the Dever School.

The WOW! festival was extraordinary, but it almost broke me. All summer long I had carried in my head the vision for this final WOW! Our children and their families deserved the best. And an amazing festival on the waterfront—a festival with the mayor, with TV cameras, with creative displays of student work, with watermelon and cotton candy as well as healthy food made by our students—was a way to give them the best, to make them feel worthy, and to put them at the center of the city's vision. The problem was that putting on a party of this scale took a lot of work—and we had a thin team. Everyone was stretched to the limit just running the program day to day and getting the students ready for their final performances. So I told the team not to worry about the WOW!—I would handle it.

In reality, what "handling" it meant was that I conceptualized the event and built momentum for it, but I didn't recruit enough other volunteers to actually make it happen. I leaned heavily on Maureen. Could she make some large posterboard signs? Could she pick up the clam chowder from Legal Sea Foods? Maureen saw how hard I was working and she pitched in heartily. But I could see she was irritated at Citizen Schools' intrusion on our family time. The day before the big WOW! I drove to a tent-rental place in the Boston suburbs to pick up three heavy tents and, with minimal help, managed to erect them. I shopped for thirty watermelons and loaded them in and out of our old station wagon. I picked up the huge helium tank and the Citizen Schools balloons. And I lugged forty folding tables and hundreds of chairs all over Harbor Point. By the time the party started, my back was in serious pain.

Adrenaline got me through the WOW! But when I woke up the next morning I could barely walk. I shuffled slowly into the shower, put as much heat on my back as I could handle, and then managed, barely, to pull on my tuxedo for that morning's graduation. John and Anita orchestrated a beautiful ceremony filled with laughter and tears. We had a closing lunch. And then, in an extreme case of unfortunate timing, I boarded a plane to San Francisco to join a conference of education entrepreneurs.

The flight was miserable. I had a three-hour layover in Newark, and by this point I was in agony. I tried to play a mind game by reflecting on the fact that sometimes I like discomfort, such as getting stuck outside and far from home in a rainstorm or walking to work on a really cold day without a hat or gloves. Maybe because I've suffered few serious discomforts in life, I feel I'm leveling the cosmic scales if I experience a little bit of pain. But nothing about this back pain was noble or uplifting. I wondered what the hell I was doing to myself and whether Citizen Schools was taking too big a toll on my health and my relationship with Maureen. The following morning on the West Coast, I saw a doctor who gave me a prescription for Flexeril, the most powerful muscle relaxant out there, a brace to support my back, and strict instructions to get back home and lie down in bed and do nothing for two weeks. That's pretty much what I did, and two weeks is about what it took before I was able to walk normally and begin to do some much-needed stretching.

By Labor Day at the end of the summer of 1995, my back was feeling better and the happy memories of the summer and the culminating festival had reestablished their primacy in my consciousness. Doctors say that mothers are genetically programmed to forget the pain of childbirth so they will be willing to endure it again. Maybe the same is true of entrepreneurs working one-hundred-hour weeks to get their enterprises off the ground. Ned and I went into full-fledged planning mode, preparing for a fall after-school pilot and starting to think about running three summer programs the following year. Ned took the lead on the program that fall, serving as campus director and directly overseeing four part-time staff members and thirty-two students drawn from the Dever and the neighboring McCormack Middle School. The program met just two days a week for twelve weeks. The McCormack kids started at 1:30 p.m., then the ridiculously early dismissal time for all middle school students in Boston; the Dever kids, who had a 9:00 a.m. start to their school day, started Citizen Schools at about 3:00

and ended at 5:30. The middle school kids began the program with ninety minutes of chess instruction and homework help, and then everyone had apprenticeships from 3:00 to 5:00, followed by a closing circle orchestrated by Ned. I was on site one of the two days to coteach a weekly apprenticeship in business in which ten students worked with me and two friends.

The "product" of our business apprenticeship was the Citizen Schools end-of-semester WOW! The idea was that the students would plan and publicize the event and charge a small admission fee, which would cover our costs, perhaps deliver a small profit, and teach the kids some business principles in the process. I am absolutely certain that the students learned at least one important lesson—which is that startup ventures need to expect the unexpected. Ultimately our WOW! was a success, with more than $2,000 of revenue from ticket sales, sales of ads in a simple program, and a raffle. But we had to reschedule the event twice because of snow!

The Citizen Schools business plan called for us to hire a full-time program director and a junior assistant in January, and I spent much of that fall recruiting for these jobs while also raising money and building relationships with new schools and neighborhood leaders where we planned to expand. We narrowed down a great list of candidates to two finalists, Stephanie Davolos and Tulaine Montgomery. Stephanie had been a French teacher on the Bayou in rural Louisiana through the Teach For America program and then became the program's regional executive director. She had a wonderful lightness to her spirit, joking, for instance, about her teaching of classical French grammar to French Cajun children who had been speaking a version of the language since they were toddlers. She was also fiercely determined and a deep believer in our "learning by doing" approach. Tulaine was a dynamo. At just twenty-four, she was program director for the House of Blues Foundation, an accomplished cellist, a brilliant speaker, and the foster mother of three teenage children. As we proceeded through the interview process I became convinced we should hire them both. "Hire ahead of your needs" was advice we had received at City Year from leveraged-buyout king Ray Chambers, and I was confident we'd have more than enough need for both Tulaine and Stephanie.

As a final interview of sorts, we took the two of them out to dinner in Boston with Anita, who was back for her final year at Harvard, and John, who was then working as a special-education teacher in Boston but was still very involved in our efforts. We were joined by Marsha Feinberg, our highly engaged board chair. This was the last stage of the vetting process and simultaneously a good chance to build the culture of our extended team. But while Ned and I knew we were likely to hire *both* Stephanie and Tulaine, we had neglected to tell either of them. Throughout the dinner, they eyed each other watchfully, looking for an edge in what they must have imagined was a *Survivor*-like reality show. Despite the circumstances, Tulaine and Stephanie were gracious and wonderful, and at the end of dinner I asked them both to join the team.

Stephanie and Tulaine started on February 1, 1996, which was also day one in our first headquarters. For the previous year Ned had been working out of his spare bedroom in Cambridge, while I worked from a basement office in Maureen's and my brick townhouse in South Boston. For meetings, we had been using the YMCA, Dever School, various law firms, and assorted coffee shops and borrowed conference rooms. But now we would have our own digs, a new "garden-level" office on South Street, a few blocks from the core of downtown Boston. The space was beneath a French restaurant, Les Zygomates, and featured a small conference room, a large back area where we could hold trainings and house part-time and future staff, and in the front, a four-hundred-square-foot room with natural light. You had to look up to see the light. But if you did, you had a good panorama of the sidewalk, including the hubcaps of parked cars and the ankles of passersby.

I spent a lot of time that winter going to meetings with Stephanie and Tulaine and working with them and Ned to build our culture. Ned was a bit of a thespian, with a love of music. One summer as a child he had lived and worked on a dairy farm in Greece, and he often shared stories of the lessons he learned there.

"When you are learning how to milk a cow in a foreign land," he would say, "you realize quickly the power of learning by doing. I spoke almost no Greek, so a lecture on milking a cow would not have been very effective. A textbook on how to milk a cow would have been, as they say, 'Greek to me.'

"But when the farmer got down on an overturned bucket and demonstrated how to milk a cow and let me practice, then I could really learn it. The language barrier went away." It was one of Ned's standards, and a great story, particularly to demonstrate the power of the Citizen Schools approach.

Apparently Ned had actually mastered some Greek, though, because he taught us all a Greek love song, "Eis ton afro," and Ned and I and Stephanie and Tulaine belted out the song on numerous occasions when we were marking important milestones, greeting new staff, or just punch-drunk after a long day at the office.

At some point that winter we wrangled an important meeting with a potential funder from New York City. "Money is the mother's milk of politics," California treasurer Jesse "Big Daddy" Unruh famously said. And money was mother's milk for us too, as for any startup, whether a Silicon Valley technology firm or a Boston-based education nonprofit. This particular meeting was with Robert Sherman, the senior program officer at the Surdna Foundation, and it was our first meeting with a significant national foundation. The Web wasn't yet a common research tool, and Google did not even exist, so I called everyone in my Rolodex whom I thought might know Robert or Surdna. People said Robert was friendly and that he and Surdna CEO Ed Skloot (later a Citizen Schools board member) had a deep interest in civic engagement. That—and the donation of my former dining room table to serve in our office conference room—was as far as our advance work went.

On the appointed day Robert arrived and found his way down the stairs into our new little office. I introduced him to Stephanie and Tulaine (Ned was away) and we headed into the conference room, where I had placed a tray of sesame bagels and a few glasses of water. We proceeded to have a meeting that struck me as fantastic. Robert shared his goals for the foundation, and we shared our vision for a new kind of school that activated community assets and turned kids into producers of things and ideas—not just passive consumers. Robert and I were both New Yorkers, and we both started talking quickly and getting more and more excited. At some point, though, I began to notice that Tulaine and Stephanie were looking at me in a funny way, as if I was somehow sabotaging our promising meeting. But I kept talking, and Robert kept talking, and the energy in the room was just exactly what I wanted. After a while Robert got up to leave and said he was impressed and wanted to think things over and would call in a few days. He left, and Stephanie, Tulaine, and I huddled to review the meeting.

"Home run," I said. "He loves this idea." Then I asked what they thought and what was behind the funny looks they had given me. Very politely, Stephanie and Tulaine explained that during the meeting I had started to lick my fingers and then use them to pick up—and then nibble on—the stray sesame seeds that had fallen off the bagels and landed on my end of the table. I cracked up. "Oh, that'll be okay. I hate to see those delicious seeds go to waste. And Robert is a New Yorker; he'll understand." We all had a good laugh, and when Robert called the next day to offer us even more money than we had asked for, I joked that sesame bagels should become the official food of all Citizen Schools fund-raising meetings.

CHAPTER FOUR

TURNING POINT

Joel Bennett had a gentle smile and a truck full of saws, vice grips, files, and other tools he used in a burgeoning carpentry and cabinetmaking business. Joel's business was stable, and he liked the feeling of tangible accomplishment he got from working with wood. But when he met Stephanie Davolos at a community event near his home in Boston's Jamaica Plain section, Joel volunteered that he had always been curious about teaching. Sometimes after completing yet another kitchen renovation or set of built-in bookcases for a home office, he wondered if teaching children might be a more satisfying way to spend his days. Citizen Schools became a way to dip his toe into the education world, and he signed up to teach a carpentry apprenticeship in the spring of 1996.

That spring we offered a Saturday program at Dorchester's Woodrow Wilson School, four blocks from the Victorian fixer-upper Maureen and I were soon to buy in nearby Ashmont Hill. We enrolled sixty-four students and offered eight apprenticeships (including Joel's) in the morning, followed by various field trips and learning activities in the afternoon. Joel's team of young carpenters set out to produce high-quality carpenter's toolboxes. They measured them, cut them, sanded them, shellacked them—the whole thing.

The kids learned plenty. Those of us observing learned a couple of things too. For starters, we learned that a few of the kids didn't know how to measure—at all. In the second week, Joel asked a seventh grader named Kiel to cut a piece of wood in half. Kiel said, "Half? What's half?"

Kiel was getting Bs at the Woodrow Wilson Middle School, and he didn't know what "half" meant. I couldn't believe it! Joel broke down the concept of half. (I remember him folding a piece of paper, then measuring his two feet compared to one, before pulling out a tape measure and actually addressing the piece of wood at hand.) Kiel and Joel cut the piece of wood together and moved forward.

Francisco was another young boy in the apprenticeship. He was eleven and a recent immigrant from Central America. His toolbox was a beautiful piece of work. Around week nine, the kids were planning their presentations and deciding what their toolboxes would be used for—gifts to their moms, or just additions to their own personal workspaces. Joel had noticed that on the side of his toolbox, Francisco had written MIGUEL in block letters.

Joel hadn't heard him talk about a Miguel, so he asked him: "Francisco, who's Miguel? I thought you were keeping this or giving it to your mom."

"Miguel is this old man who lives in my neighborhood," said Francisco. "He's always doing nice things for me. He gets me ice cream. Last summer he took me out to a baseball game. I've never had anything to give to him. So I'm going to give this toolbox to Miguel."

Francisco's story has stuck with me ever since. Even after telling his story dozens of times, I still get goose bumps imagining Francisco presenting his toolbox to Miguel. Our society embraces the giving of gifts to our children. But kids want the chance to give gifts too. Kids who grow up with the privilege of private classes—in ceramics, jewelry, woodworking, or even music—have plenty of chances to be givers of presents they created themselves. Providing kids the chance to be makers of things—not just consumers—is an important part of the opportunity equation.

Kiel's story stuck with me too. By summer 1996 we had grown to offer three full-fledged programs—one at the Dever in Dorchester, one run by Tulaine at the Timilty School in Roxbury, and one run by John Werner at the Garfield School in Brighton. The whole idea of learning by doing, and tapping the incredible resources of the city, was captivating to people. And we continued to find energetic staff members and diverse volunteers to design cool learning experiences. But our program was built on a shaky foundation, and I worried if we were doing enough for students like Kiel. We had no behavior-management system to speak of and we were naive about lesson plans and the basic building blocks of teaching and learning. We got the big stuff right: making learning interesting and connecting kids to successful and caring adults. But we got almost all of the small stuff wrong. On good days we got away with it because many of the underlying learning opportunities were powerful. But on bad days we had chaos.

The first week at Timilty that summer was particularly challenging. A handsome new staff member from Newark, New Jersey, had inadvertently created tension among the staff, several of whom, I was told in the parlance of the day, were "sweating him." And our enrollment included a larger than usual share of rambunctious seventh and eighth graders—a tougher group to engage than the preadolescent fifth and sixth graders who had been our core constituency thus far. The students, sensing weakness, ran all over us.

We released early on Fridays to allow for staff training and planning time, and on the first Friday of that summer Tulaine led her team through what became known as Frank Friday—an honest and open assessment of everything that was going wrong and a discussion of what we needed to do to make it better. The team started by brainstorming the "brutal facts": safety issues caused by kids running in the hallways, disrespect to adults by particular students followed by snickers from impressionable peers, rolling of eyes and sucking of teeth as new ideas were suggested at opening circle. They filled many pages of flip-chart paper. Then Tulaine skillfully steered the team toward a vision for the kind of community they wanted to build. "Fun-loving but respectful," volunteered one staffer. "A place that is safe where learning is fun," said another. "Energetic but tight," offered a third. As the afternoon wore on, the team turned their attention to developing protocols for all sorts of nitty-gritty program components. How would they transition from activity to activity? What would they do for bathroom passes? Who could staff a "Step-Up" room for kids who needed a quick separation from their group and a reminder of the learning opportunities they were missing? Staff agreed to call every parent that weekend and enlist them in a reset of expectations, and they made plans for an engaging series of morning ceremonies incorporating stepping and sophisticated call-and-response cheers. Their goal was nothing less than a complete restart of the campus culture.

Given the early challenges at the Timilty, my favorite memory of that entire summer came at the WOW!, again held at Harbor Point. I had delegated more effectively this time, which was a good thing because we were hosting almost four hundred parents and other guests, as well as nearly two hundred students, including the crews from the Garfield School in Brighton, the Dever, and the Timilty. The Garfield is far from public transportation, so they came to the WOW! by private bus. But the Timilty came by T. They were running late, and I remember imagining all the things that could be going wrong. Did the stars of their performance apprenticeships fail to show up? Had the students gotten involved in some sort of altercation on the T? Just as I started to get truly concerned, my pager buzzed. The Timilty team was almost there, walking up from the nearby JFK T stop at that very moment. A few minutes later I heard a faint rhythmic clapping in the distance. Then sixty-two enthusiastic young people and eight very proud staff members turned the corner, stomping their way down Harbor Point Way and yelling out a powerful call-and-response that invoked Citizen Schools and our core values of pride, joy, and respect. The Timilty was ready to roll. Frank Friday had worked!

As we launched our four school partnerships for the 1996–97 school year, we noticed a different mood among our public school partners. Teachers and principals were on edge. They described a cresting wave of pressure to improve student learning—part of a modern school-reform movement ushered in by the landmark 1983 report, *A Nation at Risk*. The report had generated front-page headlines with its rhetoric of "a rising tide of mediocrity" in US public education and its urgent call for higher standards.[1] By the mid-1990s, teachers and principals who failed to deliver better student test scores feared for their jobs.

In Massachusetts, school reform could be traced back further to an initially obscure court case, *Webby v. Dukakis*, which was filed in 1978 and alleged that the Commonwealth of Massachusetts was not fulfilling its constitutional duty to provide an adequate education for all children. A decision in the case by the state's Supreme Judicial Court forced the hand of the state legislature and ultimately—with leadership from Senate president Tom Birmingham, later our Massachusetts executive director—led to passage of the comprehensive Massachusetts Education Reform Act of 1993. The act called for dramatic increases in state funding of education and instituted a "Robin Hood" financing scheme to ensure that lower-income districts reached at least a minimum "foundation" level of investment. It also authorized up to twenty-five charter schools to push innovation,[2] instituted minimum licensure standards for teachers, and created a process to decertify graduate schools of education if too few of their graduates met those new standards. Most significantly, the new law set in motion intensive efforts to identify rigorous standards for what should be learned in each grade and created a Massachusetts Comprehensive Assessment System—the MCAS—to measure how students and schools were faring.

All of this made a lot of sense to me. The process in Massachusetts was inclusive and relatively bipartisan. Thousands of teachers were involved in setting the standards and advising on the MCAS, which, unlike tests in many other states, includes essays and short-answer responses in addition to fill-in-the-bubble multiple-choice questions. Who could be against setting higher standards and measuring progress in moving toward them? And poorer school districts got more money to make progress possible. But despite the apparent logic of reform, the new standards and tests were controversial. In Cambridge there were sit-ins and other protests organized by activists who feared reform would dumb down education by focusing only on those skills easiest to measure on standardized tests. And in 1996, when the standards started to take effect and the tests started to really count (kids could not graduate without passing the MCAS), the climate of schools undeniably did change. Some of the change was welcome—a stiffening of the spine as educators readied themselves for the hard work ahead. And in some schools educators realized they could meet high standards on the MCAS by offering engaging content and hands-on lessons. My current community of Brookline, for instance, aced the MCAS while generally keeping a rich, inquiry-based course of study. But other schools—facing the first public test of student learning—narrowed their mission, or appeared to give up. In many cases schools stripped "enrichment" classes from the curriculum because topics like art and music weren't tested. A study showed that many urban districts dramatically reduced time for science and social studies, because those tests were "low stakes," meaning there was no consequence for failing them.[3] Scores on English and math assessments did march steadily forward, but achievement gaps remained wide and dropout rates remained unacceptably high.

For Citizen Schools, the arrival of the MCAS presented a pivotal choice. On the one hand, schools were looking for more help and we were an emerging ally. But on the other, schools were deeply engaged in an examination of their own teaching practices, and these examinations were typically leading them to focus more on direct instruction by their own teachers and to eliminate anything that could be seen as a distraction from the urgent task of boosting proficiency. They had less tolerance for our rookie mistakes and seemed in some cases to lose their appetite for the enrichment-based learning we were offering.

It was in this environment, in the spring of 1997, that Nydia Mendez, our founding principal from the Dever, told us that she wanted to take a semester off from Citizen Schools. If we wanted to return, she said, we would need to retool our program to address more directly the emerging learning standards. We were a little stunned.

Nydia's decision to suspend Citizen Schools at the Dever presented us with a core organizational challenge we have wrestled with ever since. How do we keep our unique apprenticeship model intact while also doing more to build academic skills—and to help students succeed on the standardized tests that would now determine whether they could graduate from high school and whether a four-year college would be an option? At times the pendulum at Citizen Schools would seem to swing away from academic coaching and toward deep enrichment and relevant, real-world learning, but then we would hear from a parent who would say that her son couldn't do Citizen Schools anymore because, much as he seemed to love the learning activities, he had failed math in the last semester, and Citizen Schools was an "extra" the family could no longer afford the time for.

These conversations would break my heart, as I could often see the gains students were making even if they weren't yet manifesting those gains on their report cards. There was Linda, for instance, a heavyset girl who would not say a word for week after week and would not take off a thick wool overcoat even though the classrooms we worked in were overheated. During her first few months in Citizen Schools, Linda built trust with two elderly women who taught her how to knit and make dolls. One of the women, Earline, had always been upset that none of her children or grandchildren had picked up her love of sewing. She told me that Citizen Schools offered her a perfect opportunity to pass on a craft she loved, and she asked if she could teach a sewing apprenticeship with Margaret, her neighbor and friend who was born on the same day in 1921.

Most of our volunteers were young, and many were professionals who lived far from the school and arrived each Saturday by car, sometimes seeming to parachute in from a foreign land. Earline and Margaret lived just a few blocks from the school, and it warmed my heart to see them walk into the Wilson School every Saturday with their tote bags of knitting and sewing gear. It must have been wonderful for Linda, too. By week six of her doll-making class with Earline and Margaret, she'd removed her coat, which teachers from the school said she hadn't done that entire year at school. By week ten, Linda was talking. She was talking proudly about the two dolls she had sewn, one of which she was going to keep and the other of which she would give to children at a local homeless shelter.

I don't know if Linda's grades went up that year, or ever. But I think it's very likely that her doll-making opportunity, set in the middle of a difficult adolescence, was a pivotal and positive experience. It may not have been enough to propel her through high school, or on to college or career success. But I am sure it gave her the confidence of knowing she could make something beautiful with her hands, and in the process opened new doors to learning and growth.

While I was confident Linda benefited from Citizen Schools, I wondered if she benefited enough. My fears grew two years later when Linda's older brother, Matthew, a recent dropout from high school, was shot dead in front of their Dorchester home. The downward pull on Linda's life was so powerful. Taking off her coat and talking were necessary first steps. But when would Linda get her next experience with success? Would she get the academic help she needed to transition to high-school-level work? For Linda and thousands like her, would sewing, or carpentry, or law apprenticeships be a temporary oasis in a still-stifling desert, or could they become a gateway to greener pastures?

CHAPTER FIVE

ORGANIZATION MAN

We kept students like Linda in mind as, over time, we developed a series of educational innovations that maintained our focus on real-world apprenticeships taught by volunteer citizen teachers, while also taking direct responsibility for building the academic skills of our students. We launched a deeper mentoring and writing program for eighth graders (8th Grade Academy), put an increased focus on study skills and academic goal-setting throughout the program, targeted academic coaching in math and English language arts aligned with the host school curriculum, and developed a college and career connections (C3) curricula that included one or two college field trips for sixth and seventh graders and five to ten college trips for our eighth graders.

Part of the change was just a matter of time—the amount of time we engaged with our students. By our tenth anniversary, in 2005, our after-school program had evolved from two days per week to four or five days per week, from two hours to three full hours per day, and from just twenty weeks per year when we started to thirty or more weeks per year. If you thought of Citizen Schools as "get smarter" medicine, we had tripled the dosage.

Another key change was our approach to talent. Our staffing model evolved from mostly part-timers in college or graduate school to mostly full-time AmeriCorps teaching fellows, who came to us right after college and made a two-year commitment in exchange for a stipend and a $5,730-per-year scholarship to pay back loans or help fund graduate school. Since they were "only" lead teaching for three hours a day in the afternoons, the teaching fellows rounded out their day by taking on morning roles supporting teachers in the schools, or at Citizen Schools headquarters. They also worked to prepare their lessons and reach out to parents and the volunteers they helped support. We also restructured our campus director job to make it attractive to aspiring educational leaders who had taught for a few years and were looking to build management skills, potentially as a pathway to becoming school leaders. Campus directors, many of them graduates of Teach For America or of our Teaching Fellow program, served as assistant principals for the extended day, working closely with the host school's leadership and aligning our teaching to that happening in the regular day.

In addition to adding more time and creating a stronger talent profile for our front-line staff, we invested heavily in training and curriculum development. In 2004 we launched a partnership with Lesley University to offer our teaching fellows a master's degree in education through a unique blend of courses taught by our staff and Lesley professors. Teaching fellows began spending most of their summers working with us developing their teaching and outreach skills rather than running our summer program, which we began to phase out. A key role for the campus directors was observing and coaching teaching fellows, providing structured feedback based on five formal observations per year. Campus directors relied on a twenty-three-page instructional rubric that was developed by a cadre of award-winning teachers who joined us as staff or consultants. Often we would film teaching fellows and then meet to discuss teaching techniques that had worked well or fallen flat. Even our volunteer citizen teachers went through a training regimen covering the basics of student engagement and helping them adapt apprenticeship curricula that we had vetted and approved. Some volunteers still developed their own courses, but they did so according to an extensive "Getting To WOW!" guide that ensured they included best practices of apprenticeship teaching.

Students still enrolled in two apprenticeships per semester, each meeting one afternoon a week for ninety minutes, but now they also typically had one hour per day of structured homework time, which we called AIM (for Aspire, Invest, Make the grade); two to four hours per week of academic lessons led by the teaching fellows; and additional time for the C3 curricula and occasional explorations to museums and other learning venues (for a sample schedule, see the appendix). The extra time, the investment in talent, and the focus on training made us a stronger organization, better equipped to lift student learning and improve life trajectories.

An external evaluation of Citizen Schools covering Boston students participating between 2001 and 2005 helped answer the question of what happened, in the aggregate, to students like Kiel and Linda. While short-term gains in middle school test scores and grades were modest, the sophisticated matched comparison study, conducted by Policy Studies Associates of Washington, DC, concluded that participation in Citizen Schools led to greater engagement in school, better transitions into high school, and significant gains in high school achievement and completion. Starting in middle school, participants were suspended less and attended school more, gains that continued in high school, with our former participants missing five to fourteen fewer days per year than similar peers. Prior to entering Citizen Schools, our participants were among the most at-risk students in a high-poverty district, meaning they were more likely than their Boston classmates to have failed the fourth-grade MCAS test, more likely to be English-language learners, and more likely to have an identified learning disability. Yet by tenth grade, students who had participated in Citizen Schools in middle school had closed the achievement gap with *state* averages on the high-stakes tenth-grade math and English tests (the gap between passing rates for our high-poverty students and state averages), and they graduated high school on time at a rate that was 20 percent higher than their Boston Public School peers. A 2011 study of a Citizen Schools expansion site in Charlotte, North Carolina, revealed similar results and showed that our low-income participants were enrolling in college at the same rate as their middle-income peers.[1]

These results were encouraging. But we wanted to do better, and we wanted to grow. Growth would allow us to serve more students but would also create a platform for influencing policy and the ongoing education-reform debate, which was escalating in its intensity and its centrality to public discourse.

These twin goals of growth and continuous improvement set us on a never-ending quest for more money, more talent, and better systems to strengthen our organization and extend our impact. If the startup years allowed me and Ned to feel like chefs experimenting with new recipes or inventors imagining novel products, the next stage of Citizen Schools made us feel more like industrialists, debating management plans and expansion scenarios and overseeing an increasingly complex organization. In financial terms, we grew from a $1 million budget in 1997–98 to $11 million in 2005–06 and $33 million in 2013–14. The currency of the startup years was innovation and particular moments of discovery for children working with our staff and volunteers. The currency of the scale-up years was data, as we measured almost everything we did—from the grades and oral-presentation skills of our students to the quality of volunteer training and the speed with which a broken computer was fixed. As CEO and cofounder I was still supposed to be Vision Man, but I tried to also be Organization Man.

A key partner in building up the Citizen Schools organizational infrastructure was Emily McCann, whom we hired in late 2002 as chief financial officer (CFO) and who was then promoted in 2005 to chief operating officer and in 2008, after Ned left (he remained on the board), to president. The CFO search took place during a recession, and we received more than a thousand resumes. Many applicants were qualified on paper but none stood out. Then late in the game Priscilla Cohen, a founding board member who had transitioned to the staff and was running the search, introduced me to Emily. "She's too young for the CFO role," Priscilla advised, "but down the line she could be really good for something else."

When I met Emily a few days later, it was professional love at first sight. First, she was an athlete, literally. She had been an eleven-letter varsity athlete at Harvard College, demonstrating competitive grit that I find to be a great predictor of workforce success. Second, she was wicked smart, with top grades from Harvard and Harvard Business School. Third, everywhere she had worked in her nascent career she had blazed a trail forward through hard work, applied intelligence, and outstanding people skills. Currently she was working at Disney, and her reference there said she was the fastest-rising young female executive since Meg Whitman, who went on to become CEO of eBay and HP and to almost become governor of California. Wow! Fourth, in the 1983–84 school year, when I was organizing college students for Gary Hart across the country, Emily was Hart's chief spokesman in her fourth-grade mock election. Double wow! Most important, Emily was friendly and warm and passionate about making the transition from designing Disney cruise vacations to lifting opportunity for children. She had the right blend of humility and ambition and seemed a perfect fit for our culture.

The problem was that Emily was just twenty-nine and didn't look a day older than twenty-two. Besides, she had never been an accountant, a financial anything, or a chief of anything, much less a chief financial officer for a fast-growing nonprofit trying to change education in America. Nonetheless, thirty minutes into my conversation with Emily, I knew she was the one for the job. Others thought I was crazy, but within a month Emily had made a believer of everyone in the organization. Over the next ten years she would help make Citizen Schools one of the best-run nonprofits in the country. Bridgespan, the nation's leading nonprofit consultancy, has cited Citizen Schools as a best-practice organization in the domains that Emily leads, including hiring, talent development, financial oversight, and information technology.

A key ingredient of the social-change machine we were trying to build was money, and one of my jobs, in partnership with our director of organizational development, Anuradha Desai, was to raise it. We didn't take any government money for our first five years because we felt that private money would give us greater flexibility. I worked hard to attract funding from big and small companies, from foundations, and from individual donors. Eventually we would attract significant government and corporate grants, but for our first ten years of operation, most of our money came from foundations and from wealthy people, and this meant hundreds of fund-raising meetings every year.

Many nonprofits complain that funders give too little, give with too many strings attached, and usually won't continue giving for more than two to three years. That has not been my experience. I have found a significant majority of the funders we deal with to be strategic, open to general support (meaning not many strings attached), and willing to re-invest for ten years or even longer so long as we are continuing to make progress. Some of our supporters, most notably the Edna McConnell Clark Foundation, have been national leaders in engaged and strategic philanthropy and are helping to steer foundations and even government to an investment approach that is long-term, focused on results, and strategic about building capacity. Generous board members, like Andrew Balson, our chair from 2007 to 2014 and a managing partner at Bain Capital, made long-term investments in Citizen Schools similar in some respects to private equity investments in that they were tied to our business plan and our results and pooled in formal "growth capital" funds supported by other philanthropists.

But even as the giving world has slowly become more rational and focused on investing in programs with proven or promising practices—not just those where the program officer has a relationship or where the need is great—philanthropy is still a relationship game. Rule one of fund-raising, I was told in my political-campaign days, is that "people give to people." This meant that if we were to grow, I would need to meet and engage with as many philanthropists as possible. I threw myself into this work with gusto and met some amazing people who are deeply committed to building a more just world by giving away their money (or someone else's money) strategically. However, I also needed to bite my tongue during some particularly strange encounters.

There was the meeting with the young and fancily dressed foundation program officer in San Francisco who suggested that we meet at one of the city's finest restaurants, and then, after we ran up a $100+ bill on skimpy salads and seltzer water, suggested with every fiber of his body language that Citizen Schools—or me—should pick up the bill, not his billion-dollar foundation. Another time, as I prepared to meet with a prominent Boston-based executive, along with three other education-focused nonprofits, we were warned by the CEO's assistant that the CEO suffered from narcolepsy and might fall asleep briefly during our meeting. Despite the warning, it was quite unnerving when, midconversation, the CEO did indeed nod off for what seemed like several minutes. We decided to keep talking, hoping that our most persuasive arguments would find a place in his subconscious if not in his notepad.

Ever since our incorporation in Boston in January 1995, Citizen Schools had grown just in our home city. The lesson I had drawn from my City Year experience was to go deep, and I didn't see any reason to expand to other communities when there were still thousands of students and dozens of schools in Boston that needed us. As a result, in the early years we turned down offers to expand to Atlanta, New York, and several other communities. Over time, though, we heard the call of replication and reconsidered how to spread our good work. Growth in Boston had become harder because we had harvested the "low-hanging fruit" in terms of funding and motivated school partners. As a result, I felt we had reached a point where it would be easier to reach the next one thousand kids outside Boston than in Boston. I also believed that growth beyond Boston would teach us new lessons and open access to bigger pools of funding and talent and a bigger opportunity to influence the ongoing debate about how to improve public education.

A key question was *how* to grow. Should we expand in the common way for our sector—the way of the Girl Scouts and Boys and Girls Clubs and most other national organizations—which is through "affiliates" or "franchises" that are legally independent local organizations but that run similar core programs and share a brand name? Or should we just codify a set of Citizen Schools' best practices and then encourage all sorts of existing nonprofits and schools to pick up the ideas and run with them? Finally, another option available to us was to replicate as one organization, opening up what private sector analysts call "company-owned stores," or branches, in new communities.

My friends at City Year argued for the company-owned-store approach, and they had good reasons that had been articulated by, among others, former Harvard Business School professor Jeff Bradach, who founded the nonprofit consulting firm Bridgespan. Bradach had studied replication in the private sector, where many large organizations like McDonald's grow through a mix of company-owned and franchise stores, and he felt that in the early stages of replication, the company-owned approach allowed for maximum control of culture and quality. This helped young entrepreneurs hone their business model. Direct replication also allowed for a tighter learning cycle in which breakthroughs as well as lessons learned from mistakes could be shared quickly across a large network. On the other hand, brilliant thinkers like Greg Dees, who helped launch the social enterprise programs at Harvard, Stanford, and Duke universities' business schools, staked out a different point of view. Dees argued that some of the most successful examples of scale and impact in American social policy—such as Alcoholics Anonymous, the hospice movement, and Mothers Against Drunk Driving—had spread their central tenets more like Johnny Appleseed, sharing their seeds far and wide, rather than like agribusiness giants such as E&J Gallo that control the land, the seeds, the labor, and the system of production.

As we debated these options among our board members and senior staff, my bias was to avoid the company-owned-store model. I saw its advantages. But I also remembered how hard and painstaking the growth had been at City Year. I argued that there was a difference between power and control, and that by ceding some control we might actually have more power to change education. I had lots of good arguments, but I was also just stubborn. I had experienced it one way at City Year and now, in my own organization, I wanted to try a new approach.

Just as this debate was starting to percolate, Citizen Schools was approached by leaders of two groups who admired our model and our ability to engage middle school students. They wanted us to help them do something similar. The first to reach out was the After-School Corporation (TASC) in New York City, a fast-growing nonprofit that had recently made a splash when it received a $125 million gift from billionaire financier George Soros. TASC and Soros had the bold goal of bringing after-school programs to scale in New York City and then convincing the federal government to make a longer school day with extra enrichment and academics a right for all, not a luxury for the few. TASC had already helped launch or expand hundreds of after-school programs across New York's five boroughs, with the programs being delivered by a patchwork of large and small nonprofits and with a wide variety of approaches and outcomes.

As a general proposition, TASC felt that many of their programs serving younger children in the early elementary grades were working well. If nothing else, kids would stay at these programs until their parents picked them up, because the programs served as childcare in addition to providing academics and enrichment. But middle school kids could vote with their feet, and many programs serving these older children had daily attendance rates running as low as 25 to 50 percent of their official enrollment.

TASC offered to pay us $100,000 to consult on their middle school program. At first this seemed like a dream come true. We had only been in existence for a little more than five years, and I could remember when our entire budget was barely more than $100,000 and we had to hustle to raise it. TASC was getting a lot of attention because of the Soros gift, and I deeply respected its founder, the visionary social entrepreneur Herb Sturz, and his partner, Lucy Friedman. The idea that Herb and Lucy would pay us to improve services for tens of thousands of kids—more than ten times the number we were serving at that stage—was compelling. But as we visited after-school sites and talked to the organizations running TASC-funded programs, I got cold feet. In reality, the programs we would be working with already had well-established cultures and budgets and funding streams. As we spoke with leaders of the programs about adopting Citizen Schools best practices, they would initially be enthusiastic, but then when we described the staffing patterns we believed were needed, or our program design, or the budget, we would run into resistance. "That sounds good, but one of our funders requires us to run forty weeks of programming, so we couldn't have a January downtime for staff training," they would say. Or, "That sounds good, but our staffing model relies on regular day teachers, so the most extra time we can ask them to work is one or two hours, not three hours or more."

I concluded that our chances of getting these programs to shift to the Citizen Schools model—or even to successfully adopt our best practices—were slim. We thanked TASC and agreed to continue working together on advocacy for the after-school field but to defer a formal partnership for the time being.

In the middle of the TASC conversations, we were approached by another group—a for-profit consulting firm, Work/Family Directions. WFD was the brainchild of Fran and Charles Rodgers, who had taken a consulting partnership with IBM and parlayed it into a successful business that supported the family-related needs of millions of employees at Fortune 500 companies. WFD would help employees find nursing homes for their parents and summer camps and preschool programs for their kids. The business had grown like gangbusters in the late 1980s and '90s, but now it was starting to falter, and Charles and Fran and their team were looking for new lines of revenue. Their clients told them there was a dearth of programs for middle-school students, and they sensed there might be a market for a Citizen Schools–like program geared to both the children of their clients and to lower-income children who lived in the communities where the companies were based.

We started a series of conversations about a potential pilot of middle school programs in New Brunswick, New Jersey; Baytown, Texas; Tucson, Arizona; and San Jose, California, all headquarters cities for major WFD clients. Each program would be run with seed money from WFD. And this time there was an extra zero on the financial offer. We would get $1 million over two years to launch these four sites, enough we felt to fully support a small high-quality program for a two-year pilot. To address the challenges we had identified with TASC, the programs would all be new. Staffing and program design would be developed from scratch so as to more fully incorporate all of the key Citizen Schools elements. Lastly, we agreed that if we moved forward with the

WFD partnership, the programs would not be called Citizen Schools. Using our brand all across the country seemed like too big a risk at this stage, so we decided on the not-very-creative name of MAP—for Middle School Apprenticeship Program. Citizen Schools and WFD would find local nonprofits to host and run the programs, and Citizen Schools would take the lead role in hiring and training staff and developing the curriculum, the model, the school partnerships, and a learning network to share best practices across the sites.

The whole enterprise put our reputation and our capacity on the line, but we decided to take the plunge. The funding from WFD's clients mitigated the financial jeopardy, and we felt that by not using our name but still closely monitoring program quality we would minimize any brand risk while maximizing our chances of delivering a quality program, increasing learning across our network, and expanding our influence in the fast-growing world of extended-day programs. Our first step was to organize a competition in which potential local partners vied to be selected as MAP implementation partners, making commitments we saw as essential to a smooth start. In Tucson and San Jose we ended up selecting local YMCAs. In Baytown, Texas, we partnered with the local affiliate of Communities in Schools, and in New Brunswick, New Jersey, we partnered directly with the local school district.

Six months after signing the initial contract with WFD, all our nonprofit partners had been selected and we were exceeding the benchmarks we had set for staff outreach, school partnership development, volunteer recruitment, and more. We felt ready for a strong launch, and I remember inviting all the nonprofit partners to Boston and there being an air of excitement as nonprofit and education veterans from New Brunswick to Baytown shared their enthusiasm for Citizen Schools. The topic of branding came up, and someone asked an interesting question: "I understand why you might not want to call these programs Citizen Schools, but we really love the name, and we are doing everything you've suggested a Citizen Schools program should do, and we are happy to sign a contract specifying that you can withdraw the name if we don't reach quality standards. So how about letting us use the name?" It was a reasonable request and it affirmed our work. These people saw value in our ideas *and* in our brand. After a few days of consultation with our board chair, Sherif Nada, and others, we decided to brand the new programs as Citizen Schools—not MAP. We designed a special logo for the sites, giving our name in the big block letters of our logo and then, in smaller print below it, giving the name of the partnering nonprofit: for example, "Presented by the Santa Clara YMCA."

The national partnership with WFD was followed quickly by an opportunity to replicate Citizen Schools in six Massachusetts communities with funding from Chris Gabrieli, a successful Boston venture capitalist turned civic leader. I first met Chris when he ran for Congress in 1998, vying with ten other candidates for the legendary Eighth Congressional District seat. Parts of the district had been represented by John F. Kennedy; then it was held for thirty-four years by Tip O'Neill and then by Joe Kennedy, the late president's nephew. The campaign was a rollicking affair that featured twenty-five formal debates in the spring and summer prior to the Democratic primary, which would surely decide the election in the overwhelmingly liberal district. Among the best attended of the debates was the so-called Great Debate—a debate in Codman Square's Great Hall organized by two Harvard Kennedy School students and ten middle school apprentices from Citizen Schools. The Great Debate was one of my favorite apprenticeships of our early years, as it featured a recent Haitian immigrant leading the Pledge of Allegiance, middle school students helping three hundred people in the crowd register to vote, and questions during the debate asked by our middle school students and their parents.

Chris finished far back in the pack in 1998, but soon thereafter he created an organization, Massachusetts 2020, which had the initial goal of expanding after-school programs and eventually became a leading state and national voice for longer school days. Chris told me his experiences with Citizen Schools, including through the Great Debate, and his admiration for charter schools, like KIPP, that were pursuing a longer day, convinced him that a longer learning day was a key enabler of school improvement and that broader political advocacy for more learning time was needed. One of his first acts after starting Massachusetts 2020 was to fund a statewide middle school initiative, which in three years' time brought Citizen Schools to the Massachusetts cities of Framingham, Worcester, New Bedford, Springfield, Lowell, and Malden.

In the spring of 2002 we had run programs in Boston alone. Now it was fall 2004 and we were running programs in eleven cities, working with eleven school systems and ten different nonprofits. In Massachusetts we had a statewide footprint that helped us win a line item in the state budget, and we had a growing national footprint that helped us secure a $1 million AmeriCorps investment to support our Teaching Fellow program and deeper consideration from potential corporate partners. We had also launched a series of Reimagining After-School symposiums and were at the table with all the leaders of the field, pushing to transform after-school programs from an afterthought to a leading strategy for improved learning. In 2006 I coedited a book, *The Case for Twenty-First Century Learning*, with articles by leading economists, business executives, and a national teachers' union head all making the case that extended learning time was a great way to build the critical thinking skills needed to thrive in the twenty-first-century workforce.[2]

Working with affiliates helped make us national, but it also made us less agile. For example, if Citizen Schools in Tucson, where the former Teacher of the Year was running our program, discovered some new and better way to introduce math lessons, it would have taken a UN negotiator months and months of cajoling to get all of the other programs to try the same approach. Another challenge was financial. In San Jose we got a technology company involved in our work and it wanted to make a major contribution to scale Citizen Schools; but then our host organization, in this case the local YMCA, said it had targeted the same company to support its early-childhood program and asked us to back off.

The challenges of the affiliate approach mounted, and in January of 2005, right as I returned from a three-month sabbatical, I convened a Business Planning Council, a strategic planning group made up of our six most senior leaders and six more junior leaders from various parts of the organization, including from our affiliate sites. We met for a hundred hours over a five-month period and ended up making a number of key decisions, including a decision to recommit to apprenticeships as the core of our program model and to phase out our affiliate approach to replication. Going forward, all new programs would be "company-owned" branches. With existing programs, where possible we converted them to branches. In communities facing the greatest program or financial difficulties, we closed up shop. And in a few cases we continued the affiliate partnerships, until in 2010, the last of the Massachusetts affiliates, Malden and New Bedford, converted to become branches, with all of their Citizen Schools employees joining the mother ship.

As we wound down the affiliate program just a few years after launching it, there were moments when I kicked myself for my stubbornness in rejecting the company-owned approach at the outset. Replicating through branches might have ultimately pushed us further forward. But who really knows? Perhaps the approach we took worked out for the best. In just two years we went from being a one-city program to an eleven-city program operating across five geographically and politically diverse states—a nationwide initiative that caught the attention of the White House and of corporate and academic leaders from coast to coast. We had some work to do to unwind or convert the affiliates, but we also had huge new assets and opportunities that came from the fast national expansion and from the strong programs and deep local partnerships forged in so many communities.

For me, the early years of national replication were difficult. In the startup years, most of the staff had also been my friends. We cooked and ate and drank together, and though we worked our tails off to improve the program, we were also true believers through and through. We were too new to have anyone else believe in us, so we had better believe in ourselves. As we neared our ten-year anniversary, however, and as we started to win more accolades from the press and from observers outside the organization, pockets of doubt and even skepticism started to emerge on the inside. Some staff seemed to have unrealistic expectations for what the program would accomplish—finding fault if a student failed, instead of celebrating the occasions when students succeeded. Many staff also expected more guidance and handholding than we were used to providing. Sometimes I needed to channel Anita Price, our founding summer-program codirector, who would admonish potential staff to stay away if they wanted a "paint-by-the-numbers experience." In addition, there was a professionalization that on bad days could seem a little bloodless. Did we really need another database, another evaluation system, another decision-making matrix, I wondered?

A further challenge for me was that as we grew I became more isolated from the program. I didn't live in Dorchester anymore, down the street from one of our partner schools, as I had in the startup years; now I rarely had random encounters with Citizen Schools parents and kids on the T or at the grocery store.

As organizations grow, a natural tension emerges between the CEO and other top leaders, who are mostly "externally facing," and more junior staff, who are in the trenches doing the hard and sometimes messy day-to-day work. The currency for outwardly facing people is vision— the ideal the organization is aspiring to—and the stories of success and nuggets of data that illustrate the vision. Talking all day about vision and success stories reinforces the natural optimism of the externally facing people and makes them feel great about the organization. Generally this optimism is essential to their success.

The currency for inwardly facing people is challenge: the schoolteacher who is upset we left their classroom in disarray, the student who is failing math class despite our extra math lessons, or the volunteer who is struggling. Talking all day about these challenges reinforces the natural practicality and skepticism of the front-line staff and keeps them hungry and focused on improvement. Generally, this practical focus on fixing what's wrong makes inwardly focused staff better at their jobs.

The problem comes when the externally focused optimists and the internally focused skeptics take their natural proclivities too far. The skeptics forget to breathe, and to notice progress, and to celebrate positive data and stories. Meanwhile the optimists often ignore challenges and give short shrift to the long distance between idea and implementation. If this chasm is not addressed, organizational culture suffers and trust declines.

These tensions may sound highly theoretical, but at Citizen Schools—and at City Year too—we had recurring rounds in what sometimes seemed like a fifteen-round heavyweight fight between me and a few others as the externally focused optimists and a rotating cast of characters serving as internally focused skeptics.

I found a helpful refrain when trying to balance optimism and real challenges in the Stockdale Paradox, recounted by business guru Jim Collins in his book *Good To Great*, a bible to many leaders in the social sector. The paradox comes from Admiral James Stockdale, the longest-serving prisoner of war in Vietnam, whom Collins interviewed for his book.

> "Who didn't make it out?" asked Collins.
>
> "Oh, that's easy," Stockdale said. "The optimists."
>
> Collins was incredulous. "The optimists? I don't understand."
>
> "The optimists. Oh, they were the ones that said, 'We're going to be out by Christmas.' And Christmas would come and Christmas would go. Then they'd say, 'We're going to be out by Easter.' And Easter would come and Easter would go. And then Thanksgiving, and then it would be Christmas again. And they died of a broken heart. . . . This is a very important lesson. You must never confuse faith that you will prevail in the end—which you can never afford to lose—with the discipline to confront the most brutal facts of your current reality, whatever they might be. . . . I never doubted not only that I would get out, but also that I would prevail in the end and turn the experience into the defining event of my life."[3]

As a leader I had lots of people sharing brutal facts with me—or at least what they thought were brutal facts. I needed to face them and address them, but also maintain—and share—ultimate faith that we would prevail.

CHAPTER SIX

THE EDDY IS READY

In 2006, Boston's Clarence Edwards Middle School (known locally as the Eddy) was a year away from closure. The school had a strong leader and an improving cadre of teachers, but it was caught in a vicious cycle familiar to urban schools. Weak test scores and a well-deserved reputation for violence led families who could make a choice to go elsewhere. The resulting lower enrollment had two consequences. First, because the school had open seats, difficult students who had been kicked out of other schools, or who were newly arriving in the district midyear, were assigned to the Edwards. Second, lower enrollment meant layoffs of the newest and often most energetic teachers. The consequence was akin to a death spiral, and the Edwards, in spring 2006, latched on to what its leaders saw as the last best hope to save the school: a state-funded Expanded Learning Time (ELT) initiative to reimagine the length and design of the school day.

The decline at Edwards had been gradual through the 1980s and '90s and then accelerated at the turn of the century. Cindy McKeen, who started teaching arts and theater at Edwards in 1999—and was previously a private school teacher—recalled the mood in the school when she arrived. "I came here in 1999 and we had a pretty strong principal, Chuck McAfee. He was a disciplinarian, and the collegiality among adults was strong," said McKeen. "But our kids just came from so much sad and so much bad that it was tough. I remember one of my students was a drug dealer. He said he was sure that before he turned twenty-one he was going to die or be in prison. He didn't know how to reach out for anything more. The frustration and rage was just so high." McKeen saw arts and after-school programming as "a sanctuary" for many Edwards students, but one that was overwhelmed by the chaos of the school and their lives at home.

If the Edwards was challenging when McKeen arrived, it soon got worse. In 2000, Principal McAfee was reassigned by the district to lead a high school turnaround effort in another part of the city. The new principal selected for the Edwards, while academically qualified, lacked street smarts and leadership skills, according to those I interviewed. Underperforming teachers were not coached or held accountable and student frustration bubbled over. Enrollment continued to decline as parents—perhaps newly sensitized by the MCAS to the importance of school selection—increasingly steered clear of the Edwards. These years also saw a notable spike in violence, with forty-seven officially recorded assaults on teachers by students over a three-year period, according to McKeen. "I myself was punched in the neck in the cafeteria and was sent to the nurse's office three times, and the kids liked me," said McKeen.

An Edwards student at the time, Yoelinson Castillo, who now works for Citizen Schools at the Edwards, confirmed the chaos. "My first day at the school there were three fights in my class. Kids were smoking weed in the bathrooms, and I had a teacher whose main activity every day for English class was a game of hangman," Castillo recalled. Castillo's eighth-grade year was better, as he landed with a skilled teacher who told him he was smart and helped him move from a special-needs class to mainstream classes. But looking back a dozen years after leaving the Edwards, Castillo mostly remembers the chaos, and he can quickly list friends and classmates from the Edwards who are now in jail, on the streets looking for work, or barely getting by with minimum-wage jobs.

Stephanie Edmeade, a current Edwards teacher, arrived at the school in 2000. She hoped to be part of a small group of teachers who could help turn the school around, but she faced resistance.

"I remember standing up in front of a staff meeting in the teachers' lounge and suggesting we institute a community-service program and people laughed at me," said Edmeade. "Another time I talked about exemplars of advanced writing that I hoped all the teachers could use—to give the students something to stretch for—and one teacher said she didn't want her students to be discussing something they can't do."

Edmeade and others said the most tragic moments in those years at Edwards were revealed through discussions with students who, despite the environment, were hungry to learn. "I remember talking to one student who was on the student council," said Edmeade. "She turned to me and said, 'I want to pass the MCAS, and I am not being taught.'" Edmeade visited one of the student's classes and sure enough, she said, the teacher had his feet up on the desk and was reading the newspaper even as students played cards or stared out the window.

All of Edmeade's uncles and aunts were teachers, and they wondered why she was staying at the Edwards. "'Why don't you go to a charter school?' they would say."

Six years after Edmeade arrived at the Edwards—enough time for two cohorts of sixth graders to make their way through middle school—and after yet another change in the school's leadership, the Edwards embraced many of the reforms adopted by the nation's leading charter and private schools and made them work within a traditional district school. The school's dismissal time moved from 1:30 to 4:30 for every child. America's oldest public school system, which had offered about a six-hour learning day since Boston Latin School opened its doors in 1635, would now offer a nine-hour day to students in perhaps its neediest school and in two others across the city. And if that common-sense move wasn't a bold enough break with the past, the Edwards also resolved to reengineer the curriculum and the delivery system for the entire school day. Specifically, it engaged a "second shift" of paid and volunteer educators mobilized by Citizen Schools and other partners to complement the first shift of "regular" teachers.

Together Citizen Schools and the Edwards created math leagues, in which every student in the school added a daily hourlong math lesson and competed in math tournaments to practice their skills. The school also added an array of extracurricular offerings that rivaled the most elite private and suburban schools. The Edwards had a challenging past. But now through Expanded Learning Time, or ELT as it was known, the younger siblings and neighbors of those earlier Edwards students would have access to extra academic coaching, to the city's first middle school football team, to dance and theater troupes, to mock trials and filmmaking, to astronomy and Web design, and, eventually, to rocket science.

Mike Sabin was the key protagonist of the Edwards turnaround, serving as the school's principal from summer 2002 through the completion of the first year of ELT in 2007. Sabin's successor, Jeff Riley, helped make ELT at Edwards famous and took the school's achievement to the next level, but it was Sabin who wrote the playbook and coached the team through the planning year and the first critical turnaround year.

Sabin grew up in suburban Wellesley, Massachusetts, and was educated at Milton Academy and then Harvard. While still in college he committed to a career in urban education, and after graduation began work as a bilingual education teacher in Cambridge. Later he taught in and then became assistant principal of a Spanish immersion school in Lawrence while also earning his principal certification at Harvard's Graduate School of Education. By spring 2002 Sabin was looking for a school he could lead. He heard about the principal opening at the Edwards but initially didn't think he would apply as his heart was set on leadership of a bilingual school where he could use his Spanish fluency. A mentor persuaded him to show up for the Edwards interview anyway, and he ended up being offered the job. He was thirty-four.

Sabin launched his tenure as Edwards principal by meeting with every teacher one-on-one and trying in his simultaneously bookish and relentlessly upbeat manner to understand deeply the curriculum and to mold the teaching of his team. A friend at Harvard introduced him to Tony Helies, a tough-talking retired technology executive and a Harvard Business School graduate. Helies helped Sabin form an advisory board to provide management guidance and attract resources to the school.

"It was obvious from the beginning that if the school wanted to go from being the worst in the city to one of the best, that it just wouldn't cut it to have kids going home at one thirty in the afternoon," said Helies. "Mike and the rest of us started trying to raise money to build a bigger after-school program, and in some ways that helped set the stage for the ELT program that came a few years later." At the same time, said Helies, Sabin would never have succeeded if he didn't know how to move out the very worst teachers, a management task often thought futile in unionized urban schools. "We wouldn't have worked with Mike if he didn't know how to fire bad teachers and hire good ones. Principals before him were hall monitors with walkie-talkies moving from incident to incident. They didn't pick the curriculum and they didn't do anything to change the teachers."

In his first three years, Sabin stabilized the school. On a staff of about forty, he was able to make almost twenty new hires. He tightened the curriculum, lengthened core classes from sixty to eighty minutes, increased common planning time for teachers, and added a deeper focus on both math and the arts. Closer management of student misbehavior and, perhaps, the greater offerings of art and after-school electives started to reduce violence in the school. But while the climate at the Edwards was improving gradually, test scores remained abysmal. And parents and students were still voting with their feet. Every spring, parents in Boston put in for their top choices of schools, and for Sabin's first years at the helm only a handful put Edwards on their list.

As Sabin entered his fourth year, the 2005–2006 academic year, the national drumbeat for school accountability was getting louder. He sensed that if dramatic improvement didn't come soon, the Edwards would close.

It was at this time—in late fall 2005, that the Massachusetts Department of Education and a nonprofit—Massachusetts 2020—announced a grant competition to provide funding to schools that wanted to add at least three hundred hours of learning time to their schedule. Winning schools would receive an extra $1,300 per student of state taxpayer money to transform learning and results across the school day by adding more academics, more enrichment, and more planning time for teachers.

"ELT came along just as proponents of standards are saying standards-based education systems are necessary but insufficient to get all students to proficiency," said Paul Reville, then the Massachusetts secretary of education and chair of the state Board of Education. "Even an optimized educational setting is not enough to equalize opportunity for children of poverty in comparison to their affluent peers. Clearly, economically disadvantaged children need more."[1]

As soon as Sabin heard about the ELT grant, he was excited to apply. And since he believed that change in urban schools generally came through collaborative leadership, he began engaging his teachers and outside partners, including Citizen Schools, in an intensive planning process. Whereas most schools applying for the ELT grants planned to staff the extra learning time by assigning their teachers to work an extra ninety minutes per day (for extra pay), extending the length of core academic classes, and bringing in a few community partners to team up with teachers in offering new electives, Sabin engineered a solution that was bolder.[2] He extended the schedule by a full three hours Monday through Thursday and opted for a shorter day on Fridays, allowing for teacher professional development starting at noon. Whereas most other schools added ten to fifteen minutes to existing academic classes and also added a forty-five- to sixty-minute enrichment block, Sabin added a full hour of math academic league and a full two-hour elective block every day!

The changes at the Eddy were transformative, allowing students to enroll in two apprenticeships or electives per semester, including offerings such as rocket science and video game design, mock-trial classes that involved field trips to downtown law firms, and sports and a chance for full-length practices. Boldest of all, Sabin turned delivery of the extra time 100 percent over to Citizen Schools for all of his sixth graders and also deeply engaged Citizen Schools and other community partners in co-delivering the extra time to seventh and eighth graders.

An exciting development for Citizen Schools was the deep buy-in of teachers to the partnership. As stated in the school's ELT application to the Massachusetts Department of Education: "Our 6th grade teachers voted unanimously to collaborate with Citizen Schools in the Extended Day, agreeing that the entire 6th grade class of 120 students will participate in its research-based, structured model of community building, project-based learning, and community service. Leveraging this partnership provides us with appropriate programming for the students and also sets the school up for a more unified culture in subsequent years."[3]

Sabin told a reporter at the time that "Citizen Schools brought a willingness to collaborate with the school and to modify certain elements of their program as long as the big picture remained true to their vision. They brought a determination to make things work at the Edwards and a feeling that 'these are our students.' They didn't try to hand off problems to the school when they arose, but took responsibility for trying to solve them."[4]

Within Citizen Schools, the move to ELT provoked a new round of soul-searching of the type we had done back in 1997 when Dever principal Nydia Mendez suspended her work with us until we could align better with school-day academic goals. Now we needed to not only align with the school, we needed to become part of the school. In addition to helping with homework and study skills and leading field trips to college campuses and co-leading apprenticeships, our AmeriCorps teaching fellows would now deliver an hour of math lessons every day—following the same script as veteran math teachers down the hall. We would give grades too, and in an effort to create a unified culture across the full school day, we started having students address our staff more formally by their last names, rather than by their first names. Quite explicitly, Mike Sabin and his team were inviting us, and challenging us, to lift our game to a higher level and be held accountable as professional educators.

Some teaching fellows struggled with the higher expectations and the need to present a more teacherly demeanor. Many had come to Citizen Schools to get away from traditional schools. They loved our hands-on learning projects and the enrichment and community connections that infused our model. But not all felt prepared to teach math lessons for even one hour a day—and some did it poorly. On the other hand, many of our staff worked hard to become solid and, in a few cases, excellent instructional leaders. They followed the path of first- and second-year teachers everywhere, experiencing tear-inducing failures in their first months, but also moments of exhilaration when a well-honed lesson enabled a child to finally grasp how to multiply fractions, or to see the relevance of a persuasive essay to winning a law case, or of basic algebra to programming a video game.

Over time Citizen Schools would become better at supporting academics while still drawing heavily on our core competency of helping students experience success through hands-on projects that connect academics to future careers. We changed our recruiting message to prospective AmeriCorps members to be clear they would do "real" teaching along with lifting up opportunity in other ways. We discovered new ways to support teachers and to learn from them by team-teaching in overlapping blocks, sharing assessments of student learning, and more (see chapter 12 for more on this topic). As I write, Citizen Schools now graduates a majority of its AmeriCorps teaching fellows directly into full-time teaching roles. We have developed two exciting programs for certifying teachers—creating a "teaching hospital" model in which teaching fellows can earn their teaching certificate while leading extended-day classes and then transition seamlessly into full-time teaching roles.

Despite all of Sabin's good planning, it was unclear in those first months of ELT whether the school had made a good choice. There were minor conflicts between Citizen Schools and traditional teachers over damaged blackboards and divergent approaches to discipline. In mid-fall there was a racially tinged showdown between Citizen Schools students and neighborhood toughs from Charlestown, which was then fast gentrifying but still famous for its concentrated pockets of white poverty and spectacular bank robberies (such as those featured in the 2010 Ben Affleck movie *The Town*). Finally, and tragically, in December and January there were successive murders of two Edwards students, Emmanuel "Benji" Saintil, fourteen, and Luis Genera, thirteen. The two students were killed in their home neighborhoods in incidents that were unrelated to the school and occurred miles away, but that nonetheless delivered to the school what could have been a knockout blow.

Moriska "Mo" Selby was just twenty-four in that first year of ELT at the Edwards. She was in a pivotal role, acting as campus director for Citizen Schools, overseeing the final three hours of learning for all sixth graders and supporting many of the seventh and eighth graders as well. Selby, a native of the tiny Caribbean island of St. Vincent and then of Brooklyn, New York, was just two years out of Tufts University, but had already worked three years for Citizen Schools. I had pitched her on taking the Edwards job and remember seeing in her facial expression excitement for the opportunity but also concern that the experiment wouldn't work.

"Those first few months of ELT at the Edwards were so hard," Selby recalled. "Kids would just walk out on you. 'You're not a real teacher,' they would say." It reached a low point mid-fall, when an average sixth grader, a boy Selby pegged at six feet two inches tall and almost two hundred pounds, pushed Citizen Schools staffer Caroline Beasley up against a wall of lockers. "This boy was just so angry, and we tried explaining all of the opportunities we were trying to bring to the school with the longer day, but he just didn't want to hear it," said Selby. "So after we huddled with the school leadership we decided that for the safety of the students and of the staff we just needed him to go home a little earlier and we needed to focus on everyone else."

That decision, said Selby, became a turning point for Citizen Schools and the school as they realized they could work through difficult decisions together.

Another turning point came that spring, when the Citizen Schools staff formed a Student Leadership Council of thirty students and took them to a camp in rural New Hampshire, skipping three days of school in early June in hopes of cultivating role models among the school's older students. The trip was part of an effort to ease tensions between the major subgroups of the school—the general education population, students in the Chinese Sheltered Immersion program for new immigrants learning to speak English, and students with serious social/emotional and learning disabilities. The three groups attended separate classes in the regular school day and came together just at lunch and recess and in the extended-day hours with Citizen Schools.

The camp in New Hampshire was run by a Russian man named Misha, and it was a challenging and foreign experience for the Edwards kids. For starters, no electronics were allowed, no technology, not even wristwatches. There was no fast food either, and all meals came entirely from the farm on the premises, including eggs the students would collect from a henhouse. Capitalizing on the foreign environment, Misha and the Citizen Schools team introduced a series of team-building and leadership activities, including canoeing on a large lake. One Puerto Rican student, Chris, who was a good athlete and a future member of Junior ROTC, was matched in a canoe with a tiny Chinese student with serious social/emotional and academic learning disabilities. Chris suffered from his own learning challenges but told counselors he felt proud after managing to paddle six miles despite his partner paddling mostly in the opposite direction.

"It was an incredible leadership experience and it helped to draw together a group of students who normally never interacted in the school," recalled Emily Bryan, a Citizen Schools teaching fellow who helped organize the trip. (Emily later became an award-winning sixth-grade English teacher at the Edwards.)

During their three days at the Marlow, New Hampshire, camp, the Edwards kids also had a chance to work with knives, learning how to carve wood. During one of these sessions the counselors noticed that a knife had been stolen.

"Misha, the camp director, sat everyone in a circle," recalled Bryan. "He didn't yell. He said, 'It's not your fault that you live in a world where people steal, where you have to worry about your things being stolen, where you have to worry about violence. But if you are also lying and stealing then you are adding to this problem. If you want to live in a world without lying and stealing then you must be the one to change the world. You have to change yourself.'"

Misha then pointed down the field where they were sitting to his car and said to the students that if they needed anything, the car was open and his wallet was on the front seat. "The knife got returned that night," Bryan recalled, adding that she learned a lesson that day about creating an environment of trust and support and high expectations that she has carried into her classroom ever since.

Throughout the year, Sabin persisted in knitting together his traditional staff with the Citizen Schools AmeriCorps members and volunteer citizen teachers. By graduation in June, there were signs that the investment was paying off. Attendance was up across the school. Sixth-grade attendance had risen from 90 to 93 percent, an increase that may sound small but means the average student attended an additional week of school, compounding the extra learning time offered by the ELT model. Still, the Edwards had seen signs of momentum before only to be disappointed when the MCAS scores were published. This time it would be different. Math proficiency in sixth grade more than doubled, from 15 percent, the lowest in the city the previous year, to 32 percent, slightly above the city average. Test scores in almost every subject and grade were up by sizable margins.

After two more years of ELT, the Eddy was transformed. Whereas in 2005 only 17 families had chosen the Edwards in Boston's open-assignment process, in 2008 more than 450 families chose the school, creating a large wait list. By 2008 the school had a football team (the first middle school team in Boston), numerous arts programs, diverse apprenticeships offered through Citizen Schools, and an extra hour of math games and instruction every day. The Edwards had erased more than 80 percent of the achievement gap in English and science (the gap between its students and state averages), and in math it had created a reverse achievement gap, outscoring such middle-class communities as Framingham, Waltham, and Watertown. Meanwhile, the school continued to serve many of the highest-need students and families in Boston, as the percentage of Edwards students living in or near poverty had actually grown to more than 90 percent, and the share of English-language learners and special-education students continued to be high.

■ ■ ■

I recently returned to the Edwards to spend a day observing classrooms and meeting with teachers and students and with the new principal, Leo Flanagan. Principal Sabin, the ELT architect, had left after the first year of implementation to bring his family to Central America, where he helped to run a school for two years, before returning to Boston to take on another ELT partnership with Citizen Schools. Jeff Riley, Sabin's talented successor, had run ELT at the Edwards for two years and then been promoted to become Boston's assistant superintendent for middle schools, a role that allowed him to help spread ELT to other schools across the city. In 2012 Riley was tapped by the state as superintendent for the troubled Lawrence Public Schools.

I had visited the Edwards a dozen times over the previous decade, including in January 2008, when Senator Edward M. Kennedy announced the TIME Act, a legislative proposal to replicate the Edwards ELT model across the country. But I had never spent a full day at the school—a day starting at 7:00 a.m. as the first buses began to arrive and running until 4:30 p.m. as the last students left for home.

My previous visits allowed me to see snapshots that illustrated the story of a transforming urban school in a big-city district—a transformation that, while still fragile and incomplete, has nonetheless provided hope to education reformers in Boston and beyond. The Edwards success story has been touted by business leaders and charter advocates, but also by teachers' union president Randi Weingarten, who stated in a 2011 *New York Times* column that the Edwards was "one of the most impressive schools I have ever seen."[5] Now I wanted to understand the texture of the school and its makeover more intimately.

If the Edwards could turn around its fortunes, could others do the same? In a country where an estimated 50 percent of the dropout crisis and a majority of the achievement gap runs through just a few thousand middle schools, replicating the Edwards story even a few hundred times could start to move the needle on national educational results. Replicating the story a few thousand times would rocket the United States from below average in international rankings of student learning to the top tier.[6]

I got to the Edwards at seven in the morning—just as the first students arrived for a breakfast of TruMoo chocolate milk and premade sausage, egg, and cheese sandwiches. I met with veteran teachers like Cindy McKeen and Stephanie Edmeade and with newcomers like Emily Bryan. I spoke with students too, including eighth grader Adam Barriga (the student who spoke at the State House, described in the introduction). Barriga sported a mop of long and bushy brown hair but held a clear vision of his future as an engineer—a vision he said was inspired in large part by his sixth-grade rocket-science apprenticeship with David Mantus. Over the course of the day I developed a deeper sense of what made the school tick.

Leo Flanagan, the principal at Edwards from 2010 to 2013, said he was most proud that his students now feel like individuals. He described a conversation with a student who had transferred to the Edwards after experiencing bullying at another middle school. "'Mr. Flanagan' she said, 'You have black dorks here.' She is right," said Flanagan. "We have big black kids wearing pink shoes because they have been here for a while and they have found some things they are really passionate about and they are willing to be themselves. That is just huge for kids." Flanagan described a particular student he believed was gay who joined the cheerleading squad and flourished. "He would have turtled at most other schools," said Flanagan.

The Edwards's test scores have stopped rising, but the school has retained most of the gains made in the first three years of ELT. Annual student growth scores remain high in most subjects, often higher than for some well-regarded charter schools in the area. Despite calls to increase the focus on straight academics, Flanagan has insisted on continuing the school's emphasis on enrichment. "I think what we are doing is really courageous, because I believe the future of kids is really about the experiences of kids. I want kids to have the experience of being in rock bands, of conducting real experiments with scientists, of arguing a mock trial down at the federal courthouse in front of a federal judge," said Flanagan. "What would they do in the suburbs? Do you think they would ever just get rid of arts and music and other electives so they could focus all their attention on math? Part of how we drive things at Edwards is to ask, 'Would this fly in Brookline?' When we do things for poor black kids that we would never do in the suburbs, then I wonder."

Despite his faith in the Edwards approach—and in the possibility of creating good urban public schools—Flanagan says he sometimes wonders whether he made a mistake in choosing to labor in a big-city school system like Boston that has been the subject of so much criticism. "I see those charters out there offering a longer day and with full control of their teaching staff—and with kids all signing up for a lottery to get in—and I sometimes wonder," Flanagan said, "if we are on the wrong side of history here in the district schools and if we are just doomed to failure. But then I wonder if, ironically, it's more cutting-edge to have stayed in the district. And I see the work we are doing here with ELT at Edwards and see how it's now spreading to more district schools across Boston, and it feels like we are building a pathway for lifting up opportunity and achievement for the hardest-to-reach children across this city and across the country."

Among the teachers of whom Flanagan is proudest is Emily Bryan, the former Citizen Schools teaching fellow. Bryan is one of six former Citizen Schools staff members who have been hired by the Edwards for teaching or administrative roles, creating a built-in talent pipeline that has served the school well and strengthened our partnership. On a recent visit to the Edwards, I sat in as Bryan taught her second sixth-grade English class of the day in Room 102, overlooking the school's drab concrete playground and parking lot.

"Okey-dokey," said Bryan, who sports short-cropped black hair and was sucking on a bright red lollipop as she welcomed the class. "All you need on your desks right now is a pencil. The 'Do Now' is coming around." Bryan's first assignment was a short vignette from *The House on Mango Street* by Sandra Cisneros. She asked the students to read the passage and then pick out examples of metaphor, personification, and figurative speech. As the students read, Bryan played music in the background. Then after a minute or two of quiet reading she began to banter with the students as they answered questions listed on the "Do Now." "Why do you like this passage?" she asked. "What makes it good? Do you see the sensory detail we were talking about the other day?"

Bryan asked for an example of sarcasm from the text and immediately two girls raised their hands. She called on one and when the student gave a good example, Bryan affirmed her with praise and then tossed her a lollipop from across the room. "In my last class I shared a really good writing passage from one of my former students—from Emily Restrepo," Bryan announced. "Emily's younger sister was in the class"—here Bryan paused for emphasis—"and you can imagine she was *thrilled* that I was talking about her sister. That's sarcasm," Bryan continued without missing a beat. She took a few more comments on the Cisneros passage and then told the class it was time to get to work on their own writing.

As a first step, Bryan modeled the writing of a short passage herself. "Okay, I want to write about a hot day and a sprinkler," she told the class. "I want to use metaphor or simile and personification and figurative speech." Her laptop was connected to a projector, and as she began to write, every student paid attention as the first draft of her vignette began to unfold on one of the classroom walls.

"It was a hot day so we played in the sprinkler. We got really wet," Bryan wrote.

"That's not very good is it?" she asked. Twenty-two heads shook side to side, eyes still riveted on Bryan. "No, it's blah. How can we improve that with dialogue, with figurative language, and with sensory detail?"

Bryan started over, twenty-two sets of eyes darting back and forth between her and the words projecting on the wall. "It was a hot July afternoon. Eric and I danced in the sprinkler like ballerinas onstage. We screamed 'It's cold! It's cold!' as the wet grass stuck to our ankles and between our toes." In a little more than a minute Bryan had hooked the class and modeled a powerful vignette. Now the young writers themselves took pen to paper and began to work, eagerly. As they did, Bryan turned to me, saying in a stage whisper, "These guys are freakishly good."

By the time the class was over, almost every student had earned at least one lollipop, and a good measure of praise, and I had heard some quite impressive writing from a class full of eleven- and twelve-year-olds—half of whom didn't even speak English at home.

"Sometimes I go to the fountain and it calms me down," wrote Francesca. "I smell the salty waters of the ocean. Trees dancing around me. The birds watching my every move. . . . I can hear the wind whistling into my ears, the park calling my name, 'Francesca, Francesca, come to play.'"

I was inspired. I had heard that Bryan's students had improved more in their MCAS writing and reading comprehension scores in the previous year than all but four other sixth-grade classes in the entire state, and now I knew why. She built relationships with her students; she challenged them to do great work, first modeling excellence and then coaching as students practiced their skills; and she made learning fun—all principles at the core of the Citizen Schools approach.

Full-time teachers like Bryan and leaders like Sabin and his successors as principal were critical to the Edwards turnaround, and a key part of the value that Citizen Schools added was the full-time AmeriCorps teaching fellows—a job held right after college by future educators like Emily Bryan and Moriska Selby and dozens of others. Yet equally important factors in the school's turnaround were the hundreds of volunteer citizen teachers who led apprenticeship courses—people like David Mantus. Mantus taught rocket science seven times at the Edwards, forging hundreds of relationships with students like Adam Barriga. Tony Helies, the retired businessman who advised Principal Sabin in the early years of the Edwards turnaround, taught astronomy at Citizen Schools fifteen times, including multiple times at Edwards; and Alan Su, a whiz kid engineer at Google's Cambridge office, taught computer programming classes five times at the Eddy.

Su is such a talent that even as a relatively young engineer Google tapped him to help lead the team that made YouTube (a Google subsidiary) faster, helping the company "live-stream" every event at the 2012 London Olympics. But teaching was tougher than Su expected. He taught his first apprenticeship at the Edwards the first year of ELT, and Su remembers "feeling a little naive" when he realized the Web design curriculum he had put together was over the heads of most of the students in his class and that many of the students didn't seem motivated to learn.

Despite the challenge, Su committed to teach again. His next course involved creation of a public service app for the Android phone—an app that would enhance the experience for participants in First Night, a popular Boston arts festival. "The idea was to make First Night more interactive and drive up attendance. You could imagine a clue on the ice sculptures and then people would have to take a picture to show they were there," related Su. "The students learned the basics of putting together a user interface and basic computer programming, and by the time they were done they had the bones of a really cool app."

Su has since come back to teach three more times and said he has seen a transformation at the Edwards and in its students. "It's palpable, the difference in the attitude of the kids. It's night and day. There is no more 'too cool for school,' and now the students see that learning can be really fun." Su said that his personal motivation to volunteer has grown too. "The thing I love is the combination of the boots-on-the-ground experience—the experience of introducing kids to something out of the ordinary and helping them realize that the Web is not just something to consume from, they can be creators too. I love the combination of getting to know the kids and also seeing the results at the Edwards, which are incontrovertible. I also love that I have a role in addressing one of the greater inequities in our society."

Helies and Mantus also stood witness to the transformation at the Edwards. Mantus's first course was in 2007 at a Citizen Schools campus in Boston's Brighton neighborhood, and it was an ill-fated effort to get the students to develop a pathway for bringing a new drug to market. The course was authentic, as that's what Mantus did for a living, but the lessons lacked pizzazz and didn't appeal to students. Mantus remembers several co-teachers from his firm vowing they would never return.

"The only part of the class that really resonated was the day we had a paper airplane contest and the kids all learned about the physics of flight," said Mantus. "I realized that what I was really going for was to get kids jazzed about science and technology, and the key to that was just getting them excited about the fundamentals of chemistry and physics. I had a friend who worked at the Challenger Learning Center in Wheeling, West Virginia, and I called her up and she said she would love to collaborate with me on a course." Mantus went to work and designed a class in which his students learned the fundamentals of space travel and ended the semester with a live video hookup with astronauts from the Challenger Center. It was an instant hit. Mantus and his colleagues have now taught the class to more than one hundred students from the Edwards over the last five years.

I knew that Mantus's motivation for teaching came from his desire to spread the wonder that he first experienced launching rockets in the backyard with his dad and going on trips with his grandfather to the New York Hall of Science in Queens, near their Long Island home. When I met with Helies, a retiree who had taught fifteen apprenticeships and volunteered in other ways to help the Edwards, I wondered what had motivated him to get so involved.

"Part of why I do this," Helies said, "is that I was raised by a single mom who had four kids in a tough neighborhood in Brooklyn, and she just worked incredibly hard to get all her kids scholarships to private schools. I didn't get a lot of hugs growing up, but I got an education that changed my life. I am here today because of that, and God bless my mother for the aggressiveness she had in helping her kids get a good education."

Helies graduated from the Trinity School on Manhattan's Upper West Side and then went to Northeastern University, where he earned a degree in electrical engineering. He worked on the Apollo project from 1967 to 1971 and then was laid off as the space program began to downsize. He earned a degree from Harvard Business School, married, and started raising a family, while also founding a company that did network management for large corporate computer systems. Helies never got involved in nonprofits during his professional life, but after selling his company, his interests turned to K–12 education. He hoped to provide to others the education that his mother provided for him. Soon he met Sabin and helped him with management advice, but he also began tutoring kids in math, which he loved and was good at. When Helies asked to do more with students, Sabin suggested he get involved with Citizen Schools.

Helies decided that at Citizen Schools he would teach astronomy, a topic that had always fascinated him. He organized a course in which the students used the same simple instruments as the ancient Greeks to measure the size of the planets, their distance from each other, and the orbits of their moons. Helies was a good teacher, so he usually was assigned more than his share of discipline challenges. Maybe as a result, he found the classes difficult but also rewarding enough to keep coming back. "Tutoring one or two kids is easy," said Helies. "Teaching fifteen or twenty kids is much tougher. You need to develop a relationship with the kids, because people treat people who they have a relationship with much better." Helies also found ways to weave in exercise to his classes, which he found kids hungry for more of. "I would have the girls race the boys to map out the solar system and they would just go nuts. They were so excited and they needed that chance to blow off steam."

Looking back, Helies recalled a number of students for whom astronomy provided a breakthrough during their difficult middle school years. One student who was failing several of his classes initially told Helies that astronomy was stupid. Then at the end of the semester he handed Helies a note saying: "Dear Mr. Helies, I used to hate astronomy. Now I like it."

A few days after we spoke, Helies wrote me with another example of a rewarding experience from his class.

"One of our more challenging assignments is to determine the orbital period of Charon, Pluto's large moon. This is pretty sophisticated stuff for sixth graders," Helies wrote. "We used photos taken by NASA of Pluto three days apart, showing that Charon had moved halfway round during that time. From that data we figured out the period, six days. For our WOW! we were having an 'Astronomy Conference' in the Boston College physics department, with the students serving as the conference presenters. BC does a wonderful job setting up the conference, with badges, conference programs, even cookies and juice. Professor Michael Graf and his grad students are the attendees. One of our quieter students volunteered to present about Charon's moon and its orbit. He had been quite shy during the apprenticeship, so I was pleased to see him take the initiative. Charon's orbit is six days, but the data we had could also be interpreted as a two-day orbit. (Can you see why?) Professor Graf challenged the six-day number and soon he and the student were both up at the white board, with the student drawing orbits! The student was able to explain why the data was inconclusive, show that both six days and two days were possible, and proposed that we could find out for sure with more photos. I felt like I was at a real astronomy conference. Well, I guess I was."

The Expanded Learning Time model we piloted at the Edwards sparked a transformation at Citizen Schools. We stopped opening new after-school programs, formerly the bread and butter of our organization, and instead looked to replicate ELT programs where we could work with every student in a middle school, or at least every student in one or two grades. While in 2006 I had been nervous to make the jump from optional to required programming at Edwards, by 2009 I was convinced that ELT—done right—could become an essential new paradigm for schools in the twenty-first century.

In the four years since the Edwards success was established, we have scaled ELT to a national cohort of twenty-four formerly struggling schools—from East Harlem to East Palo Alto and from the west side of Houston to Chicago's South Side. Results in individual schools have varied, but on average ELT schools partnering with Citizen Schools have significantly increased student engagement (attendance, staying out of trouble, and seeing the link between school and careers) and increased proficiency rates on state tests by more than ten percentage points within two years. Teachers and parents give the program high ratings for academics and for offering a well-rounded education. The progress at ELT schools means that for students who attended these schools, who started middle school about two years behind their middle-income peers, half or more of that gap has been cut while they are still in middle school. Our hope is that students have also learned better school navigation skills like how to ask for help, how to advocate for themselves, and how to work toward a goal on diverse teams. We believe the academic momentum as well as the social skills and social networks Citizen Schools students build will help close most or even the entire remaining achievement gap before adulthood. In fact, in the two locations where we have longitudinal data through high school—Boston and Charlotte—low-income Citizen Schools graduates fully eliminated gaps with their middle-income peers in on-time high school graduation and in college enrollment, though not yet in college completion.

In Oakland, where I started my career as a journalist, the fastest-improving middle school in 2011–2012 was a Citizen Schools ELT school. And in our home base of Boston, Orchard Gardens, formerly one of the lowest-rated schools in the entire state, had such a dramatic turnaround through ELT and other reforms that it recently boasted the highest scores for student-learning growth of any middle school in all of Massachusetts.[7] The latest report on our ELT work from external evaluator Abt Associates indicates that, on average, Citizen Schools ELT schools are delivering an extra three months of learning in math per year and an extra five months of learning per year in reading and writing compared to similar schools, while also boosting engagement in learning and interest in careers.

The second section of this book starts to unpack the key success factors of Citizen Schools—the key components of the opportunity equation—and suggest how we and others might bring them to millions more children.

CHAPTER SEVEN

SCALE, SPREAD, AND THE PURSUIT OF SYSTEMIC CHANGE

In the early days at City Year, founders Alan Khazei and Michael Brown and I would sit around our partially renovated warehouse space and discuss ways that City Year and national service could change the world. We talked a lot about Steve Jobs and Apple Computer. This was in the early 1990s, before the iPod, the iPhone, and the iPad. Apple had nowhere near the commercial success it has today; in fact, Jobs had been booted out of Apple by his board of directors, and the company was in trouble. Nonetheless, we loved the Macintosh computer and had used it, literally, to create City Year—from our logo, to every proposal for support, to our database of applicants looking to join the City Year corps. To young social entrepreneurs,[1] the Apple brand and the vision of Steve Jobs to "make a dent in the universe" was immensely appealing.

Apple, as its advertisements trumpeted, thought differently. While our parents worked in offices powered by huge IBM mainframe computers, we were the first generation to create and share ideas on personal computers. Apple stood for creativity and innovation and the little guy. Its design was intuitive, with dropdown menus and point-and-click

visual icons instead of the slashes and dashes of computer code. It married the power of computers with the beauty of design and put control in the hands of average citizens, not experts and specialists. But
while we thought of Apple as inventing personal computing, the truth
is that for most of the 1980s and '90s—as personal computers became
ubiquitous—Apple's market share was generally stuck in the mid to low
single digits. IBM evolved, and it sold more personal computers than
did Apple; so did Hewlett-Packard. And there were Compaq and Dell
and Atari and a whole host of companies—old and new—that for most
of those years held about 95 percent of the personal computer market,
while Apple captured about 5 percent. What Apple and Steve Jobs did
do—and this is what fascinated us at City Year and fascinated me and
my team as we developed Citizen Schools a few years later—is change
the vector of an entire industry. IBM, as iconic a mainstream company
as there has ever been, adapted to the new standard that Apple had set.
Hewlett-Packard adapted too. Microsoft changed its operating system
to become more intuitive and personal, taking a page from Apple's playbook. An entire industry improved, and Apple led the way.

As we looked in 2008 to recalibrate our strategy at Citizen Schools
and to build from the ELT breakthrough at the Edwards, we too
wanted to change the vector of an industry. We wanted to change the
vector of K–12 education, everything from its agrarian-era schedule to
its industrial-era delivery system. When I wrote the Citizen Schools
concept paper in my basement office in the summer of 1994, I sketched
a business plan to create just six programs in Boston, but my hope was
to catalyze a paradigm shift and to mobilize citizen teachers by the
millions—the "sleeping giant of education reform"—and to get school
districts and communities to think differently about the length of the
learning day.

Now in the Edwards ELT model we had a proof point that wasn't
just a cool after-school program for select students but a full-school
turnaround that offered a new vision for how schools could operate in
the twenty-first century. We had an opening to argue for a whole new
day for learning: a day with more time, more caring adults, more support for teachers, and more chances for students to be successful and to

be creators of things, not just consumers. The question facing us was *how* to grow and *how* to change the vector of education. Should *scale* be our focus, with success measured by how quickly we could grow the Citizen Schools footprint? Or should we focus instead on *spread*, helping to create the conditions for our ideas to disseminate by influencing public policy and by sharing best practices at conferences and trainings and through the Internet?

This same conversation about scale and spread was happening at every other entrepreneurial social service organization I knew, and we were all talking with each other. Leaders at City Year and JumpStart, and Year-Up, and Teach For America, and others were wrestling with the same issue of how to grow our ideas, our brands, and, ultimately, our impact. We had all seen technology firms like Google and Amazon go from startup to market dominance within a decade, but our world of direct-service nonprofits with human-powered delivery systems wasn't scaling that fast. Not even close. Barry Harrington, an advisor with the consulting company Bain, had told me that human service businesses like Bain, or like law firms or accounting firms, generally can't maintain growth rates faster than 20 percent per year once they have gone through their initial startup period. While you might exceed 20 percent some years, Harrington said, the human challenges around hiring, training, and integrating talent—all while maintaining or hopefully improving quality—are too great to exceed it consistently.

If Harrington was right—and even 20 percent growth is wildly higher than typical in the nonprofit sector[2]—we had a long way to go before our scale would be significant relative to the challenge we were addressing. In the 2008–9 school year, Citizen Schools was serving twenty-five hundred students. There are about twelve million middle school students in America, about four million of them in schools that are majority low-income, which are our target. At a growth rate of 20 percent per year it would take us a quarter-century to get to a point where we were reaching just 5 percent of the students in our target group. If we wanted to really change the vector of education, wouldn't we need to spread our ideas through policy work and through other organizations, and not just scale them directly as Citizen Schools?

In February of 2005 one hundred leading social entrepreneurs gathered at the Mohonk Mountain House in upstate New York. New Profit Inc., the venture philanthropy group, convened the meeting. Our goal was to think about how our community of social entrepreneurs and a few of our leading champions could collectively do more to address the urgent challenges of the day. I was commissioned to write a paper for the group, which I titled "Realizing the American Dream: Historical Scorecard, Current Challenges, Future Opportunities."[3] In the paper I made the case that after two centuries of steady progress in reducing poverty and increasing opportunity, America—including those of us gathering at Mohonk—had just witnessed the first generation in American history in which opportunity had declined. Poverty had gone up and high school graduation rates went down. Paraphrasing Dr. Martin Luther King, I described our recent pursuit of opportunity in America: "Rather than rolling down like a mighty stream, justice trickled forward."

The solution I urged us all to consider was a three-part strategy for social change: organizational reform, meaning efforts to grow promising organizations like Citizen Schools; political reform, such as efforts to change laws and policies to encourage broader adoption of best practices; and cultural reform, by which I meant initiatives to change beliefs and behavior among citizens, such as the designated-driver campaign in the 1980s that helped to reduce drunk-driving deaths by one-third.

David Gergen, the CNN commentator and senior advisor to four presidents, also spoke to the group at Mohonk. In a memorable after-dinner talk that didn't start until almost midnight, Gergen told us that social entrepreneurs were doing the most exciting work for the country since the civil rights movement. But he warned us that sometimes we looked like the little Dutch boy with his finger in the dike, trying to prop up a crumbling infrastructure rather than leading efforts to replace it with a different and better structure, a systemic change. Gergen urged us to think beyond creating independent charter schools and after-school programs and college-access programs and to work more with government. "You need to transform islands of excellence into systemic reform," he told us.

There were two stories that we discussed that spoke to Gergen's challenge and examined the possibilities of big change through the scale and spread of effective interventions.

The first story is about Head Start. It begins in the small Michigan community of Ypsilanti, where in 1962 a local school administrator named David Weikart created the Perry Preschool Project. Perry enrolled the poorest children in the community and gave them access to caring adults who read to them and provided all kinds of enriching learning experiences to get them ready for first grade. The program was intended to lift student IQ, something thought impossible at the time, and was connected to an ambitious research effort. Directors of the project received 123 applications, and they randomly selected fifty-eight children to be in the treatment group. These children would enroll in the program. The other sixty-five applicants were assigned to the control group, meaning they would not be able to access the program but would agree to share data on their lives with researchers.

The evaluation of Perry Preschool caught the attention of policymakers far and wide. An initial study conducted two years after the program began showed student IQ for participants growing by an average of fifteen points, and other school-readiness measures rising sharply as well. Later studies showed that the IQ gains washed out over time but that other gains were deep and long lasting. Perry Preschool students earned significantly higher grades in school, and 71 percent of them graduated on time from high school, compared to just 54 percent in the control group. As the Perry kids grew up, the benefits of the positive preschool experiences kept compounding. By the time the graduates were twenty-seven years old, they were almost three times as likely to own their own homes as students in the control group and half as likely to receive public assistance.[4]

Among the people captivated by the project and the early research was Edward Zigler, a professor of child psychology at Yale University. President Lyndon Johnson had asked Zigler to develop a strategy for early-childhood education as part of Johnson's War on Poverty. With Perry as an important inspiration, Zigler and his colleagues created Head Start, one of the most ambitious social programs of the last fifty years.

In many ways the Perry Preschool Project and its influence on Head Start is a social entrepreneur's dream. It's what David Gergen was calling for as a better alternative to the little Dutch boy sticking his finger in the dike. A new program in Ypsilanti, Michigan, offered a vision of what was possible and evidence it could work: a proof point. Key opinion leaders learned of it and proposed policy based on its success. The president of the United States and his team supported it enthusiastically. A new law was passed to provide funding and spread the idea. The program then attracted bipartisan support and funding grew, through Democratic and Republican administrations, from a few million dollars in 1965 to $8 billion today. Head Start now serves one million three- and four-year-old children, which is roughly half of all the children living in poverty in that age group in the entire country!

The problem with this seemingly dreamy story is that while many studies of Head Start point to modest benefits of the program, such as slightly better health outcomes for participants and modest academic gains in elementary school, most studies also show that the gains eliminate only a small fraction of the achievement gap and washed out over time. Everyone agrees that great early-childhood programs—programs like Perry and like the Abecedarian Project in North Carolina—make a big and lasting difference for children. But the difference made by average Head Start programs is much more modest, and in the view of skeptics is negligible over time.

The moral of the story is that spreading high-quality programs by government adoption is difficult. One reason is that small proof-point programs tend to be relatively expensive. There are no economies of scale, and the founders are biased toward investing whatever is needed to produce results. But when Congress or school districts look to scale up a demonstration, they face pressure to reduce costs. Scaling to more schools, or more congressional districts, sometimes becomes the most important metric, with program impact taking a back seat. This happened with Head Start, and when the program grew from Ypsilanti to the rest of the country, it got watered down. The original program had a 1:5 teacher-to-student ratio, which is similar to the ratio of preschool programs in upper-income communities. But to get the program to more communities at what was deemed a reasonable cost, Congress funded Head Start at a 1:10 ratio.

More fundamentally, the Head Start case illustrates the challenge of spreading ideas that will be implemented locally by very different organizations. It's important to understand that the federal government doesn't actually run Head Start, just as it doesn't run most social programs. Instead the government holds a competition and makes grants to thousands of local nonprofits that run the programs. Some of those nonprofits—just like some local schools and some local hospitals and some local after-school programs—are really good. They excel at hiring people and occasionally firing people and training and managing people. But other nonprofits that operate Head Start programs are not so effective at hiring and firing and training people, and children who attend those programs lose out. When we try to spread ideas, like those proven so effective in Ypsilanti, Michigan, we need to think not only about the programmatic models we want to replicate, but also about how we can replicate and grow effective *organizations* that will bring the model to life and fulfill its promise. Even a great idea will founder without a strong organization to implement it.

The Head Start story as I've told it feeds distrust in government. When I tell this story to conservative friends, they nod their heads and talk about the challenges of getting entangled with government. But there are promising new efforts to improve Head Start's delivery system and an exciting push across the federal government to establish new criteria in funding competitions to steer more money to organizations with proven and promising track records. And there is another story that needs to be considered: the story of Habitat for Humanity.

Habitat is an amazing organization that serves as the poster child for scale in the nonprofit arena. While particular companies often scale quickly in business, and nine of the thirty largest companies in America, including Apple and Amazon and Google, were started in the last forty years, change in the nonprofit sector is much slower.[5] When I wrote the American Dream paper in 2005, of the thirty largest nonprofit organizations in the United States, only one had been started in the last forty years, and that was Habitat.[6]

Habitat was founded in 1976 by Millard Fuller, a lanky Southern businessman and a member of the Disciples of Christ, a large evangelical church. Habitat has a mission of increasing home ownership among the poor and eliminating substandard housing. Its model is to recruit volunteers to team up with low-income families to build new homes or renovate existing ones that the low-income family can then move into as owners. Habitat's model is a twentieth-century barn raising, and with the help of Fuller's church, it took off. In 1982 former president Jimmy Carter volunteered with Habitat and gave its work credibility and stature, accelerating its growth.

Habitat grew through a franchise model, empowering local leaders to build their own Habitat organizations, but following best practices shared by the national office and benefiting from national marketing efforts and partnerships with major companies, which donated materials and encouraged their employees to get involved. In 2013 the organization built its six hundred thousandth house, and there are now more than three million people around the world living in Habitat homes.[7] All this was accomplished with minimal help from the government (though Habitat is a recipient of AmeriCorps funds and deploys AmeriCorps members to advance its work) and with a maximum of old-fashioned community compassion.

Habitat is a great nonprofit success story and its mission and methods offer valuable lessons for social entrepreneurs. But the problem with the story is that while Habitat was scaling like gangbusters, the percentage of low-income Americans who own their own homes actually went down.[8] Habitat scaled rapidly and cost-effectively, but the policy climate and the business climate changed, and Habitat ended up further from achieving its mission than when it got started.

My point is not to criticize Habitat or Head Start but to acknowledge that really big change—truly systemic change—needs to come both from the scaling of particularly effective organizations *and* from spreading the best ideas through policy and cultural change work.

The election of President Barack Obama in 2008 had all the markings of a sea-change event not just for American politics writ large, but specifically for the nonprofit sector and for the growing community of people within it who identify themselves as social entrepreneurs.

By 2008 social entrepreneurship was a hot topic around the world. Every spring since 2004, thousands of social entrepreneurs and members of their supporting ecosystem have journeyed to Oxford University for the field's top gathering, the Skoll World Forum on Social Entrepreneurship—sponsored by eBay cofounder Jeff Skoll. The forum, which I've attended every year since 2005 when I was awarded a Skoll Award for Social Entrepreneurship, features keynotes by the likes of Bishop Desmond Tutu, Vice President Al Gore, and President Jimmy Carter, as well as by celebrated social entrepreneurs who have used innovative strategies to bring clean water, health care, electrical power, and books to the most remote regions of the world. Social entrepreneurship is hot in the United States too, with social enterprise clubs becoming the most popular and fastest-growing student groups at Harvard and Stanford Business Schools in the early 2000s.

Obama's election held great promise for social entrepreneurs for at least three reasons. First, as the nation's first black president, elected just two generations after the milestone events of the civil rights movement, Obama's election sent a message that big change is possible. If an African American could be elected president, maybe other dreams deferred could come true too. Second, in many ways Obama and his wife, Michelle, were social entrepreneurs themselves. Obama had been, famously, a community organizer on Chicago's South Side trying to establish innovative job training and after-school education programs. Later Obama served on the Chicago advisory board for Public Allies, a pioneering AmeriCorps program, and an innovator in deploying skilled mobilizers into the nonprofit community. Michelle Obama served as Chicago executive director for Public Allies in the early 1990s—the same years I served as Boston executive director for City Year. Finally, the policies Obama spoke about in the campaign were policies that resonated within our community of social entrepreneurs and in some cases policies we had actively promoted during the campaign.[9]

In his first inauguration, speaking at a time of rising economic crisis, Obama called on the country to move beyond a debate over the size of government to a discussion of how government can help us accomplish our public purposes most effectively. "The question we ask today is not whether our government is too big or too small, but whether it works—whether it helps families find jobs at a decent wage, care they can afford, a retirement that is dignified. Where the answer is yes," Obama stated, "we intend to move forward. Where the answer is no, programs will end."[10]

Within one hundred days of taking office, Obama signed the Edward M. Kennedy Serve America Act, which passed the House and Senate with substantial bipartisan majorities. The Serve America bill aimed to triple the size of AmeriCorps to 250,000 members and put a special focus on education, an emphasis inspired in part by the teaching fellows bill Kennedy had sponsored and announced at the Edwards School almost two years earlier. The Serve America Act also created a new Social Innovation Fund in which the federal government would partner with private philanthropy to scale up proven and promising solutions and programs. When the White House put out its press release explaining the initiative, Citizen Schools was one of four examples given of the types of organizations the program was designed to expand.

The Obama administration also teamed up with private funders to initiate a series of competitions to crowdsource creative solutions to persistent public problems. The Department of Energy, for instance, offered prize money to anyone who could make solar energy cheaper than coal, and the EPA offered funds to groups that could develop technologies to clean up oil spills faster and more completely. Both efforts stimulated new technologies that dramatically improved on the status quo and generated additional billions in private research and development spending.[11] Robert Gordon, a friend to many in the social enterprise world, was named associate director of the Office of Management and Budget and pushed efforts to "fund what works," trying to put more federal money behind programs and organizations with the strongest record of impact.

Of all Obama's new approaches to activist and results-focused government, the boldest and most controversial was his Race to the Top initiative and a companion measure, the Investing in Innovation (i3) program, run by the Department of Education.

Race to the Top was a $4.35 billion initiative funded by the 2009 emergency stimulus bill that allowed Obama and his secretary of education, Arne Duncan, to drive systemic change in education.[12] Federal funds account for only about 10 percent of all that's spent on public schools (with the rest coming from state and local sources), and most of the federal funds are allocated to states and districts by formula to support low-income students, teacher training, education for disabled students, and a few other specific programs. Historically, federal money added to the school-funding pot but didn't do much to stir it. With Race to the Top, that was about to change. Using the $4.35 billion in stimulus money as leverage, Duncan told states and districts they could win a share of the money if they developed a bold vision to improve student learning, including adopting policies the administration favored, such as allowing more charter schools and evaluating teachers based at least in part on student test scores.

I don't agree with all of the policy priorities Race to the Top emphasized (for example, "merit pay" for individual teachers based primarily on test scores seems like a bad idea, and certainly an unproven one), but as a strategy for driving change at the local level, Race to the Top was unbelievably successful. To date, through three rounds of Race to the Top competitions, nineteen states and sixteen school districts have won more than $4.5 billion in awards.[13] Even many states and districts that did not win the contest for federal funds made major changes in their policies, such as allowing more charter schools and adopting more rigorous teacher-evaluation systems.

Citizen Schools benefited from Race to the Top in a few states. For instance, North Carolina made a particular push in its successful application to improve science, technology, engineering, and math (STEM) education, and some of these funds ended up supporting our work in Durham. And Massachusetts created a "preferred partner program" as a centerpiece of its winning application and then used the money to support a small set of organizations, including Citizen Schools, with strong track records of lifting student achievement.

But for Citizen Schools, as with most nonprofits, Race to the Top was small money. The big opportunity for us was the i3 competition, which was designed to help school districts and outside partners scale promising and proven programs. Throughout 2009 and early 2010 we waited impatiently as finishing touches were put on the competition design.

The basic idea for i3 was to create a tiered funding opportunity where the more evidence of impact you had, the more funding you could qualify to win. There were several categories within the competition, with one focused on teacher training and preparation, for instance, and another focused on turnaround of the lowest-performing schools. Applicants with the strongest evidence of success, usually multiple rigorous external evaluations, could apply for up to $50 million. Initiatives with shorter track records but still a strong evidence base could apply for up to $30 million, and more experimental efforts but with promising strategies and a commitment to track outcomes could qualify for up to $5 million. The whole initiative was funded with $650 million in stimulus money and an expectation that only fifty or fewer grants would be made across the entire country.[14] In addition to scaling aggressively during the initial five-year grant period, applicants were required to sketch plans to eventually spread their innovations to hundreds of thousands or even millions of students.

Citizen Schools decided to apply for $25 million to scale the ELT school-turnaround work we had begun at the Edwards to twenty-five schools across ten school districts. For three months this became a principal focus for me and several other senior staff. We forged partnerships with ten school districts, from New York to Oakland, and from rural Henderson, North Carolina, to the Apache community of Mescalero, New Mexico. We convinced Bain to commit $3.5 million of in-kind consulting support to help craft our strategy. WGBH, which in partnership with PBS runs an educational website that reaches 77 percent of all the schools in America, agreed to build a curriculum and training repository that could help us share best practices across schools and to spread the ELT idea broadly after the initial direct replication. The competition provided us with a unique opportunity to push the scale and spread of our idea, and provided me with a powerful lever to drive change within Citizen Schools. With the Edwards we had piloted ELT. Now we would bet the farm on it. While we would still run some optional after-school programs, our entire focus and all new programs would now be ELT. Adopting this strategy would mean that again we'd need to raise our game in order to be an effective partner to school districts in helping turn around some of their lowest-performing schools.

I knew we were competing with the nation's top school districts, school-reform nonprofits, and research universities, and I also knew that only a few of many excellent applicants would win. Despite all those caveats, my competitive juices were flowing and I had high hopes we would be selected.

It turned out that the 13 winners were revealed prematurely in an e-mail unintentionally released by the Department of Education on August 4, 2010. I was at a Red Sox game that night, enjoying an evening out in the Bank of America skybox with Kerry Sullivan, the head of the Bank of America Charitable Foundation, and Lynn Wiatrowski, a bank executive we were recruiting to the Citizen Schools board. There were a few other nonprofit leaders there as well, including Michael Brown, now the CEO of City Year. Near the end of the game, people started to buzz about the i3 news. Michael stepped outside to call his team. I checked my e-mail and saw that the list of i3 winners had been sent. There were sixteen winners at our level of funding, but Citizen Schools was nowhere on the list. Teach For America and KIPP (Knowledge Is Power Program) had won the big $50 million awards. And City Year, which had teamed up with Johns Hopkins and Communities in Schools on a $30 million school-turnaround proposal, had been selected for funding. We had scored in the top 4 percent of all proposals submitted but not quite high enough to win.

I was devastated and deflated. The baseball game was not close and the group was starting to break up, so I excused myself and headed outside into the August night. I began to walk home, about a half-hour journey and one I completed with as deep a feeling of melancholy as I had experienced in a long time.

When I got home I e-mailed our staff and partners, putting the most positive spin I could on the announcement. "Although the news is disappointing," I wrote, "I am extremely proud of the Citizen Schools staff and partners today and know that we have a lot to be excited about moving forward. The i3 fund was intended to spark innovation and partnership not only among those who receive funding, but among all working in education. For Citizen Schools, it did just that. Together, in partnership with fifteen partners, we've developed a tremendous plan for helping schools innovate and expand the learning day for students." I went on to share that missing out on the grant would not change our budget for the upcoming year (we had hoped for the money but not counted on it) and recounted the ways in which the application process had sharpened our thinking and our strategy and built our partnerships with districts and others.

The next day I went into the office early and looked up our scores, which were posted online. Ratings on the strength of our evidence of impact had been perfect—15 out of 15 from both the evaluation experts brought in to assess that part of the application. Of the three judges who had rated our application for clarity of vision, power of design, and strength of implementation and sustainability, two judges had given us almost perfect scores and the third had given us solid scores but ones just low enough to pull us below the top tier. I joked about "the Russian judge" and tried to rally the troops around a vision of still implementing our i3 plan, but without the money from the Department of Education.

As I write this, it is now almost three years from that frustrating night at Fenway Park. In fact we did move forward with the i3 plan, even without the $25 million. We have grown from just two ELT schools when we wrote our i3 application in the spring of 2010 to twenty-four schools for the 2013–14 school year, with plans to reach twenty-six to twenty-eight in 2014–15. We are on target with the growth schedule we proposed in i3. In our proposal we asked school districts to provide $600 per student, with the rest of our costs coming from the i3 grant and private support. Now districts are providing an average of $1,200 per student, drawing from a variety of funding sources, including school-turnaround dollars, Title I funds, and, in Boston's case, a smaller i3 award that the district won in 2011 to replicate the Edwards ELT model. In 2012 Citizen Schools won a smaller i3 grant to scale our apprenticeships in STEM education, and private funders have done more too. Even though we didn't initially win, the i3 competition, while bruising, did catapult us forward.

Legendary business consultant Peter Drucker described entrepreneurship as the rearranging of existing resources to higher and better uses. Since that first journalism class in 1994, I had hoped that Citizen Schools could make even a small contribution to rearranging how American schools and communities use the resource of time by putting afternoons and summers to better use, and I hoped we could help rearrange the use of our public school buildings, activating these public spaces—an estimated $2 trillion resource—to engage children beyond the regular school day. But the really big resource we have always hoped to rearrange is the talent and time of average citizens. If we can get architects and engineers and lawyers to carve out a few hours a week in which they get out from behind their desks and into American schools—and also offer more Americans the chance to devote a year or two as full-time AmeriCorps members at the start or end of their careers—we will move America forward and restore public schools to their historic role as engines of opportunity.

The next section of the book further explores five drivers of the growing opportunity divide that separates wealthier and poorer children. As mentioned in the introduction, too much of our national dialogue about education is focused on two convenient bogeymen: poverty (even though there are plentiful examples of poor students learning and achieving at high levels when given high expectations and support) and teachers and teacher unions (even though only 20 percent to 30 percent of the rich-poor achievement gap is explained by differences in school quality).

In my view, we can give low-income children a fair chance of competing with upper-income children (from around the world as well as

across town), but to do so we need to focus on the following five building blocks of childhood success:

1. More mentorship by caring and professionally successful adults
2. A longer learning day, allowing more time to master the aca-
    demic basics and chances to participate in sports, art, and music
    as part of a well-rounded education
3. More chances to practice creativity and innovation—critical
    skills in the modern economy
4. More chances to build the social networks and social skills that
    help drive professional and life success
5. Better support of full-time teachers and parents, the primary
    caregivers for lower- and moderate-income children.

The five chapters of section 2 each explore one of these success drivers in depth, sharing surprising research as well as illustrative stories
from Citizen Schools and other programs.

HOW CITIZEN POWER AND AN EXPANDED LEARNING DAY CAN NARROW ACHIEVEMENT GAPS, BROADEN OPPORTUNITY, AND STRENGTHEN AMERICA

JOYCE KING THOMAS, VOLUNTEER

The secret sauce of Citizen Schools is the volunteer—the caring and talented adults, from all walks of life, who teach apprenticeships that our middle school students choose. Volunteer citizen teachers are part of a proud American tradition of citizen power that has strengthened the country since its founding, and that will be discussed in this section of the book. Here is the story of one of our volunteers, Joyce King Thomas, in her words.

I never learned how to say no to my oldest son. He always won our biggest debates.

At eleven, he came out on top in our knock-down, drag-out fight over listening to R-rated rap lyrics. (He needed to experience the Beastie Boys uncensored; it was part of a Brooklyn boyhood, he effectively argued.) He used his relentless charm to persuade us to make room for a parakeet, a second parakeet, a turtle, three lizards, a two-foot-long live-cricket-eating Komodo dragon, and, finally, a dog.

Lest I sound like a wimp and Aidan sound like a monster, you should know that I was the chief creative officer of a huge New York ad agency, and my son is a Colgate University graduate aiming for a master's in education at the Bank Street school.

Years of honing his skills at getting me to do things I had no intention of doing culminated when Aidan asked me if my company and I would volunteer for Citizen Schools, the organization he worked for. No, I didn't stand a chance.

The mission of Citizen Schools is to provide middle school kids in disadvantaged areas with an educational after-school experience. What makes the program unique is its twelve-week "apprenticeships." Citizen Schools recruits companies like Google, the Food Network, and AOL to teach apprenticeships that give the kids hands-on experience in fields they might not otherwise be exposed to. Each apprenticeship culminates in something called a WOW!, where the kids literally wow their parents, teachers, and friends with what they've accomplished in those twelve weeks. While all the school reformers are debating what should happen in the six or seven hours kids are in school, Citizen Schools is busy filling up those three lonely after-school hours; the hours kids fill with either random TV watching or potentially dangerous hanging out.

As I mentioned, when Aidan made his pitch, I was the creative director of a gargantuan New York ad agency. We were in the middle of one of the most challenging economies in history. Clients' businesses were hurting, which meant we were hurting. Teaching a two-hour class in Harlem every Wednesday for twelve weeks, and investing hours in prepping for those classes, wasn't really a smart career move. But it turned out to be one of the smartest life moves I ever made.

For our apprenticeship, my team of volunteers divided the class into three "mini agencies," gave them an assignment, and let them develop a strategy, brainstorm ideas, present their ideas, and, finally, film and edit a real commercial.

■　■　■

We even recruited the Ad Council, which creates advertising for important national issues—like Smokey Bear's "Only YOU can prevent

*forest fires"—to join us. The kids would present their ideas to the Ad
Council, who would pick the ones to film.*

*So what could the kids make ads about? In the past, the Ad Council
and our agency had created communications to help fight childhood
obesity. Who better to create ads to convince young people to eat healthier and exercise more than a bunch of middle schoolers?*

Our homework was done. And we were off.

*Day one we showed up at Isaac Newton Middle School on 116th
Street in Manhattan, a big, classic old school with wide hallways.*

*I'd passed it a million times driving down the FDR, but never
imagined I'd be teaching there with the most impressive team I could
draft from our agency: Vann, an African American creative director
who won a Purple Heart in Iraq; Craig, a dad/creative director with
a real knack for working with kids; Sallie, our indefatigable head of
creative human resources; an energetic admin named Kim, who kept
us focused and made sure we had it together each week; and me. Over
the course of the program, we also wrangled a young editor, two junior
producers, and an assortment of other agency personnel to join our
naively overambitious mission of producing three commercials. It took
a village. And then some.*

■ ■ ■

*The first class wasn't easy. Okay, none of the classes were easy. But
armed with techniques we learned in the Citizen Schools training program (like, "If you hear my voice, clap your hands twice") we muddled
through. The kids loved looking at commercials and explaining what
the strategy of each piece of communication was. Aidan worked with us
to create the right bite-size curriculum and helped us control the class,
since we were middle school neophytes.*

*The kids were so quick and bright that the team leaders fell in love.
My team included Hakeem, a brilliant kid with a truancy problem
that had him skipping school thirty-five days one semester. The amazing thing was he didn't skip one single day of the apprenticeship. I was
also lucky enough to work with Aaron, a mosquito of a kid who buzzed*

around keeping everyone laughing; Miguel, a charming boy whose quiet demeanor belied his quick mind; Dontea, a bright girl who seemed to have some serious personal issues; Aaron, a born actor and close friend of Hakeem's; and Michael, a talented artist who needed a lot of reassurance about how good he was.

The kids brainstormed ideas to convince their peers to eat healthier and exercise more. Then, they came up with a winner: a talking apple that would literally hit someone over the head with the point that they needed to eat more fruit. We scouted for locations within walking distance and picked a spot just east of the FDR Drive. The kids made most of the decisions, from shooting to editing.

A hundred or so people attended the WOW!, where we screened the behind-the-scenes film and the three commercials (available on YouTube: see ADLab Citizen Schools), including the school's principal and assistant principal, parents, Citizen Schools staff, and an assorted group from the agency. I stood in front and watched the crowd watch the kids present their work. It was a beautiful sight.

Around that time, I decided it was time for me to leave my company and explore some other possibilities, including helping in the education arena. I'm working with Citizen Schools to encourage other agencies to step up and teach. Sixth and seventh graders can learn so much from the process of creating communications. They learn it's possible to have a good career being creative. They learn that creating requires order and discipline. They learn that they can do it.

And I learned how important it is to listen to your children.

CHAPTER EIGHT

CITIZEN POWER AND THE IMPORTANCE OF MENTORING

While countless education reformers have suggested we improve schools by recruiting and training more effective teachers, developing better tests, and adopting stronger curricula—all within the confines of a traditional six- to seven-hour school day—what if the holy grail of educational advancement lies outside this box? What if closing opportunity and achievement gaps requires an entirely new approach to our schools, including their hours of operation, the ways they define success, and the talent pool they draw upon in pursuing their goals? I think it does.

Better full-time teachers and better tests and better curriculum are all important things, and we should pursue them actively. But providing equal educational opportunity to all children will require us to address the root causes of our growing educational inequality: unequal access to extra learning time to master the academic basics, unequal access to enrichment and opportunities to practice innovation and problem solving, unequal access to social networks, and unequal access to well-supported parents and teachers. The only realistic way to equalize access to these essential assets is to mobilize America's greatest resource: citizen power.

Citizen power lies at the heart of the American experience. From the citizen soldiers who fought for independence to the citizen activists who fought for civil rights, America has met its biggest challenges when its citizens have gotten directly involved. Citizen power built the settlement houses of the early twentieth century that welcomed and trained new immigrants and helped make America the world's first majority-middle-class nation. And citizen power drove the civil rights movement, which, while incomplete, has in the last two generations increased African American college completion from just over 1 percent to 20 percent and reduced poverty among African Americans from 55 percent to 27 percent.[1]

The distinctively American impulse to join together with neighbors and make things better is what French aristocrat Alexis de Tocqueville chronicled in his 1835 classic, *Democracy in America*. Tocqueville noted that unlike citizens in his native France or other European democracies, when Americans faced challenges they banded together in associations of mutual self-help. He wrote of Americans on the frontier and in larger cities coming together to create libraries to share knowledge, firehouses to promote safety, granges to promote farming, Sunday schools to teach religion and reading, and social clubs to promote quality of life. Tocqueville called Americans a "nation of joiners" and, without using the term, described social capital as a unique facet of American life. Tocqueville has been in the news recently as evidence mounts that social capital in America is now in decline (see chapter 11).

You may think of citizen power as political, concerning sit-ins, marches in major cities, and calls to Congress. Citizen power does include these things. But citizen power can also be exerted through direct action. It's the families along the Underground Railroad who sheltered fugitive slaves seeking freedom in the North. It's progressives like Jane Addams starting Hull House in Chicago and hundreds of her peers devoting a few hours each week to tutor new immigrants there. And citizen power is college volunteers on their summer vacations heading to Mississippi to teach former sharecroppers to read and register them to vote. On the American frontier in the early nineteenth century, before public schools were established, citizen power was the volunteer Sunday school teacher who taught children to read so they could study the Bible and also conduct basic commerce and follow the events of the day. Citizen power has always been able to get big things done in America. Amazing as it may seem today, it is likely true that for three generations after the formation of a government by the newly independent United States, more Americans were taught to read by volunteers, usually in Sunday school, than by paid public school teachers.[2]

Citizen power is not naive optimism. It works, and it *is* working in communities across America. Citizen power today looks like the National Academies Foundation (NAF) high school initiative, which uses corporate volunteers from more than twenty-five hundred companies as the backbone of a model that serves more than sixty thousand students across thirty-nine states. Business experts from the industries of finance, hospitality and tourism, information technology, and health sciences volunteer in NAF classrooms and engage NAF students through paid internships at their companies. Most NAF students are low-income, but they graduate high school on time at higher rates than middle-class kids. And according to a rigorous external evaluation, 52 percent of NAF graduates earn a bachelor's degree in four years,[3] compared to 32 percent of all students nationally and just 8 percent of low-income students.

Citizen power helps fuel the Met School of Providence, Rhode Island, and High Tech High of San Diego, networks of schools whose students are asked to identify their passions and then meld them into internships and substantive projects that serve real-world purposes. The schools rely heavily on community participation by volunteers for the rich, real-world learning opportunities their students enjoy. One of the core design principles of High Tech High is "Adult World Connections," and all students complete substantial internships where they have the opportunity to learn from and work with real-world experts. Students create projects for an authentic audience and have the opportunity to present their work in a professional setting. The assumptions behind High Tech High and the Met's school-to-work strategies mirror those behind Citizen Schools' WOW! events. Long-term student interest can be driven by providing students the opportunity to be successful with successful adults. Both schools deliver strong results with high graduation rates and more than 90 percent of the primarily low-income students going on to college.[4]

Citizen power can also look like FIRST, prolific inventor Dean Kamen's effort to mobilize engineers to work with high school students to build robots and then enter them in regional contests that have the feel of March Madness basketball games, complete with well-coached teams and screaming fans. Or like iMentor, which connects college-educated mentors with thousands of high school students through virtual and in-person mentoring, increasing graduation rates by 18 percentage points. Or like City Year, which places near-peer mentors into Elementary and High School classrooms in twenty-four cities across the country and has set as its goal reducing by half the number of students who are off-track to graduate high school on time in each of the cities where they operate.[5] Citizen power can also shine further from the schoolhouse doors, such as in Girl Scouts, which increasingly offers badges in robotics and science in addition to babysitting and quilting, and in 4H, which reaches six million students and deploys 540,000 volunteers annually, with a majority serving in urban areas like Los Angeles, Washington, DC, and Atlanta.

Like Citizen Schools, many of these citizen-power solutions are delivering compelling results, often in partnership with local schools. Our collective success does not absolve government of the responsibility to adequately fund and support a high-quality education for all children—an investment that will pay dividends to our society for generations to come. But Citizen Schools and others are showing that any successful effort to improve education in America at scale will have to include a broad effort to get citizens off the sidelines and into the action as coaches, tutors, mentors, and teachers.

I have seen again and again how real-world experiences and exposure to role models with real careers can be transformative for young students. I remember a Boston seventh grader named Lin-Ann, who loved the idea of being a doctor based on what she had seen on her favorite TV shows. In Citizen Schools she enrolled in a Cure Cancer apprenticeship, working with a researcher from a local cancer hospital and studying the behavior of cells when observed under a microscope. As part of the apprenticeship, Lin-Ann and her peers received white lab coats, and on school days when she had her apprenticeship, Lin-Ann would wear her lab coat all day long, from six thirty in the morning, as she prepared to board the bus to school, to five thirty at night as she headed home from her apprenticeship. She was proud, and her very identity changed, from drifting middle school student to future medical professional.

Another young student in Citizen Schools, Stephanie, took a different medically oriented course, Drugs on the Brain, which was led by Harvard University postdoctoral fellow Marcus DeLatte. Stephanie said that she was excited to be in the Drugs on the Brain class, because she was definitely planning to become a doctor. One day when Stephanie reiterated her interest in the medical profession, Marcus asked her to bring in her report card so they could discuss it and help plan her pathway to medical school. The next week Stephanie brought in her most recent report card—a mix of Bs and Cs, with one D, in math. Marcus shared some feedback. "Stephanie, I know you want to be a doctor, and I can see in our class that you have a good mind, and when you work hard you do excellent work. I know you *can* become a doctor. But you need to know that you won't be able to become a doctor if you don't bring your grades up, particularly in math and science, to at least a solid B and eventually to an A." It was an essential message, but no one had ever delivered it to Stephanie before she heard it from Marcus, who had navigated his own way from inner-city New Orleans to Harvard Medical School.

A third student—also enrolled in Marcus's Drugs on the Brain class—was Jonathan, a special-education student who was struggling in middle school. As an African American boy who was assigned to separate special-ed classes (often offered in the school's dingiest basement classrooms), Jonathan's chance of finishing high school was about 40 percent, and his chances of completing any kind of a college degree was in the low single digits. But while Jonathan's low test scores and grades and his special-education status would jump off the page to any future teacher who read his transcript, what would not be seen was his love of animals. If you spoke with Jonathan, however, you quickly learned of his passion for animals of all types. He sometimes fed stray cats and often asked after the dogs and hamsters and other pets of his friends and relatives. Once when a bat flew into the brick wall of his mother's apartment and collapsed on the ground below, Jonathan nursed it back to health in a little shoebox he hid under his bed without his mother ever knowing. Jonathan loved animals. But he knew nothing about careers in veterinary medicine. He had never made the connection between animals and biology or math. Jonathan started to make those connections through his apprenticeships at Citizen Schools and the opportunity to spend time with successful professionals like Marcus DeLatte. He had the chance to hold a human brain in his hands, to handle a boa constrictor, and to examine slices of sheep brain tissue under a microscope, recording what happens when a few droplets of alcohol are added. The experiences were transformative. When I last checked, Jonathan was a senior at a top high school in Boston, a mainstream education student getting Bs in math and science. He was hoping to go to college to study marine biology or veterinary medicine.

Lin-Ann, Stephanie, and Jonathan all benefited deeply from citizen power—from active mentoring by volunteers who offered new perspectives and opened doors to new professions. Their mentors helped these young students see the connection between school and exciting future possibilities—a link that is fundamental to successful education but often overlooked by traditional educators. For some children it is easy to imagine the pot of gold at the end of the educational rainbow—the job as a doctor or lawyer or engineer—and the path they need to travel to reach it. They see the pot of gold around them every day in the form of parents with good jobs and good incomes, nice houses and nice cars. Lower-income children, however, are less likely to believe that hard work today will yield tangible rewards in the future. Real-world mentors help make the pot of gold real—and they help their apprentices understand the path to get there.

Citizen power comprises more than just current professionals. Lester Strong and his team at Experience Corps have capitalized on a growing and undertapped citizen-power resource: older Americans.

Experience Corps and similar programs like ReServe and the Retired and Senior Volunteer Program engage older adults who have retired from their "main jobs" but who are eager to find part-time or even full-time "encore" careers. Strong himself is serving in an encore career, having worked previously as a television reporter and news anchor in Boston. Joining forces with AARP, Experience Corps puts thousands of senior citizens to work as volunteers in public schools across the country. The volunteer mentors meet with children in small groups, providing individualized instruction during regular class time. Currently in nineteen cities and reaching twenty thousand students, Experience Corps is now in the process of scaling up and expanding its reach by adding more than ten thousand volunteers to their corps in hopes of serving one hundred thousand students per year by 2017.

For Strong, mentoring is personal. He grew up in South Carolina in the crucible of the civil rights years, and he tells a story now of how mentoring saved his life.

> I got interested in mentoring because three amazing people mentored me. When I was in third grade, my teacher told my parents that basically I was unteachable, her term was "mentally retarded," and told my parents that they really shouldn't have high expectations for me academically. But fortunately for me there were three people in my community that didn't believe in that and in fact really mentored me. They were a barber, a minister, and a mother of a friend of mine. And they mentored me literally from third grade through high school. And as a result of their amazing care and attention, I graduated with honors, hundreds of scholarships, got an undergraduate degree from Davidson, went to Columbia Business School, had a wonderful career, and now I work for one of the most recognized and respected nonprofits in the country. All because those three individuals really saw something in me and believed in me. The interesting question for me is what is it that they saw? What is it that they saw that my teacher and in fact even my parents couldn't see? I think it's because they were looking through the lens of love. And for me love has three central qualities. Number one, that you want the

best for a person, place, thing, or idea. Second, is that you're willing to make a sacrifice in order to achieve that best. And third, you're not asking for anything in return. There's no condition attached to it. And that certainly was the reflection back to me of these three individuals. They just totally cared about my success, and my future and my opportunity to grow.[6]

Experience Corps has advanced achievement at the schools with which it partners. Focused on improving the five components of reading, a rigorous external research study found that students with Experience Corps mentors made 60 percent more progress in critical reading skills than control group students who did not have mentors.[7] In addition, teachers report improvements in the learning environment and overall school culture, as well as reduction in behavior problems, in schools with Experience Corps members.

CEO Strong describes his volunteers as coming from a "place of passion and wanting to leave something that is of value and is sustainable. By changing the life of one child they are influencing something that ripples out through multiple generations."[8]

While Experience Corps members are seeing real and measurable results in their schools, they are also serving themselves in the process. Senior citizens who volunteer with Experience Corps report feeling better about themselves, expanding their circle of friends, becoming more physically active, and seeing improvements in their health, strength, and cognitive abilities. Members tell Strong that the reason they get out of bed in the morning is because they "know they are going to make a difference in the life of a child that day."[9]

At Citizen Schools we've also seen this deep impact on the volunteer citizen teachers with whom we work. It's no longer surprising to hear volunteers say: "I got much more out of this than the kids did." But when I ask the volunteers what they gained, I realize that their statement is heartfelt and what they "got" is important. Sometimes volunteers gain hope that inner-city kids are not a lost cause, or they gain pride that they are engaged in helping their community address the civil rights issue of our time, or they gain networks when they team up with colleagues and other citizens from the community. Often they gain a deeper understanding of themselves, a renewed appreciation of their profession, or a rediscovery of a forgotten passion.

Britton Picciolini, an advertising sales leader for Google in Chicago for eleven years and now a volunteer citizen teacher, taught photography, which had been her college major. She realized she was happier when she introduced what she called "a philanthropic angle" into her life. Rachel Schachter, who taught music in an inner-city Newark school, said it felt great to remind herself how much she loved music as a kid. "Teaching [at Citizen Schools] has also let me remember how much I wanted to grow up to be a musician when I was younger, and let me realize how proud the person I was in middle school would be of the person I am now," said Schachter. "Whether I continue to teach or take my career path in a whole different direction, I will always have singing and songwriting in my life, and I am incredibly glad that this apprenticeship has reminded me how important it is to me."[10]

An early Citizen Schools board member, Karen Webb Campbell, told me that she became a better mother after volunteering to teach a business class in which a team of middle school students designed and sold T-shirts. Campbell said that as she got better at setting clear expectations for a team of teenagers she had never previously met, she also got better at setting expectations for her own children. Other volunteers who have team-taught with their college-age children described it as a "do-over" opportunity in their own parenting and a welcome chance for bonding.

Bob Mersereau, a retired scientist, has taught twenty courses, more than any other Citizen Schools volunteer. Some semesters he traveled between campuses in three different cities each week to offer classes in astronomy. He even continued teaching through a recent bout with cancer. In the past couple of years he has teamed up with his son Bobby, a chef, to teach pizza science. The students make pizza from scratch and learn the scientific principles involved in making pizza taste great.

"Years ago I would have classified myself as not very emotional—taking a psychology test, I scored low in the 'needs affection' category,"

Mersereau wrote recently to a Citizen Schools volunteer coordinator. "My wife calls me insensitive. But Citizen Schools has become a very emotional experience for me. Being a part of such a philosophically solid enterprise has been fulfilling to say the least. Hauling my teaching materials into the Garfield [a school in Revere, Massachusetts] and New Bedford while undergoing radiation and afflicted with double pneumonia was simply a test of how important this new 'occupation' has become for me. Not only is this 'keeping me alive' it is a real source of personal value. I am not sure if there is any other reason to get up each morning other than the sense of being of value and Citizen Schools affords that opportunity to every one of us.

"This idea you had of pairing me up with my son Bobby is more of the same," continued Mersereau. "I am so proud of him for 'following in my footsteps'—he has expressed himself in those terms—not easy for a father and son to talk like that."

Citizen Schools and other citizen-power programs also deliver value to early-stage professionals. Supervisors at some of America's leading companies—places like Google, Fidelity, Cisco, and Cognizant—report that employees who volunteer at Citizen Schools improve their skills at leading teams, at communicating expectations, and at planning multidimensional projects. A whiz-kid engineer like Alan Su (introduced in chapter 6) learns how to be a more effective manager when he leads fifteen kids of diverse academic abilities to create educational video games over ten ninety-minute sessions. Cognizant, a technology firm with a large foreign-born workforce, noted an additional benefit. Teaching an apprenticeship, says Mark Greenlaw, the firm's former vice president for Sustainability and Educational Affairs, helps Cognizant employees gain confidence in their English skills even as they help transmit confidence in technology to the middle school students they teach.

Recently, Citizen Schools commissioned University of Vermont Business School professor David Jones to examine in a methodologically rigorous way the potential impact that volunteering has on citizen teachers and their companies. Jones studied more than one hundred volunteers across four companies and a control group of similar employees who did not volunteer. He concluded that volunteering at

Citizen Schools delivered significant gains in employee satisfaction and loyalty to the volunteers' companies and gains in specific job skills, including communication, leading and motivating others, and providing performance feedback.[11]

The fact that well-designed mentoring and teaching experiences can benefit adult volunteers is exciting. But the reason I am so excited about citizen power is that it represents the key to lifting up opportunity and achievement for more children.

Human beings learn best through relationships and experiences. Some children get a wealth of rich, catalyzing experiences courtesy of their parents and in their schools and neighborhoods. Other children get little access to these experiences and are poorer for it, and they stay poorer because of this disparity. The good news is that successful professionals and successful retirees and successful graduate students—all potential mentors—are not a scarce or limited resource. We spend trillions searching for scarce natural resources like oil. We'll need to spend far less to mobilize citizen power—a plentiful and renewable resource that has the power to advance opportunity for all, strengthen our workforce, and restore the American Dream.

CHAPTER NINE

IT'S ABOUT TIME

When Citizen Schools opened in North Carolina, I had a chance to meet former governor Jim Hunt. I knew that Hunt was a skilled political leader who had led the Democratic National Committee in the 1990s. And I knew that he was a leader among a cohort of southern governors trying to lift expectations and funding for schools to build a more educated workforce and thereby help compete for good jobs. Hunt recognized that plentiful mill jobs were gone for good and that the economic future of his state lay in the big-city banks of Charlotte and the emerging biotech and computer technology companies of the Research Triangle. I did not know that for both his terms as governor, Hunt insisted on devoting a portion of every Thursday to tutoring a student after school at a struggling Raleigh public school.

"I remember one boy I worked with," Hunt told me. "And he said, 'Governor, I'm not stupid. I can do the work. But I just need a little more time to understand it.'" Governor Hunt is a big believer in extended-day learning, because he knows that kids learn at different paces and in different ways and that for many kids, all they need is a little more time.

Hunt recognized that the great inequity in our education system has less to do with differences in teacher quality between the suburbs and inner-city neighborhoods of Charlotte and Raleigh and more to do with the different amount of time devoted to extra learning opportunities. Sure there are some differences in teacher quality. Better teachers often stay longer in wealthier districts, which offer better working conditions, though not better pay. We urgently need to address these differences. But differences in teacher quality are more pronounced within schools than between schools, and, as described in the introduction, school quality only explains 20 to 30 percent of the rich–poor achievement gap.[1] Hunt wondered why we maintain an education system where time for learning in school is fixed and achievement is wildly variable, instead of a system of consistently high achievement where time for learning is variable.

When my own children were entering fourth and first grades, my wife and I decided to move from Boston to neighboring Brookline and enroll our kids in the William H. Lincoln School, a great K–8 public school. The house we bought was more expensive than the one we sold, just a ten-minute walk away, in Boston's Jamaica Plain neighborhood. But more than a house, what we bought was access to a school and neighborhood that is economically diverse but weighted toward professionals, including architects, academics, doctors, lawyers, and business leaders. I see every day how upper-middle-class communities like mine powerfully organize afternoons, weekends, and summers full of formal and informal learning that propel our children past those living on the proverbial "other side of the tracks." Brookline doesn't have a longer school day than Boston. But when you add up formal and informal learning, most kids in Brookline have a learning day that's almost twice as long.

Children have fundamentally unequal access to learning time, just as they have unequal access to successful mentors, two things we must change if we are to narrow our nation's huge and growing achievement gap.

As I write this, I am missing my daughter, Orla. She is eleven now, prime Citizen Schools age, and in the middle of an eighteen-day singing tour in Argentina, where she is performing seventeen concerts, riding horses, sightseeing in thirteen cities, and having the experience of a lifetime courtesy of Boston City Singers, a youth choir she joined last year. My son, Ronan, sixteen, had his own adventures this summer. In the past eight weeks he traveled with his AAU (Amateur Athletic Union) basketball team to Philadelphia, Portland, Hartford, and Orlando, where he played at the ESPN Center at Disney World, notching twenty-six points in one game. He also attended specialized basketball camps at Harvard and Yale, receiving high-level instruction and getting exposure to campus life in the Ivy League.

When Orla and Ronan were younger, we invested in academic tutors on a few occasions, not because our kids were behind, but to prevent them from getting behind. In Ronan's case the tutor was Catholic and wore a necklace with a large cross. She told us one day that Ronan said he appreciated her wearing the large *T* around her neck. "If you could just start wearing the other letters, then reading would be a lot easier," Ronan told her. We all had a good laugh, and as parents we felt good that we had a concerned and sympathetic ally helping us raise and educate our son. When Ronan was in third grade we conducted some testing and found that he was struggling with sensory integration. We signed him up for sessions at a state-of-the-art center that effectively addressed the issue. Like most upper-income parents, we organize our lives—and never-ending car pools—to put opportunity in front of our children. We write checks left and right to underwrite these opportunities.

The voracious appetite for supplemental learning in wealthier suburbs has spawned a fast-growing cottage industry of tutors, enrichment programs, and specialized camps. Just in our immediate circle in Brookline, children enroll in fee-based programs that offer piano, pottery, theater, choir, dance, voice lessons, guitar, robotics, architecture, video game design, filmmaking, ballet, gymnastics, Hebrew school, Suzuki violin, Russian math, Chinese language, cooking, capoeira, sailing, rowing, rock climbing, martial arts, Girl Scouts, Boy Scouts, Junior Achievement, all manner of team sports, and hip-hop dance. Collectively, our friends employ dozens of tutors, coaches, and counselors.

Demand for extra learning is so strong in communities like Brookline that some education companies have gone beyond cottage-industry status to become big business. For instance, Kumon, a popular tutoring service in math and reading, is now the twenty-second-fastest-growing franchise business in the world, right up there with the fast-food burger chains. Kumon started in Osaka, Japan, in 1954. Toru Kumon, a high school calculus teacher, was tutoring Takeshi, his second-grade son, when he noticed the benefits of giving short, bite-size assignments in math and getting total mastery and lots of repetitions before moving to the next challenge. By sixth grade Takeshi was solving calculus sets. Toru and his wife, Teiko, opened the first Kumon Center in Moriguchi City in 1958, and today the company operates in forty-eight countries around the world, with two thousand Kumon franchisees in North America (startup costs are about $100,000) serving 340,000 students. Kaplan, Sylvan, and Princeton Review are additional giants in the supplemental education market, which is overwhelmingly aimed at middle-class and upper-middle-class communities.

I love the vibrancy of Brookline's after-school learning ecosystem and would love to see it replicated in Boston, Oakland, and other big cities across the country. But until parents in Boston and Oakland have the money to pay for all that is offered in Brookline, their after-school options are going to remain significantly less dazzling. As a result, I have come to believe that while Brookline should keep its formal six-hour day, which for most kids works effectively in combination with the town's array of school-based and parent-guided extra learning opportunities, Boston and other lower-income communities need a whole new day for learning. They need an equally dazzling nine- or ten-hour public school day with more time for academics, more time for enrichment, and more time for social and emotional development—all built into the publicly funded core school day. By building extra learning time right into public schools, we can transform the current patchwork of programs that help a relative handful of kids beat the odds into a system of programs that helps whole neighborhoods of children change the odds. The students mentored by Governor Hunt needed more time for learning, but so frankly do most students in high-poverty schools.

They need more time with successful adults to help them build their social skills, social networks, and social capital. They need more time to create and innovate. And they need more time to master the academic basics. In middle school—which Education Secretary Arne Duncan has called "the Bermuda Triangle of American education"[2]—the need is particularly acute, as children require more help navigating a set of challenging years when the brain is changing and developing faster than at any point except right after birth.[3]

Put yourself in the shoes of a middle school principal in any lower-income neighborhood in America and consider the challenge presented by today's typical school schedule—a schedule invented for an agrarian age and too often implemented with an industrial-age sensibility. Imagine your district has assigned you six hundred sixth through eighth graders, typical for middle schools, and most of them arrive by bus, many from other neighborhoods in the city.

On the first day of sixth grade, your students arrive on average two years behind grade level. Several are so far behind that you wonder if they have been attending school at all. Ninety percent of your students live below or just above the poverty line and about half are learning English as a second language or have been identified as having a significant learning disability, or both. Roughly 10 percent of your students will turn over every semester, meaning that when you prepare for state testing in the spring and for graduation in June, about 120 students will be newcomers to your school. Now assume that your district has a traditional school day, in line with national averages, meaning that your students arrive by bus at about 8:00 a.m. and start lining up to go home at about 2:15. Once you account for lunch, a lightning-quick recess, and take time for recording attendance in the morning and transition time between classes, you have about five hours left for academics and enrichment. How will you use the time? And how might citizen power help you expand it?

Let's assume you are a believer in arts and sports and music as ways for students to build teamwork skills, and to practice creativity, and as an alternative way for students to shine and build their confidence. But let's also assume that your school doesn't have much in the way of art and music and sports facilities—and that you don't have time to travel off campus. You decide to provide one hour per week each of art, and music, and sports—for every student. On the fourth and fifth days, you provide students with an hourlong study hall block instead of enrichment because it's easier to staff and can be scheduled in the regular classrooms, which helps with logistics. You just scheduled your first hour. You have four left.

The district has prioritized math instruction in large part because last year half of the eighth graders failed the new Common Corps–aligned statewide math assessment, and only 18 percent were proficient (actual numbers from New York City in 2013).[4] Plus, middle school math is a gateway skill for higher education and for life (more so than high school math for all but the highest-level STEM jobs). If your school is in California, you need to get your middle school students through Algebra 1 by the end of eighth grade or else they may be unable to enroll in a four-year college even if they have good grades in high school due to the state's A through G course requirements, which require starting Algebra II by ninth grade. Eighth grade seems awfully early to give up on a four-year college, so you decide to schedule a double block of math for two hours each day in hopes you can get your students ready for college-track courses in high school. The double block gives students lots of opportunities to work on math problems, but classes are still operating on a 1:28 teacher-to-student ratio, so there is little time for individualized instruction or for tutoring of particular students. Still, focusing on math seems like a smart move. But now you only have two hours left.

You would like to offer a foreign-language block, as you have heard that learning a foreign language builds brain capacity and is increasingly important in the modern global economy, but there are only two hours left in your schedule and you haven't yet gotten to English or science or social studies. You'll have to skip offering any foreign-language instruction, at least for this year. You would also love to provide a double block for English language arts (ELA), because this could allow a deep dive in both reading comprehension and writing and oral expression—key skills in the modern economy. But if you schedule a double block in ELA, you will have zero time left over for any science or social studies classes, nor any time for theater or library or computer science. You decide to go with a single English class per day. Since 80 percent of the state test is focused on vocabulary and reading comprehension, with just a few short sections testing student writing skills, your teachers too will focus mostly on vocabulary and reading and just do a few writing units, mostly focused on how to write a five-paragraph essay.

Now you have one hour left. You decide to split that time between social studies and science, offering each student a chance to study one of those core topics for an hour a day in the fall and then switch to the other in the spring. A new study says that reducing time for science in school actually undermines student performance in math and reading.[5] And you worry less time on social studies will yield less engaged and informed citizens. But you have hard decisions to make and you stick with the schedule you've crafted. You certainly wouldn't want the schedule for your own child. But you feel stuck between the proverbial rock and a hard place, and without more time you don't see how it's possible to provide the time needed for academics and for the well-rounded education that you know your students deserve.

These are the types of bad choices that our agrarian-era school schedule forces even the most progressive and creative school leaders to make. Without sufficient time, principals routinely choose academics *or* enrichment; extra time for English *or* math; social studies *or* science. The short days work in the suburbs because the students arrive at or above grade level and their education is massively supplemented in the afternoons, on weekends, and in the summer. But for schools serving primarily lower-income students, the traditional school schedule is obsolete.

Now imagine you are that same principal but that your students stay in school from 8:00 a.m. until 5:15 p.m. instead of 2:15. You are a practical person, so at first you would probably throw your hands up in despair because you don't know how in the world you can staff the extra time. Your teachers are already working full-time to run the six-hour day, so you can't just put the extra three hours on them. What will you do?

Here is where Citizen Schools—and citizen power more broadly—as well as artful efforts to schedule teacher time more flexibly can make a longer learning day feasible, affordable, and productive. Keep in mind that while teachers typically teach students for five or fewer hours per day, most studies indicate that they work nine or ten hours per day or more.[6] The additional time is devoted to lesson planning, reviewing and grading homework and tests, meeting individually with students and/or parents, serving on committees, overseeing lunch or recess or student arrivals and departures, collaborating with other teachers, and reviewing interim assessments.

Despite the long days, your teachers know their students need more learning time, and with the help of Citizen Schools, they want to make this work. Some teachers elect to work a different shift—starting and ending their day a few hours later than normal, which can work well for teachers who need to get their own kids off to school in the morning. A few other teachers agree to add an extra hour of teaching time in exchange for a little additional pay. But the bulk of the coverage for the extra time comes from Citizen Schools. Specifically, by partnering with Citizen Schools, our principal gets an entire second shift of educators. The Citizen Schools team is led by a campus director—someone who has already taught for three or four years, and who essentially serves as the school's assistant principal for ELT. The campus director will be an additional right hand for you as principal and will sit on the school's leadership team. His or her name may go on the school stationery, below your name and next to those of the assistant principal and director of instruction. Reporting up to the campus director are one or two deputies and as many as two dozen full-time AmeriCorps members—all recent college graduates, most aspiring to be full-time teachers. Also included in the package are a few part-time staff and about one hundred trained citizen teachers—volunteers from local industry—enough so that every student in the school can take four apprenticeships over the course of the year, each offered one afternoon a week for a three-month span.

Citizen Schools is not the only way to staff a longer learning day. There are promising models being developed by TASC in New York,

Baltimore, and New Orleans, in which teachers cover one hour of extra learning and community partners provide an additional one to two hours of enrichment. Other organizations such as BELL, Breakthrough, City Year, College Track, Communities in Schools, and Higher Achievement are starting to move beyond offering optional after-school programs to more robust partnerships that change the structure of the school day and year. Many charter schools build into their model AmeriCorps-type fellowship positions, allowing them to staff a much longer learning day while keeping teacher workloads to manageable levels. The MATCH charter school in Boston, for instance, has Match Corps, a team of aspiring teachers who tutor six teams of two to three students every day; this is a smart strategy for expanding the day without burning out teachers. Some other charter schools have scheduled much longer days and staffed them without benefit of a second shift. When I speak with funders and leaders of these charter groups they generally concede that relying on teachers to routinely work twelve or more hours is a recipe for burnout and is not sustainable or scalable.

With a longer learning day and a second shift of talent, our principal can now take a fresh look at the schedule. Now Citizen Schools can take the lead for that second hour of math, allowing teachers more time to collaborate, or plan, or pull out individual students for extra tutoring. And now students can take both science and social studies all year long, and they can add a full two hours of enrichment every day, allowing for special classes like rocket science and slam poetry, allowing for field trips to local colleges and museums, and allowing for the relational time that adolescents need to navigate middle school.

Extra time is particularly important for English-language learners, who need more chances to use English in real-world contexts, and for special-education students, who often need expert intervention from trained professionals as well as more personal attention and guidance and extra time to master academic content. But the extra time can be stressful too, adding more opportunity for conflict and challenge. Tyriq, a special-needs student enrolled in one of our Boston ELT schools, is a case in point.

In many ways Tyriq fits my favorite description of a middle schooler as having "the full emotional range of an Italian aria, packed into the attention span of a gnat." Tyriq has the *capacity* to show that full emotional range, but when our staff first encountered him in the fall of 2012, most of what we saw was anger. He spent most of his first semester in middle school getting kicked out of the classroom at all times of day for swearing, breaking things, and fighting with other students in his separate education group, the Therapeutic Learning Community (TLC). He could often be seen storming down the hallway to the time-out room, paraprofessionals hurrying behind to help calm him down and redirect his behavior so that he could reenter the classroom. Tyriq lacked the patience and emotional skills to cope with his frustration in a healthy way and he lacked the desire to do well in his classes. He ripped up tests and broke pencils to avoid performing academic tasks. His grades and scores were rock bottom.

I have met a lot of kids like Tyriq over the years and, typically, school does not work out well for them. They have emotional issues, or attention issues, or organizational issues, or reading issues, or all of the above. For medical reasons—and sometimes because of severe daily trauma in their lives—tasks like listening to instructions, and following directions, and working in groups, and doing multistep problems are really hard. Some days they just can't do it. They are so angry they feel like their head is going to explode. It gets even harder because classmates in their special-needs clusters have similar problems, so they reinforce and add to each other's challenges. Further, they all notice that they are in the "Therapeutic Learning Community" or the "Learning Adaptive Behavior" cluster or just the "special needs" class, and they feel ashamed. In the cafeteria, other students call them the dumb kids or the weird kids or use "SPED" as an epithet and avert their gaze as they walk through. When they sign up for a sports team, which is rare, they often get kicked off the team for yelling at the coach or not following a play or for some other transgression.

Tyriq's school had some uncommonly good special-education teachers. But his lack of emotional control and intense struggles with executive function were on full display when he entered his Citizen

Schools classroom at the end of each day last fall, the first year of mandatory ELT at the McCormack Middle School. When he was assigned to the soccer apprenticeship on Thursday afternoons, he refused to enter the classroom the first week, and the second week he entered reluctantly, unleashing a torrent of curse words. It was the same story when guests would come in to help teach the apprenticeship, such as Pat Kirby, then the executive director of Citizen Schools Massachusetts. Kirby, a college-level soccer player, remembers casually ignoring Tyriq's initial stream of foul language and encouraging him to participate, to share his knowledge of sports statistics, and to play in the scrimmage at the end of the lesson, something he had never done in any previous week.

Kirby arrived in the fourth week of the apprenticeship, and his presence marked the first in a series of turning points for Tyriq. According to his Citizen Schools team leader, Tyriq talked about his positive experience in soccer all week long. In a world devoid of positive male role models, Tyriq came to depend on Kirby, his new mentor. He started to open up in his soccer apprenticeship, looking forward to it each week and earning the title of "Team MVP" in the final WOW! Bowl Tournament. He went from literally standing on the sidelines of the game, reluctant to enter the fray, to running into the chaos and helping to score the winning goal. In the spring Tyriq rejoined the soccer apprenticeship and served as the team captain. He took his new role very seriously, rarely swearing and impressing teachers with his growing emotional maturity and his kindness to other students on the field. For someone who initially seemed unable to display any empathy, actions he now took, such as using the word "we" to refer to his teammates and helping people up when they fell, were big developments. Tyriq's improved behavior started to spread to his regular Citizen Schools team too and eventually to his performance in the classroom. He started to improve his grades. One day when Pat Kirby came in to visit him, Tyriq bragged about earning a perfect score on a recent math test.

Tyriq's only hesitation in playing on the soccer team in the spring was missing the opportunity to be in the camping apprenticeship, which was held at the same time. To build on Tyriq's momentum, however,

Citizen Schools staff agreed that after the soccer apprenticeship ended he could join in the last few weeks of camping and, if his behavior kept improving, could participate in the camping WOW!—an authentic overnight camping experience in the Blue Hills Reservation about ten miles outside Boston. Tyriq was initially wary of the many deprivations involved in camping, but when the camping day came he was eventually laughing and running around with new friends. He recruited others to watch the sunset over Ponkapoag Pond, which he described as "peaceful and beautiful," slept through the night in his tent, and completed an eight-mile hike the next day. Tyriq told his team leader during a quiet moment on the trip that during the past year, having more time to work with people like her and Mr. Kirby "helped me work on my behavior, and now Mr. White [the coordinator of the TLC program] wants me to do regular education classes next year." She asked him, "Are you scared for next year?" and he replied, "No, I already have friends that are older than me," and he named several of the other students on the camping trip and from his sports apprenticeship teams.

For Tyriq and other students, ELT gives them time to slow down, to literally and figuratively watch the sunset and soak in some extra time with a mentor, a teacher, or an interesting assignment.

ELT is such a powerful idea—and so full of common sense—that it's worth pondering why it has not been adopted more broadly. The National Center on Time & Learning lists more than one thousand ELT schools, but that's less than 1 percent of the schools in the country, and many of these schools have added just an hour a day of extra time, which is a good start but far from sufficient.[7]

I think there are two main reasons we haven't yet adopted ELT on a more ambitious scale.

The first reason is inertia and the difficulty of shifting paradigms that govern our thinking. When I was in my twenties and working as a journalist, I took night courses in the history of science at the Harvard Extension School. One of the people I read was Thomas Kuhn, who wrote *The Structure of Scientific Revolutions*.[8] Kuhn noted that old paradigms—like the idea of the earth being flat or at the center of the universe—die a slow death. For an old paradigm to fade away, Kuhn believes, it not only needs to be proven wrong but an alternative theory needs to be persistently proven right. The flat earth idea didn't become passé just because people realized that boats weren't falling off the edge of the earth. It took a new theory of a spherical globe that rotated on its own axis and around the sun for the old theory to truly enter the trash bin of history. In education it's a similar process, except maybe even slower. That's why we need a vision for what ELT can look like. We need to create more ELT success stories that people can learn from and be inspired by. For the old agricultural-era schedule and industrial-era delivery system to truly wither away, we need to create an alternative theory of how to organize schools, and we need to prove the theory over multiple years in multiple locations.

The second reason society isn't moving faster to ELT—and I am going to say this in stark and honest terms—is a deeply ingrained and thoroughly incorrect belief held by too many people that poor kids, and particularly poor black and brown kids, can't learn at high levels. This belief makes it easier to accept poor kids not getting access to opportunity. If kids like Tyriq can't learn, and their parents didn't learn—this usually unstated line of reasoning goes—then it is okay for society to give up on them.

A great deal of expert research, however, has challenged this genetically driven talent frame and pointed to other explanations for success, whether in academia, the workforce, or in other pursuits like sports and music. The new research doesn't entirely discount the power of inherited genes to influence future outcomes, but in the age-old debate between whether nature or nurture plays a bigger role in setting our destiny, the new research gives the nod to nurture.

Malcom Gladwell has become the great popularizer of this research. Gladwell, a British-born Canadian journalist who writes for the *New Yorker* and recently had three books on the *New York Times* best-seller list at the same time, writes in his book *Outliers* that the two greatest factors in driving achievement are luck and the time to practice, not inherited talent.[9] Whether you look at the Beatles in music, or Bill Gates in software design, or all-stars in hockey and other sports, notes

Gladwell, great achievers generally log ten thousand or more hours of practice before they get great at what they do.

As a seventh grader, Bill Gates was lucky enough to be enrolled by his parents at Lakeside, an excellent private school in a wealthy Seattle neighborhood. The Mother's Club at the school held a fund-raiser every year to provide extra resources to the school, and in Gates's eighth-grade year, the mothers decided that in addition to supporting a summer scholarship program and a training fund for teachers, they would invest $3,000 in a state-of-the art ASR-33 Tele-type computer with a direct link to a large mainframe computer in downtown Seattle. This one investment provided Lakeside students a computer-programming opportunity that went far beyond what most college students had access to at the time. Gates himself reported log-ging thousands of hours on the Lakeside computer. Then, in high school, he gained access to two computer centers at the University of Washington. Just as the world of coding was opening up, Gates was one of the few anywhere who actually had access to practice it.

"It was my obsession," Gates told Gladwell. "I skipped athletics. I went up there at night. We were programming on weekends. It would be a rare week that we wouldn't get twenty or thirty hours in."[10] With his ambition, his intelligence, and his parents' support, Gates made the most of his differential access to computer time, and by the time he was nineteen he was ready to drop out of Harvard and start Microsoft.

Some of the most convincing evidence for the importance of extra learning time involves hockey players. In Canada and many other coun-tries, January is the cutoff date for youth hockey teams. To understand what this means, imagine that it's October and you and a friend show up to play youth hockey in Manitoba. Your friend is going to turn six in December and you are just a few weeks younger and will turn six in January. Based on the age cutoff, your friend gets assigned to the six-and-under team, where he will be the youngest player and probably just a little slower and smaller than most of his teammates; you become the oldest player on the five-and-under team. Age differences of six or twelve months don't matter much once you get to high school or college. But at age five, a six-month difference is 10 percent of your life! And that 10 percent turns out to provide a real advantage.

At age five or six, the slightly older kids—the kids born in January, February, and March—are, on average, slightly better players. They get placed on the first line. They play twenty minutes a game rather than ten. And they are more likely to be selected for the all-star game. As the kids get a little older, the extra time and the competition against better players pays off, and the kids born in the early part of the year are now more likely to get selected for the better travel teams. That means more games, and more practices, and a bigger competitive edge. Canadian psychologist Roger Barnsley was the first to study this effect of relative age, and he found, according to Gladwell, that in any study of elite Canadian hockey players, right up to the National Hockey League, about 40 percent of the players will have been born in the first quarter of the year, 30 percent in the next quarter, 20 percent in the third quarter, and just 10 percent between October and December.[11]

The kids coming into Citizen Schools are like hockey players born in the late fall. They need extra learning time to catch up.

Why should Bill Gates and his classmates at a fancy private school be the only ones to get access to thousands of hours of computer time? How much faster would our technology industry have developed, producing how many more jobs, if all schools had a computer like his did and a mechanism to allow students to learn for extra hours? How much better would we be as a country if instead of just a few kids getting extra ice time, or extra tutoring time, or extra enrichment time—all kids got it? Some kids would still rise to the top, and others would still bring up the rear. But we would have something much closer to a true meritocracy than we do today, and our average educational attainment would rise, boosting the economy for everyone.

FROM A NATION OF CONSUMERS TO A NATION OF MAKERS: INSPIRING CREATIVITY AND INNOVATIVE THINKING IN OUR SCHOOLS

Tinkering seems to come naturally to McCalvin Romaine, who is now in his twenties and pursuing a career in technology at Digitas, one of the world's top online marketing firms. On Tuesday afternoons he can often be found at the Washington Irving School in Roslindale, Massachusetts, volunteering with teams of sixth and seventh graders and teaching the young students how to pull apart computers, install more RAM, and identify and fix software problems.

Reflecting on his childhood, Romaine's eyes open wide and he smiles broadly as he remembers the time he turned his Mom's hair dryer into a flashlight. All it took, he remembers, was duct tape, copper wire, and a little ingenuity to connect the dryer's batteries to a small light bulb rather than a heating coil and blower. That the flashlight operated and looked like a gun, turning on as you pressed the plastic trigger at the base of the dryer, added to the excitement felt by the nascent inventor. But Romaine also remembers a dark side to his project. He brought his flashlight into school one day and his teacher threatened to throw the whole project in the trash if he didn't put it away. Then she reprimanded him for straying from his assigned work.

Romaine was a Citizen Schools student in middle school, and his favorite apprenticeships were in hip-hop dance, law, and a technology class not very different from the one he teaches today. "I was always a curious kid growing up," Romaine told me. "But it wasn't until I joined Citizen Schools that I really understood where these math and science courses that I took in school could take you in the future. Just seeing so many volunteers who were real professionals in my apprenticeships, it gave me an outlet for my creativity and it gave me some insight as far as the career paths I could pursue."

Across America we face a giant and growing mismatch between what our schools are teaching and what our children need. Creativity and scientific thinking and innovative problem-solving are skills increasingly in demand in today's job market. Yet too many of our schools focus on teaching students how to follow rules, memorize facts, and master basic arithmetic and reading. Schools persist with an old paradigm despite mounting evidence that the scientific thinking of American students lags that of students in most other industrialized countries and new evidence that the creativity and innovativeness of American students—which had formerly set the United States apart—is in decline.[1] Some of the mismatch is due to the short agrarian-era school day discussed in the previous chapter and to the limited time allocated to scientific learning in schools in the era of high-stakes math and reading assessments. One study showed that in the last fifteen years there has been a 23 percent decline in time devoted to science instruction in schools, down to a low of 2.3 hours a week in 2011–12.[2] In my experience, the decline has been most dramatic in schools serving the lowest-income students.

Compounding the time-on-task challenge, too few schools have the equipment or orientation to offer significant time for hands-on science projects, the type most likely to spark interest in science or engineering as a career and to build creative-thinking skills. Researcher Robert Tai and his colleagues have demonstrated that interest in science in middle school is a stronger predictor of who goes into careers in STEM fields than is math or science proficiency.[3] And the Lemelson-MIT Program sponsored research indicating a majority of teenagers reported they may be discouraged from pursuing STEM careers because they do not personally know any engineers or know what engineers do.[4] Yet despite looming talent shortages in all sorts of STEM disciplines, we persist with a school system that is offering kids less time for science, less time to conduct experiments and build things, and in most cases no time at all to meet and work with real scientists and engineers like Marcus De-Latte and David Mantus. Where is the interest supposed to come from?

Too often the shortage of exciting STEM opportunities in public schools means that the only kids who get cool STEM opportunities are kids who already have STEM-savvy role models in their lives. These are mostly the children of engineers and doctors and scientists, most of whom are white, male, and middle class. No wonder our homegrown STEM pipeline is drying up like an old riverbed in a drought. Among students who took AP (Advance Placement) computer science classes in 2010–11, for instance, a gateway into one of the fastest-growing segments of the STEM workforce, just 2 percent were African Americans and only 16 percent were girls. In California that same year, 51 percent of all K–12 students were Latino, but among those taking AP computer science, just 7 percent were. We shouldn't be surprised that just 14 percent of engineers in America are women,[5] and only 5 percent are African Americans.[6]

As I was launching Citizen Schools in the mid-1990s, there was a lot of talk in education circles about creativity and higher-order thinking skills. Of course, I wanted Citizen Schools to promote both. Who wouldn't? But we also had pressure from parents and school partners to make sure their children were progressing on the basics—arithmetic, reading, and writing—and that seemed like a key priority for Citizen Schools too. We were stuck in a raging debate between back-to-basics purists and advocates for twenty-first-century skills such as higher-order problem solving, teamwork, and creativity. The focus on basics was often associated with E. D. Hirsch, who wrote a series of books outlining what all Americans should know. The second approach was associated with an unusual alliance of corporate leaders and educational progressives.

As I tried to navigate Citizen Schools through this educational debate, I often turned to a slender volume called *Teaching the New Basic Skills*, published in 1996 by educational economists Richard Murnane and Frank Levy.[7] Instead of guessing what skills graduates needed—and would increasingly need in the future—the authors studied in detail the actual hiring practices of eight large American companies, including Northwestern Mutual Life, AT&T, and Mitsubishi Motors of America. By starting with real data about the skills workers needed to get good entry-level jobs, Murnane and Levy cut through a lot of the ideological abstractions. I also appreciated that the "new basic skills" Murnane and Levy described as necessary for the modern workforce were also a good inventory of the skills active citizens need to thrive in a democracy. Schools need to prepare students to earn a living in the work world but also to contribute to their communities.

Murnane and Levy drew three central conclusions. First, companies hiring for entry-level middle-class jobs have an increasingly clear set of standards. To be hired, applicants need ninth-grade-level math and reading skills, but they also must possess the ability to communicate nuanced ideas orally and in writing, to work well on diverse teams, to form hypotheses and test them, and to use technology to solve problems. These are what Murnane and Levy call the new basic skills, a subset of what others call twenty-first-century skills.

Second, Murnane and Levy's research indicated that half of the eighteen-year-olds in the country, even as they are poised to graduate from high school, do not possess the new basic skills and therefore are not eligible to get hired at entry-level jobs at companies like those named above.

Third, the authors concluded that the new basic skills can be taught, and that just as with traditional academic skills, they can be learned through practice. Murnane commented: "These skills need to be practiced and after-school and extended day programs provide a great way to practice them."[8]

At company after company they visited during their research, Murnane and Levy learned that hiring managers had adopted a multistage process for winnowing their applicant pools. In every case the hiring process took into account cognitive and analytic skills taught in school but also tested for other abilities. At Mitsubishi Motors of America, for instance, prospective employees were first given a drug test and the General Aptitude Test Battery (GATB), an IQ-like test that assesses nine different skills including verbal and numerical aptitude. Depending on the exact job, the company set minimum thresholds for the GTAB, typically near the fiftieth percentile. Prospective employees who passed the drug test and scored at the required level on the GATB would be invited back to take a mechanical aptitude test and then to engage in two expensive hands-on assessments. In the first of the hands-on tests, the authors explained, each applicant was assigned to a small team composed of men and women with various ethnic backgrounds. Their task was to assemble circuit boards, wires, and modular components on a large frame according to a blueprint. The team members could pursue the work in any fashion they chose. At the end they held a *kaizen* meeting (a continuous-improvement approach pioneered by Japanese corporations) to discuss how they could have done the job better. Then they assembled a second board. Throughout the ninety-minute activity, trained evaluators assessed the applicants on teamwork, communication skills, and creative problem-solving abilities.

I was deeply influenced by Murnane and Levy's work and found it highly relevant to our own. They had pinpointed a mismatch between the goals and values of schools and the requirements of the workplace. But rather than business being the bad guy, representing soul-crushing conformity and slavish obedience to the profit-driven dictates of "The Man" while education offered a high-minded vision of learning and discovery, somehow things had been reversed. Schools were the ones following the industrial-age playbook, and many in the corporate world were looking for something new.

The biggest mismatch between what schools are offering and what the workforce needs concerns creativity. In 2010 IBM released a poll of fifteen hundred CEOs, who identified creativity as the number one "leadership competency" of the future.[9] The next year the social-networking site LinkedIn reported that "creative" was the most commonly used word in the profiles of its members. Clearly creativity is hot in the business world. But there is new evidence that the creativity of America's children—long the envy of the world—has been in decline since the mid-1980s. The decline was brought to light by Kyung Hee Kim, who analyzed fifty years of data from the world's most established creativity assessment: the Torrance Test of Creative Thinking.[10] In 2010 *Newsweek* magazine trumpeted the topic on its cover, calling it a "Creativity Crisis."

Kim and others who have analyzed the data say that creativity in America started to decline sometime between 1984 and 1990. In Kim's words, the data indicate that "children have become less emotionally expressive, less energetic, less talkative and verbally expressive, less humorous, less imaginative, less unconventional, less lively and passionate, less perceptive, less apt to connect seemingly irrelevant things, less synthesizing, and less likely to see things from a different angle."[11] The change has been significant, with 85 percent of students in 2008 scoring below the level for the average student in 1984.

As the nation thinks through how to prepare more young people for the innovation economy of the present and the future—for jobs that require a strong grounding in basic academic proficiencies *and* a bent toward innovation, tinkering, and team-based problem solving where there are no rules—we need to rethink how we build those skills and who is best positioned to teach them.

These were the key questions posed in 2004 at Reimagining After-School: A Symposium on Learning and Leading in the 21st Century, organized by Citizen Schools at the Harvard Graduate School of Education. Prolific author and Harvard Business School professor Rosabeth Moss Kanter kicked off the conference with a call for "kaleidoscope thinking," which questioned who should teach twenty-first-century skills and when and where they should be taught. I spoke and urged my colleagues in the after-school and Expanded Learning Time fields to lift our sights beyond the low standard of keeping kids safe during potentially risky afternoon hours and instead see extended learning time as a front-burner solution to America's educational and social challenges, such as how to teach creativity and innovative problem solving.

The Reimagining After School conference drew two state commissioners of education, numerous district-level leaders, national policymakers, multiple foundation presidents, and extended-day leaders from across the country. A surprise attendee—and a presenter—was Tyeisha Bogy, an assertive sixth grader from the Grover Cleveland Middle School in Boston's Fields Corner neighborhood, a school so challenged that it would close for good five years later. Tyeisha was one of ten sixth and seventh graders who had enrolled in a Citizen Schools apprenticeship I taught called Power Learning Out of School. The course was my effort to question the paradigm around where and when learning happens, while also introducing my students to interesting people. I also wanted the students to apply their middle school math skills in a real-world pursuit with an authentic audience.

This was an unorthodox Citizen Schools apprenticeship with no toolboxes, video games, rocket launches, or mock trials. But my students did important work. Our goal: to interview as many CEOs and other senior executives as possible, ask them about the key skills they needed to get to the top, and find out where they had learned those skills.

We started with in-person and conference-call interviews, and we completed some great ones with Jeff Taylor, CEO of Monster.com, and the heads of the Boston Children's Museum and a fast-growing beauty products business. These interviews helped me and my ten apprentice research assistants to build a questionnaire that we posted on SurveyMonkey.com. We then recruited nonprofit and for-profit CEOs to fill out the survey online, eventually getting more than two hundred responses. While I am quite sure our sampling techniques did not meet the standards of the Gallup polling group, what we learned was interesting.

We discovered that of the nine skills that helped executives get to the top (ranging from math to teamwork to creativity), just three of them were learned primarily at school, with three learned primarily at home and three learned primarily through after-school and summer activities. The three most important tickets to the top, our executives said, were perseverance, teamwork, and creativity. Further, they said that these skills were primarily learned outside of school, either at home or in various enrichment experiences like those described in this book.

Looking back at the results of the survey and at the urgent challenge of teaching creativity and innovation, I am convinced we need to embrace both in-school and extended-day (and year) strategies. Within the core day we need to stop giving science and related topics short shrift. And we need to recruit new teachers who are familiar with the wondrous things that can be done in physics and biology and chemistry labs and who have the ability to link basic math and science facts to cool new discoveries. I'm involved in one exciting national effort called 100Kin10, which is designed to promote the hiring and support of one hundred thousand excellent new science and math teachers over the next ten years.[12] The effort was launched by the Carnegie Corporation (the same foundation that brought us the public library) and is supported by the White House and CEOs from some of the top technology companies in the world.

But the real game changer for STEM education and for boosting innovation and creativity is to recruit one million scientists and engineers to team up with those one hundred thousand full-time math and science teachers. Getting STEM professionals in every classroom, and giving students of all ages a chance to make things with STEM professionals after school, would make science classes more fun, more engaging, and more connected to the creative discoveries happening in the real world. Most schools in the country are within a few miles of a university, hospital, or industry lab brimming with science, engineering, and medical professionals, some portion of who are interested in advancing the learning of young people.

Imagine being a student in a school in which real chemists joined your regularly scheduled science class every Monday to conduct real-world experiments, and where every Wednesday you could choose among electives taught by video game designers, medical researchers, and astronomers. Imagine if a requirement of your sophomore year was to complete an internship in a local lab and conduct an experiment and gather evidence to prove or disprove your hypothesis.

In an effort to build a movement around just this type of STEM mentoring, Citizen Schools is incubating a new organization, US2020, which is designed to coordinate and promote efforts to mobilize STEM professionals. We aim to match individual mentors—most drawn from corporate members like Cisco, HP, Tata Consulting Services, Raytheon, and Salesforce—with schools and nonprofits that know how to coordinate real-world projects, like Citizen Schools, FIRST, 4-H, Spark, and others. I am serving as executive chairman of US2020, which we plan to spin off as an independent organization in late 2014.

US2020 was launched by President Obama at the White House science fair in April 2013 and has set a bold goal of mobilizing one million STEM mentors by the year 2020, creating millions of "moments of discovery" for children. "We would never teach football by having students study it in a textbook," said President Obama's science advisor, John Holdren, noting that football players only get good by putting on pads and getting on the field. Similarly, students need to get into the lab and grapple with real-world experiments and projects. At the US2020 launch, President Obama said we need "all hands on deck" to improve STEM education.[13]

When the president says we need all hands on deck, he is talking about people like Steve Robinson, a molecular biologist. In 2002 Robinson and his wife adopted a child, and the couple agreed that Steve would take a year away from full-time work and take the lead on child care. Robinson was excited for a sabbatical and eager to dig into life at home, but he decided he'd also love to teach one course as a volunteer, spending one or two mornings a week at the local high school. He approached the school principal and asked if given his credentials as a PhD in molecular biology, he could develop and teach an optional advanced course for some of the older students in the school. The principal was intrigued, but said that because Robinson was noncertified, he wouldn't be allowed to teach even one elective. Disappointed,

Robinson took his offer to the leaders of a nearby private school and they eagerly snapped him up.

It turned out that Robinson loved teaching and was good at it. Midway through his year as a part-time volunteer, he applied for a full-time job at the same private school and was hired on the spot, turning his career upside down but allowing him to pursue a passion and share it with dozens of new students every year. In 2007, after just four years as a full-time teacher, Robinson was awarded an Einstein Fellowship, given to the very best math and science teachers in the nation. Robinson was born in Illinois, and for his fellowship he was assigned to work with the freshman US senator from Illinois, none other than future president Barack Obama. Robinson became a key advisor in the Obama campaign, and until recently he served in the White House as President Obama's senior science education advisor. Now Robinson is back teaching science full-time at a Democracy Prep charter school in Harlem.

For every Steve Robinson who volunteers to teach science and then is so excited by the challenge and opportunity that he switches careers, there will be a hundred people like David Mantus and Alan Su, who take great pleasure in teaching—and are good at it—but want to continue doing science, or engineering, or law as their full-time job.

America's schools need to open their doors wide to more Robinsons and more Mantuses and Su's too. If we want children growing up on the South Side of Chicago to become chemists for Abbott Labs, which is located in suburban Chicago, or electrical engineers for Boeing, which is located downtown, we need these children to meet chemists and engineers at these companies and do real-world projects with them.

One of the most interesting recent developments in the informal learning space is the maker movement, a fast-growing effort to stimulate more backyard inventing and to showcase the work of tinkerers and artists and inventors. Makers are people who might be the next Steve Wozniak, who hung out with other tinkerers at the Homebrew Computer Club in a friend's Menlo Park garage before teaming up with Steve Jobs to create Apple Computer.[14] Or they could be your neighbor who organizes a day for the kids on the street to make tie-dye shirts, or who designs a pedal-powered green TV that allows her to exercise while watching her favorite show and maintaining a carbon footprint of zero.

If there is a leader of the maker movement it is Dale Dougherty, a middle-aged technology entrepreneur and the founder of Global Network Navigator, or GNN, a Web portal and the first site on the Internet to be supported by advertising revenue. Dougherty is now the publisher of *MAKE* magazine, a quarterly publication that highlights DIY (do it yourself) and DIWO (do it with others) projects and hawks the building blocks of the maker movement, including 3-D printers and Arduino microcontrollers, the brains of small, electronically controlled gadgets that can tell lights when to turn on and off or control the movements of a small robot. Simple 3-D printers are now available for less than $1,000, and many believe they could radically decentralize manufacturing in the coming decades.

If you are a technology CEO, makers are the type of young "creative class" workers you want working with you. And if you are a mayor, you want more makers in your city. In fact, when makers are present in critical mass, they drive innovation and economic growth for an entire city, as powerfully documented by Richard Florida in his book *The Rise of the Creative Class.*[15] Recently, people active in the maker movement have been thinking about how to insert maker thinking and maker activities into schools. Dougherty and *MAKE* magazine teamed up with Pixar, Intel, and Cognizant, three leading technology firms, to launch the Maker Education Initiative, or Maker Ed as it is known, and Maker Corps, efforts to open and support more than one hundred new maker spaces in schools and community centers around the country. The maker spaces are essentially arts and crafts rooms with soldering irons, parts to build robots, and 3-D printers or industrial design tools. In a parallel effort, DARPA, the Defense Advanced Research Projects Agency, made a 2011 grant of $10 million to Maker and Otherlab, a San Francisco firm, to create industrial design labs in one thousand schools, although sequestration budget cuts have slowed the rollout.

US2020 and Citizen Schools are working closely with Maker Ed and Maker Corps, and I see the maker movement as a way to scale the apprenticeship experience much faster than could be done just through Citizen Schools. But I also know that the maker movement, like FIRST, is primarily white and Asian, middle class, and suburban. If you go to the Maker Faires that Dougherty organizes at the San Mateo Fairgrounds, and at the Henry Ford Museum in Detroit, and in New York, you see incredible creativity. You also see lots of people (one hundred thousand plus in San Mateo every spring). But you don't see a lot of kids. And you definitely don't see many kids or adults from the inner city. You are much more likely to see a young David Mantus with his rocket scientist father than an Adam Barriga or a McCalvin Romaine. I sometimes wonder if the maker movement will contribute to a renaissance in creativity but mostly among those already on the right side of the opportunity divide.

In September of 2012 my eleven-year-old daughter, Orla, and I headed to the New York Maker Faire, held outside the New York Hall of Science in Queens on the grounds of the 1964 World's Fair. The gathering was beautiful, like a high-tech Woodstock. Huge puppets from the Bread and Puppets group in Vermont paraded around the fairground. Long-haired engineers in tie-dyed shirts biked around on old three-speeds outfitted with huge butterfly wings. Thousands of burritos were being eaten. There was a workshop featuring a young inventor from Sierra Leone who had made an entire FM radio station, including the batteries to power it, out of scrap materials and a 3-D printer. He was now employing three journalists and three DJs and making plans to build a windmill to bring electricity to his community.

The ingenuity was inspiring. Several of the Maker Ed corporate partners were there, and they had brought young inventors from across the country. Orla and I met Joey Hudy, who was not much older than Orla and had designed a hydraulic marshmallow cannon that he had demonstrated the previous spring to President Obama at the White House Science Fair. We also met with Anthony Rodriguez, a young inventor from Newark who said he hoped to become an industrial designer or a multimedia producer. "My favorite part," he said, "is you see a problem or a need and then you can just make something for it."

There was lots of stuff for sale at Maker Faire. You could buy robotics kits and rocket launchers, arts and crafts materials, dressmaking kits, and even 3-D printers. Orla and I checked out one of the 3-D printers and were fascinated but a little disappointed. The concept is cool but the reality of the production process is it's slow. The printer we saw was creating a pocketsize bottle opener, maybe two inches by one inch by a quarter-inch thick. The printer went back and forth for about half an hour spraying layer after layer of red plastic according to the template that had been programmed into the attached computer.

As Orla and I headed back to Manhattan on the elevated Number 7 train, we passed graffiti-covered bodegas and Laundromats, open-air vegetable stands, and check-cashing stores in the Willets Point neighborhood near the Hall of Science. The handful of passengers coming from Maker Faire stood out in sharp relief from the locals sharing the same subway car.

We noticed a Jamaican man with a Pittsburgh Steelers cap and an energetic three-year-old son who hopped from seat to seat and stared curiously out the window. There was a middle-aged Chinese man with a shopping cart filled with thousands of sheets of roasted dried seaweed. And there were a half-dozen young Latino men with Rocawear T-shirts, jeans, and Adidas sneakers. None of these folks had been to the faire, and if they noticed it as the train rumbled past, it was only with a fleeting glance.

Standing out on the train, as did Orla and I, was a middle-aged father and his three young children. The dad had tired eyes, and I imagined him up late at night writing computer code. His young son held a lightsaber he had bought at the faire and was engaging in an imaginary sword fight with a subway pole. The eldest child, a girl, was recounting the Maker Faire project that most inspired her. I imagined David Mantus as a young child taking this same train with his technician grandfather or his rocket scientist father to go to the New York Hall of Science, and I was reminded anew of the power of relationship and the power of experience to imprint any number of characteristics, including creativity.

I was inspired by Maker Faire. The crowd was overwhelmingly white and middle class, but there were a significant number of immigrants from India and the Far East and a small number of African Americans and Latinos. With effort, these numbers could grow. The event made me hopeful. But as I headed away on the Number 7 train, I was equally humbled by the challenge of equalizing access to all it has to offer.

CHAPTER ELEVEN

SOCIAL NETWORKS AND SOCIAL SKILLS

Robert Putnam has a gentle, pious demeanor befitting the son of a Methodist small-businessman from the Midwest, which he is. But on the Fourth of July weekend of 2012, Putnam, author of the best-selling 2000 book *Bowling Alone* and described by the London *Sunday Times* as "the most influential academic in the world today," gave a talk at the Aspen Institute's annual Ideas Festival that was shocking.

"The American Dream of equality of opportunity is destined to decay in the years ahead," Putnam told the assembled power brokers. "Whether or not you care about inequality in wealth and income, we should all be worried about growing inequality in opportunity."[1]

Putnam has made social capital—the relationships we all have with family, close friends, and extended networks—his lifelong obsession. He believes that human productivity, quality of life, and professional success are determined as much or more by *who* you know, and the depth and quality of those connections, as they are by *what* you know, or even by your family's relative wealth.

Putnam's research raises a trio of imposing challenges for educators trying to reduce opportunity and achievement gaps. First, as Putnam and his research team document exhaustively in *Bowling Alone*, and have continued to demonstrate, social capital has been declining steadily since its high point in the 1960s. People may have more contacts on Facebook or Instagram, but we spend less time with our friends, we trust people less, and we have fewer people we feel comfortable turning to for a favor.[2]

Second, social capital and social skills are becoming more important to success in the highly networked twenty-first-century economy, an assertion also convincingly made by Richard Florida in *The Rise of the Creative Class*. Not good for Americans to have less social capital just as its importance to both individual and community success grows.

Third, social capital is more and more unequally distributed. This was the focus of Putnam's talk in Aspen, in which he described a "sharply growing class divide among America's youth."[3] Most Americans have less social capital today than they did one or two generations ago. But the decline has been steepest for Americans with lower incomes and less formal education.

Putnam helps us see that the opportunity divide is not just a divide in access to good teaching of math, science, or writing, but a divide that is much more fundamental: a divide in access to positive experiences and relationships *that are foundational to almost everything we do.*

Putnam and other researchers, including famed sociologist James S. Coleman, have documented a variety of ways in which access to childhood social experiences and networks that are proven to support adult success has become more unequal. Thirty years ago, for instance, upperincome children were slightly more likely than lower-income children (67 percent rather than 62 percent) to participate in extracurricular high school clubs like chess, theater, or community service.[4] Today, that modest gap has almost quadrupled. Thirty years ago children of parents with a college degree and children of parents with a high school degree attended church at about the same rates. Today, on any given Sunday, children of better-educated parents are 50 percent more likely to attend church and to build the associated social networks. Today if you are an upper-income child in high school, your likelihood of serving as captain of a varsity sports team—a proven chance to strengthen leadership skills—is 27 percent, whereas just 12 percent of lower-income students will get this same opportunity. Gaps have also grown in overall levels of trust, in time spent with parents, and in participation in high school sports.[5] And, as we discussed in the opening chapter, the investment gap has tripled between what upper- and lower-income families spend on out-of-school tutoring and extracurricular activities like piano lessons and robotics camps.[6]

Sociologist Coleman was one of the first to clearly document the impact of social capital on educational and career outcomes in his influential 1988 article, "Social Capital and the Creation of Human Capital."[7] It's not just nice to participate in extracurricular clubs, or in a faith community, or to spend more time with caring adults, he argued; these experiences drive students to entirely different places.

Coleman documented, for instance, that children who attend church regularly are half as likely to drop out of high school compared to their peers who rarely or never attend church. This holds true even when the peer families have the same levels of education and financial resources. When a child has weak social networks, less time with caring adults, and lower expectations from those adults, he or she is almost four times more likely to drop out of high school compared to peers whose families have the same education and financial standing but have weaker social networks. Other more recent research has drawn causal links between social capital and math and reading scores.[8]

The case for social capital's influence on career (as opposed to academic) success is strongest of all, and its influence is on the rise. In an *Atlantic* article titled "Where the Skills Are," Richard Florida argues that we are going through a second seismic change in the orientation of our economy and the abilities it values in its workers.[9] For much of human history, Florida says, the differential ability that drove variation in human success was physical strength and dexterity. People who could plough more land, catch more fish, make more shoes, or lay bricks better and faster were rewarded for it. By the middle of the twentieth century, Florida argues, the world economy transitioned, and analytical brainpower became the skill that was increasingly prized by employers and recognized in the marketplace. This was the first seismic shift, and it meant that the difference in the earning power of someone with strong analytical skills and someone with weak analytical skills was now much larger than the difference in earning power between a skilled and not-so-skilled bricklayer.

Florida believes that we have now entered a third phase in our economic history—one in which social skills have become more important than analytical skills. In his *Atlantic* article he describes how an examination of US labor market job listings and average wages led to his conclusion.

Florida went on to describe the implications for education: "Given the rising demand for social skills in our economy, it is curious that we devote so few of our educational resources to building them. A growing chorus has noted the failure of US schools to adequately teach math, science, and technology, but social intelligence is equally important, and we need to cultivate it more systematically."[10]

Updating our schools with more time for learning and more citizen power will create a foundation that enables schools to more effectively build the social capital and social skills crucial for student success. If we instead continue to ignore social capital as a systemic driver of opportunity and achievement gaps, we will contribute to the current vicious cycle in which families and communities with lower levels of income and education provide their children with less exposure to the relationships and opportunities that drive adult success, which will in turn leave their children with even less income and an even lower likelihood of achieving academic and professional success.

As Citizen Schools was getting started, my colleagues and I got to know Robert Putnam, and in 2000, when he published *Bowling Alone*, he included a nice shout-out to Citizen Schools, calling our efforts an effective way to "serve civic ends" and to "strengthen the civic muscles of participants."[11] For a young and mostly unknown organization, this was welcome recognition.

As we got to know Putnam, we learned that there were two types of social capital and that each was critical to helping individuals get ahead. "Bonding" social capital involves close connections to people like you— such as the people from your church or neighborhood or from people who share your same ancestry. People who have strong bonding social capital reinforce shared social norms and often do favors for each other, making what Tom Wolfe, in his novel *The Bonfire of the Vanities*, called "deposits in the favor bank."[12] In communities with high levels of trust, you expect that favors will be repaid, and this helps the community operate effectively. "Bridging" social capital is equally important and, Putnam taught us, even more important to individuals from low-income communities. Bridging social capital is when you form a relationship with someone who is different from you—from another side of town, a different class, and with an entirely different network.

Putnam's ideas resonated with me. It was my mom's network that helped me set up that summer camp when I was just fifteen. And it was the fact that my dad knew Senator Gary Hart that opened the door to a summer internship on his campaign when I was just nineteen—an internship that became the turning point in my life. For my wife, Maureen, strong bonding social capital gave her initial access to the world of work. Then, as her jobs evolved, she built bridging capital with the "Jewish mother" whose hair she cut and with others. New doors opened.

But how would this work at Citizen Schools? Can social capital be transferred, or does it just reproduce, cementing inequality? Can a few young educators and a few hundred community volunteers build social capital for low-income children stuck in struggling schools, while building their own social capital in the process? And if volunteers can build social capital in tough schools and tough neighborhoods, will it really make a difference for the kids? Or is social capital such an elusive and hard-to-measure asset that we'd be wiser to bet all our chips on building academic skills? After reflecting on my early experience at Citizen Schools, I concluded that social capital *can* be imparted and *is* life-changing. It's not easy to build social capital for a thirteen-year-old kid. But it's not easy to build reading skills either. And both are vital to the future success of our students.

In some cases, social capital is clearly transferable and transformative. Consider the examples of Chrystal and Col, two former Citizen Schools students. Both were born in Haiti, the poorest country in the Americas, and came to Boston as young children.

Chrystal was a charmer, the type of student who attracts adults to her because of her eloquence and bright smile. Her home life was difficult, though, with Dad remaining in Haiti, Mom severely ill, and an aging grandmother struggling to keep up with the young children. When Chrystal was in sixth grade at the Woodrow Wilson Middle School in Dorchester, she enrolled in Citizen Schools. She would sometimes show up at our Saturday program with all her belongings in a trash bag. She would say she was moving from her grandmother's house to an aunt's house, or to another location. Deb Daccord, a lawyer with Mintz Levin who was one of her teachers, recalled that "Chrystal was a standout student in our mock-trial class. She had a way of attracting role models to her because of her intelligence, but it was a patchwork of role models in a life with very little stability."

When Chrystal's mom died during her high school years, she and her beloved younger brother initially went to live with their grandmother. But the grandmother was aging and couldn't handle both children, so they split up. Chrystal moved in with one aunt in Dorchester, and her brother joined a different relative in Brockton, almost an hour away. It had been five years since Daccord and Chrystal had met, though they had stayed in touch sporadically. Daccord herself had been orphaned as a teenager, and when she heard about Chrystal's latest move, she resolved to be a more active mentor. She remembers buying Chrystal a computer and going to her aunt's apartment to help her set it up, and then returning months later to fix it.

When Crystal turned eighteen, government benefits that had been coming to her since the death of her mother ended, and her aunt kicked her out of the house. She was homeless, just as her senior year at English High School was supposed to begin. Daccord said her immediate impulse was to reach out. She consulted with her husband and two daughters, the eldest of whom had just gone off to college, and they were enthusiastic about helping. The Daccords decided to offer Chrystal a room in their home for the year and to help her navigate the college enrollment process. Chrystal happily accepted the offer, and with Deb's ongoing mentorship and support, Chrystal finished high school successfully and gained admittance to and enrolled in a four-year college, the University of Massachusetts at Dartmouth. Chrystal is now working as a waitress at a restaurant in Boston while continuing to work toward her degree. While this level of generosity is not an everyday occurrence, there are many more examples of Citizen Schools community members going out of their way to help students.

Col was another student of ours in Boston at around the same time. He lived with his dad and one sibling while his mom and two younger siblings remained in Haiti, where Col had completed the early years of his schooling. Col enrolled in the Citizen Schools 8th Grade Academy (8GA) program in the fall of 2003, and as part of 8GA he took two apprenticeships and visited ten colleges and universities, including an overnight trip to my alma mater, the University of Vermont. All 8GA students also wrote essays during the year with volunteer writing coaches drawn from the city's top law firms. Every other week, each student would meet one-on-one with their writing coach (they referred to their coach as "my lawyer") and at the end of the year they each published an essay in a glossy magazine called *Bridging*. Col's essay was about the high cost of college and his concern that it might discourage kids from pursuing a college education.

After completing his 8GA year at Citizen Schools, Col enrolled in TechBoston High School, a small and supportive "pilot" school that we had encouraged him to consider. He enrolled in Upward Bound, a federal college-access program, and stayed connected to Citizen Schools through occasional alumni reunions. Four years later Col graduated high school on time and with solid grades and enrolled at the University of Vermont as part of the class of 2012. Hundreds of Boston eighth graders had trekked north to UVM through Citizen Schools, taking classes from great professors like Huck Gutman, visiting the university art museum, meeting admissions officers, scrimmaging with the women's basketball team, and braving the cold weather and the culture shock of life on an almost all-white campus. Col would be the first Citizen Schools alumnus to enroll.

Social capital certainly played a role in prompting Col to apply to and enroll at UVM. He had met students and faculty and staff on the admissions team back in eighth grade, and this made him more confident to apply, even though the school was far away and no one in his family had ever attended a college. The relationship with Citizen Schools was likely a plus on his application too, as UVM hoped the partnership would help it build a more diverse student body. But whatever role social capital played in Col's application and acceptance, it would become even more important after he enrolled.

Col completed his freshman year, but his grades were low and he found it difficult to bond with his roommates. They were from wealthy families in the Boston suburbs and had never met anyone like Col, and they had little understanding of the academic and social challenges he faced. In Col's sophomore year his struggles grew. Like many first-generation college students, he couldn't pay all of his tuition. UVM's costs are high—they were close to $45,000 in his freshman year—but the university had provided Col with a substantial financial aid package. He had tuition relief worth close to $20,000 from UVM's general scholarship fund. Plus Col was eligible for a federal Pell grant of about $5,000, and he personally took out a subsidized Stafford student loan for another $6,500. He also served as a federal work-study student, earning money for school and picking up job skills as a computer technician at the business school. Rounding out the package were two special UVM scholarships. One of them, at $3,750 per year, was covered by the Minnie Parker Charitable Trust, a New York foundation chaired by Citizen Schools cofounder Ned Rimer, who had been my roommate for two years at UVM. Col was able to cover most of his tuition for his sophomore year too, but he had lost one of the smaller UVM scholarships (not the one from Minnie Parker) and tuition charged by the university had gone up more than $1,000. There was a gap of close to $5,000 between what he owed and what he could pay. In December the university froze Col's account, meaning that he couldn't register for spring courses, couldn't take out a book, and couldn't even log on to a computer.

The university thought the solution was simple. The gap was only a few thousand dollars, and they suggested that Col's parents take out a federal PLUS Loan at 8.5 percent interest. But Col's father wasn't willing to do this, as he was sending every penny he could back to his wife and two children in Haiti. Col was stuck in a quagmire that snares hundreds of thousands of first-generation college students every year and causes them to drop out of a four-year college. Six years after they enter college, only 11 percent of first-generation college students have earned a degree, compared to 55 percent of their more advantaged peers.[13]

Col reconnected with friends on the Citizen Schools staff, who in turn alerted Ned, the Citizen Schools cofounder and chair of the foundation that was funding UVM to support students like Col. Ned called a friend of his in the development office and made two suggestions: First, if this situation could be resolved, maybe the Minnie Parker Trust would make an additional contribution to the university, again targeted to helping students like Col succeed. Second, Ned, who along with me had recently received a distinguished alumni award from the university, appealed to their sense of justice. Col had already covered more than 90 percent of his tuition. Please solve the problem and let Col continue his studies, Ned asked.

Ned's appeal worked. Col was a long way from home. His roommates couldn't relate to his situation and his immediate family didn't have the money or the know-how to help. But because of Citizen Schools, Col's network at UVM also included an influential graduate of the university and a donor—someone in Col's corner who was willing to make a call on his behalf. Three years later—and after additional tuition scares again resolved through interventions by Ned and members of the Citizen Schools staff—Col graduated on time with a degree in business.

In Col's case, social capital worked just the way it sometimes does for rich people. You have a problem—like needing an introduction to someone who could offer you a job—and someone you know helps you solve the problem. The connection doesn't *get* you the job. You have to perform in the interview and be a strong candidate, just as Col had to get the work done and pass his courses. But when your connection has juice with someone in power, they help you get your foot in the door, which is often half the battle. Not every graduate of Citizen Schools or similar programs is going to be fortunate enough to receive scholarship funding via an influential leader like Ned. But what is scalable is the building of relationships so that hundreds of thousands of students like Col have someone in their corner, someone they feel comfortable calling who in turn can pick up the phone and get people in power to help.

Nancy DiTomaso, vice dean at Rutgers University, wrote an intriguing article in the *New York Times* last year in which she stated that a major driver of employment inequality between blacks and whites is that whites have more connections with people in hiring roles and are therefore more likely to get the friendly introductions that lead to jobs. "Getting an inside edge by using help from family and friends is a powerful, hidden force driving inequality in the United States," she wrote, basing her findings on thousands of interviews she has conducted. "Inequality reproduces itself because help is typically reserved for people who are 'like me': the people who live in my neighborhood, those who attend my church or school or those with whom I have worked in the past. The mechanism that reproduces inequality, in other words, may be inclusion more than exclusion."[14]

Social capital helps Citizen Schools kids get access to good high schools, to good summer programs, and as we've seen with Col, Chrystal, and others profiled in this book, to homes, colleges, and job interviews. Professionals like Deb Daccord and Ned Rimer have lots of social capital. Through Citizen Schools they get the chance to use it not only for their own children and the children of their friends but for other people's children too.

Social capital also helps students in more subtle ways. For sure it helps students get their foot in the door; but it also helps students see new doors, and sometimes it helps them develop the confidence to walk through the door and ask for help when it's needed.

Jadine Yarde, for instance, grew up in the same low-income Boston neighborhood as Col. She navigated her way through high school to college at St. John's University and into a good job as ad sales coordinator for DISH Network. She's a young professional in New York City and has become a skilled networker with a bright future. But Jadine told me that her newfound confidence was hard-won. In middle school, as she enrolled in Citizen Schools and started talking with her friends about her apprenticeship classes, such as one in entrepreneurship, some of them distanced themselves and said she should stop acting so high and mighty. "I was fighting outside influences like peer pressure, and at the time I couldn't conceptualize what exactly Citizen Schools could do for me because I saw it as what stood in the way of me being a 'normal' middle school student who hung out with friends on Saturdays and went downtown to cause trouble after school."

Jadine said that Citizen Schools staff members and volunteers kept pushing her and became instrumental to her academic and professional development. "Being able to meet through Citizen Schools with top execs at some of the most successful businesses and share my goals and aspirations is an environment that Citizen Schools created and it has helped me beyond measure. Now I am excited, motivated, and determined to be as successful as those I met as a twelve-year-old."

As I finished a recent conversation with Jadine, she wanted to reinforce one final point. Apprenticeships, she said, helped give her confidence *in her own ideas* and the comfort to approach strangers at a cocktail party or in an interview and engage with them as intellectual and social peers. "At Citizen Schools I was constantly reminded of my abilities. I realized that color and your academic standing do not define you and you should never fall victim to believing that they do. You are just as smart as a billionaire, you just have to give your dreams your undivided attention. Confidence is something that should be worn proudly."

When a student builds a network of advocates, they not only have more people to open doors for them but more people willing to stand up for them in difficult situations. Let me give an example. For many years I taught a master's degree class to young teaching fellows at Citizen Schools, and as part of the class, we devoted one evening to watching clips from education-themed movies such as *Children of a Lesser God*, *Dead Poets Society*, and *Stand and Deliver*, the last the story of real-life math teacher Jaime Escalante, who led a class of inner-city Los Angeles students to take and pass the AP calculus test. We always keyed in on the scene when Escalante, played by Edward James Olmos, visits his star pupil in her parents' restaurant after the parents have asked her to drop out of school to work at the family business. In the movie, Escalante brusquely confronts the hard-working immigrant parents and tells them their daughter should return to school. Every year we viewed the clip, our young staff would react the same way. They would be disappointed the girl had dropped out of school but would say that Escalante had crossed a line and should have left the decision about whether to attend school to the girl and her parents. But on two occasions when we asked our young student alumni—kids like Chrystal, and Col, and Jadine—to join us in watching the movie, they took a different point of view. They were glad Escalante intervened. They loved their families, but they wanted fiercer advocates for their interests, even if those advocates might occasionally cross lines and break from their parents' views.

There has been a growing recognition recently of the importance of social networks and of nonacademic skills such as grit and persistence, and suggestions that schools should try to build these skills and attributes.[15] But too many schools and school reformers remain stuck in an obsolete paradigm. They focus on the traditional Three R's and generally see learning as something done in a chair and behind a desk and with a single teacher in front of the room. In most schools, students have too few chances to work on teams, too few chances to meet and work with successful adults, too few chances to learn about the world of work through internships, and little explicit training in how to give or ask for feedback. Activities that provide these skills—like playing on sports teams, acting in plays, participating in internships, and building robots on a team—are rare at most schools and only available to a small number of students.

For children like Chrystal and Col and Jardine, citizen power and an expanded learning day can build nonacademic skills and narrow social-capital gaps by giving kids chances to practice relating to many different adults while building confidence, higher levels of trust, and stronger social networks.

Working with very-low-income students in some of the toughest schools and neighborhoods in America, Citizen Schools has gotten our graduates to finish high school and enroll in college at rates that are the same as or higher than in middle-class communities. Some of the success comes from the academic boost we give students when they are still in middle school. But I believe an equally big success factor is the social capital we help our students develop.

CHAPTER TWELVE

SUPPORTING TEACHERS, AND PARENTS TOO

Of all the questions I get about Citizen Schools, perhaps the most frequent is: "Do the teachers like you?" Many questioners seem conditioned to expect the worst of public school teachers and assume that a second shift of educators, offering different approaches and taking less or no pay, will inspire resentment from the full-time teachers who lead classes for a majority of the day.

Generally, however, America's teachers have embraced Citizen Schools and embraced an expanded learning day and citizen power in their schools. While a few teachers may react defensively and hide behind the closed door of their classrooms, the best teachers welcome any help they can get. Teachers' unions as well have generally embraced Citizen Schools. As stated earlier, American Federation of Teachers president Randi Weingarten visited the Edwards ELT campus and declared it in a *New York Times* column, "one of the most impressive schools I have seen in America."[1] The Boston Teachers Union has gone so far as to explicitly advocate for a nine-plus-hour learning day for all students, with the extra time delivered either by teachers receiving extra pay or by outside programs like Citizen Schools.[2]

Adding a second shift of educators in schools could fundamentally change the teacher's job for the better, making it more sustainable and enjoyable while bringing more resources to kids and engaging families more deeply in their child's education. Suburban teachers often get this support from active families and well-organized extended-day programs. But most teachers in high-poverty schools feel overworked, undersupported, and unsuccessful. As a result, many of them leave teaching too soon, creating a higher-than-necessary teacher churn and more challenges for students.[3] Many rigorous "no excuses" charter schools have been successful at lifting test scores, but they have even higher rates of teacher turnover than district schools because of the long days and breakneck pace. For district and charter schools, a second shift can make a full career in teaching more attractive.

Erin Dukeshire, a middle school science teacher at the Orchard Gardens K–8 ELT school in Boston, illustrates the point. Orchard Gardens, formerly one of the lowest-performing schools in Massachusetts, became a "turnaround school" in 2010 with new leadership, mostly new teachers, and an expanded learning day. Very quickly Orchard Gardens became one of the strongest schools in Massachusetts. In 2011–12 its middle-grade students had the highest rate of student learning growth of any middle school in the state. All of these students received an extra three hours of learning from Citizen Schools every day. Some students even had a chance to travel to the White House and meet with the president.

By the time Dukeshire came to Orchard Gardens, she was a relative veteran in the ed-reform world. She had taught for two years in Miami through Teach For America and then had joined a charter school in Boston that offered students a nine-hour day with core teachers covering the entire time. At Orchard Gardens, Principal Andrew Bott recruited her to be part of his turnaround team of teacher leaders.

"I was ready for a change and I was looking for leadership opportunities beyond the classroom," said Dukeshire. "Also, I personally wasn't able to sustain the intensity at which I was working for that number of hours in a day. Since I was coming to Orchard Gardens at the start of the turnaround, the work was still intense and I was working just as hard that first year, but the difference was that the work with students ran until about two-twenty, and then Citizen Schools took over and I could use that afternoon time to work with my colleagues." Dukeshire, a 2014 winner of the Presidential Award for Excellence in Math and Science Teaching, said that having a high-quality partner extend the day for students while teachers prepare the next day's lesson with colleagues "means that we have more time to create better outcomes for kids and it makes the profession of teaching more sustainable."

At the Isaac Newton School in East Harlem, New York, sixth-grade teacher David McKinney can teach his math class every morning knowing that every student in his class has done their homework from the previous day, because every student participates in the extended day with Citizen Schools and gets an hour of supported homework time from a second-shift teacher while still at school. Imagine this difference alone: Before ELT maybe half of your students completed their homework, since many had no structured time and place to complete it. Now all of your students, or almost all of them, complete it. Imagine how that changes your job as a teacher.

For Sara Sheckel, a former sixth-grade English teacher at the McKinley Institute of Technology in Redwood City, California, a second shift means that she can coordinate with five AmeriCorps teaching fellows, who collectively support the ninety-six sixth graders, a majority of them from Spanish-speaking families, enrolled in her four English classes. While Sheckel has one hour per day with each of her four classes of twenty-four students, the teaching fellows have three hours every day with one team of eighteen to twenty students. Sheckel benefits from the extra practice her students get building vocabulary skills with the teaching fellows, and she also gets help engaging parents and providing individualized guidance to her students. With so many students, it's not realistic for Sheckel to call every parent every week, or even every month, or to sit down one-on-one with all of her students. But in the course of just one week it *is* realistic for the Citizen Schools teaching fellows to call every parent with an informative update and to have one-on-one conversations with every student on their team. Now

Sheckel has a conduit to pass on key messages to students and parents and also a way to receive information back from them.

Increasingly, Citizen Schools ELT schools include a thirty- to sixty-minute block where first-shift and second-shift teachers lead a class together. At Elmhurst Community Prep in Oakland, which in 2012–13 had the most student learning growth of any middle school in the city, the teachers and teaching fellows co-teach an advisory block focused on goal-setting and on increasing students' ownership for their own success. Most days each adult in the room takes an advisory group of ten to twelve students, allowing students and adults alike to build meaningful relationships and trust, a sort of school-based social capital that often helps students advance. When students get better at asking for help, at speaking up when they don't understand something, and at holding give-and-take conversations with adults and peers, they are better positioned to move forward academically, socially, and professionally.

The more overlap time there is between first- and second-shift teachers, the more opportunity there is to re-create the core learning day in a way that supports teachers and improves student learning. In our ELT schools in East Palo Alto and San Jose, California, for instance, teaching fellows lead three hours of extended learning time but also support two to three "regular" classes each day. Before ELT, a typical school-day class was fifty minutes long and consisted of the teacher sharing a new concept for about twenty minutes and then giving students thirty minutes to practice the new skill as the teacher tried simultaneously to manage behavior across the full class while circulating for mini-interventions with students, a majority of whom are typically stuck on one or more steps in the lesson. With a teaching fellow in the room, the master teacher can introduce the lesson and have the class work through a few sample problems as a group. Then the teaching fellow can oversee the class, keeping students on task, while the lead teacher takes a succession of small groups to the worktable at the back of the room to unpack a new skill until each student has mastered it.

"Teachers and principals are telling us that having a teaching fellow support core classes is allowing teachers to close the instructional loop," said Katie Brown Rothschild, the Citizen Schools managing director of program in California and formerly a teaching fellow and campus director. "They used to preassess for understanding, then teach and practice, and then assess again. Now they can preassess, teach and practice, assess again, and then remediate as needed. They love it."

Allowing teachers time for pull-out tutoring, giving students extra academic practice time, and engaging parents in their child's learning are all important ways that Citizen Schools supports teachers. But the most important way we support teachers is by motivating students to try harder in school. By exposing students to exciting real-world projects, Citizen Schools helps make traditional school subjects become more relevant and enticing. All of a sudden a topic sentence becomes a key skill to win a mock trial, not just another academic standard on a long list that needs to be mastered. A student becomes motivated to learn the Pythagorean theorem because it helps unlock the secret of programming a video game.

"In education we can test kids, we can have progress reports, data reports, but the bottom line is if learning is not meaningful for a student they won't truly learn," said David Baiz, a former teacher and now principal at Global Technology Prep public school in East Harlem. "Citizen Schools makes that connection possible and allows kids to see how learning is meaningful for their lives." Baiz described a student, Kamarthy, who did a Citizen Schools presentation with NBC iVillage. "He is a student who struggled a lot in the school day and was never engaged. But he was very engaged in this presentation and it was a wonderful presentation. He felt so comfortable up there talking to these executives, presenting his products to board members, and giving a mini-speech. We saw his potential in a whole new way."

Citizen Schools also supports teachers by allowing them to be mentors and master educators. With a second shift of eager young educators on the scene, experienced full-time teachers can not only *get* help in the classroom but can *give* help by mentoring the young teaching fellows sourced by Citizen Schools.

As an example, Kendra Engels, who served as campus director at the De Vargas Middle School in Santa Fe, New Mexico, which in two years of ELT was able to raise math proficiency by eighteen percentage points and ELA proficiency by eight percentage points, described the relationship her team built with a strong teacher at the school.

"We had a teacher who taught English and who was really skilled at ELL (English-language learner) instruction techniques," shared Engels. "She was often in the classroom when we were teaching and she ended up working with our Academic Program Lead to help her rewrite some of the lessons to better align with where she saw gaps in student learning and with how she taught in her class. We rearranged our staffing so that our three teaching fellows who worked most often with ELL students could observe her teaching. It was great, because it showed students that we were all colleagues and that the teachers and Citizen Schools staff were in it together. It was great for the teacher to see the planning that went into our programming and to have input into our instruction. And of course it was fabulous for our staff to have great techniques modeled by a pro."

Engels said the same teacher also led a four-hour training session for the Citizen Schools staff that many deemed the best they'd had all year. They loved the new perspective, and she loved the opportunity to teach her craft.

Engels and her team also partnered with teachers to use assessment data more effectively. Together they reviewed interim test results and came up with plans to boost student understanding and performance. "The school led several half-day data-analysis sessions," Engels recounted, "to strategize about how to best adjust instruction based on what the data said about student learning. This was the first session of its kind for the school in quite some time, if not ever, but was the type of thing we do at Citizen Schools all the time. Our staff was able to attend and contribute a lot of great ideas and strategies. It really helped the teachers to see us as colleagues and for them to see that we felt equally responsible for the standardized testing results and equally driven to improve them. We became partners toward one goal rather than just two entities working in the same space."

ELT also provides teachers with a pathway to leadership, often a tough road in schools where the typical management structure for a school of six hundred students is one principal, one assistant principal, a director of instruction or dean of discipline, a secretary, and fifty teachers. In the second and third years of ELT at her school in Redwood City, Sara Sheckel actually split her time between the school, where she taught two instead of four classes, and Citizen Schools, where she served as the part-time instructional coach, providing feedback and professional development to the first- and second-year educators in the teaching fellowship. The experience allowed her to continue adding value as a teacher while building management skills, ultimately leading to Sheckel's appointment for the 2013–14 year as assistant principal of the Roy Cloud K–8 school in another part of Redwood City.

In many ways, the job of teacher as currently constructed is an outmoded relic of an industrial age. The teacher works mostly alone, putting equal attention into tasks he or she is great at and ones he or she struggles with. The job in year one is similar to the job in year ten or year forty. Just as students are treated too much like widgets in a factory, receiving the same dosage of multiplication tables and the same serving of Mendel's peas, regardless of their understanding and interest, teachers are asked to teach the same topics and in basically the same way regardless of their skill and experience and the needs of their students. It's as if students came into a hospital and received the same medicine and the same fifty-minute examinations from doctors and nurses who followed the same script regardless of the ailment and regardless of the particular specialty and previous training of the medical professionals.

The United States has roughly 5 million medical professionals but only 624,000 doctors who care for patients.[4] At its best, the medical system leverages each of those 5 million professionals to do what they can uniquely do best, with the role of an intake nurse different from that of a nurse practitioner, and different still from the X-ray technician, the medical resident, and the attending physician. Surely education could learn something from this differentiated approach.

Right now there are approximately 3.5 million full-time teachers employed to teach about 50 million US students enrolled in about 100,000

K–12 schools.[5] There are another 2.5 million public school employees, ranging from special-education paraprofessionals to lunch monitors, librarians, secretaries, principals, custodians, and administrators. Whereas in the 1950s the ratio was one teacher for every twenty-eight students, today, in part due to growing numbers of special-education students, it is one to fifteen, and in urban districts it's one teacher for every twelve students.[6]

The sheer volume of teachers creates real problems for professionalization of the craft, as Rick Hess of the American Enterprise Institute, among others, have described. Even with modest rates of turnover, schools across the nation need to hire 280,000 new teachers per year, many more than the 120,000 full-time registered nurses hired each year, or the 26,000 new lawyers.[7] As Hess notes, hiring 280,000 excellent teachers every year when there are only 1.5 million college graduates per year—and just 500,000 from competitive colleges—is an impossible task.[8] A lot of people coming out of college don't want to be teachers, and yet we are trying to recruit almost one in five recent college graduates year after year. Imagine if we had slightly fewer teachers and paid them better and supported them with hundreds of thousands of teaching fellows, many of them training to become teachers but others taking a year or two to contribute to a local school before going on to careers in business or science, or the arts. Most teaching fellows would be right out of college, but some might be older professionals transitioning to a new career in education.[9] This more flexible talent model would provide more continuity with better-supported master teachers staying longer, while also infusing schools with fresh energy and additional talented and caring adults.

A model in which there were varying levels of teachers in a school would support educators at every level of experience, increase efficiency, and allow for more differentiation of student learning. Master teachers who had demonstrated excellent teaching over a sustained period of time could earn 50 percent more than typical teachers today and could teach one or two fewer classes per semester so they had time to coach their younger peers. Core teachers might have a similar teaching load to teachers today but would receive help from a teaching fellow, offloading work such as grading of homework and tests, supervising student practice sessions, and management of field trips. This would allow core teachers to put more time into the development of great lesson plans. Teaching fellows and volunteer citizen teachers could support the master and core teachers while also extending the learning day, providing more time for academic practice, more time for personalized learning (through online programs such as Khan Academy or software-based learning), and significantly more time for students to make and do things with real professionals. Together, this American Dream team of talented educators could build academic and social skills while also helping students discover the real-world applications of school-based knowledge.

In some respects this multitiered approach would look like the Isaac Newton Expanded Learning Time Middle School in East Harlem, which is located in the same building where my Mom taught freshman English more than forty years ago. After many years of disappointing performance, Principal Lisa Nelson adopted ELT in 2011–12 for all of the school's sixth graders and saw proficiency jump by twenty-six percentage points in math and seventeen percentage points in English. Nelson, a veteran administrator, also saw a new spirit in her school. Her teachers and her leadership team felt buoyed by the energy of the Citizen Schools second shift, and she increasingly turned to Citizen Schools campus director Seth Miran as a trusted partner. Her school was infused with artists and engineers and financial professionals. My mom even came back to her old school building and taught an apprenticeship in organic farming and said she learned a few new teaching tricks she wished she'd had decades earlier.

Isaac Newton is now in the process of expanding ELT to all students in sixth through eighth grade. As part of this year's plan, Principal Nelson has asked her Citizen Schools teaching fellows to take the lead on interim assessments, including the administration of "exit tickets," which are two- to three-question assessments to check for understanding at the end of a single lesson. Teaching fellows will score the various interim assessments, load the data onto a spreadsheet, and conduct initial analysis that they can then share with Citizen Schools and school-day colleagues. The core teachers will have more time to focus on instruction and lesson planning and other high-value activities.

ELT with Citizen Schools is one compelling way to reorganize the talent strategy of a school, but it's not the only way. Generation Schools in New York City delivers smaller class sizes and a longer day and year to its students—while working within the New York City teacher's contract—by eliminating most administrative and specialist positions. Many charter schools have developed junior-teacher models that allow rookie teachers to extend the learning day without burning out core teachers, while also developing needed bench strength for the school. As mentioned in chapter 6, a majority of Citizen Schools teaching fellows now transition directly from their two-year assignment to a full-time teaching role, in many cases after having earned a teaching certificate with one of our alternative certification partners.[10] All the programs mentioned in chapter 8, including the National Academies Foundation, High Tech High, and the Met School, have found ways to creatively engage a second shift of educators to support core teachers, engage students, and build a bridge to parents.

Infusing citizen power and extra learning time into schools also supports parents. For starters, and to state the obvious, a day that ends at five or six o'clock instead of two or three lines up better with the end of the workday, meaning children have fewer hours home alone or on the streets. Keeping kids off the streets is a low standard for extended-day programs, but it's an important first step. According to the Afterschool Alliance, more teens are victims or perpetrators of crime between 3:00 and 6:00 p.m. on school days than at any other time of the week.[11] School-day afternoons are also a time of experimentation with drugs and with sex and, most commonly, a time for mind-numbing TV shows and violent video games.

Citizen Schools and programs like it also create a bridge that helps parents connect with their children and the public schools they attend. Sometimes this bridge comes from the simple act of calling parents (or grandparents) at home just to check in and name something a student is doing well and something he or she could do better. Community police officer Denis Rorie had advised us to "catch kids doing things right." That advice is reaffirmed every time I see parents beam with pride as they watch their children showcase a new skill. These WOW! moments open doors to new careers as well as to new conversations around the kitchen table.

Sometimes the extended-day staff serve as translators, literally. Our work in Revere, Massachusetts, an immigrant city with fast-changing demographics, is a case in point. When we started working in Revere, we learned that a majority of the students in the school spoke a language other than English at home. But not a single one of the school's thirty-eight full-time teachers was fluent in any foreign language. When the principal wanted to translate a flyer into Spanish, the most common language of the school's parents, she needed to send the text to the district and sometimes wouldn't get a translation back for three weeks! Fortunately a majority of the Citizen Schools staff was fluent or conversational in Spanish, and one staff member spoke Haitian Creole. We became an essential conduit for communication.

The sometimes-difficult relationship between urban parents and schoolteachers was driven home to me in 1999, when a few colleagues and I traveled with twelve parents and teachers from a Boston middle school to Camp Kiev, a high-end summer camp in Maine. We ventured all the way to Camp Kiev because it had an Outward Bound–type ropes course, and camp director Dick Kennedy had lined up funding to pay his instructors to lead us in team-building activities. It turned out we needed all the help we could get.

On the first day of the retreat, when asked to suggest ways to improve the school, teachers quickly defaulted to complaining about parents, saying they needed to get their children to complete their homework and to get to school on time each day. I cringed. Parents blamed the teachers—not those who had volunteered to attend the retreat but others they felt were not serving their children well. As parents they were entrusting their children's learning to the school but they were seeing disappointing results.

On the second day of the retreat, the facilitator asked participants to remember who held a vision for them when they were twelve years old.

Most people had a story of a teacher, or a parent, or a helpful neighbor. But one father said that when he was twelve, no one had a vision for him, and he broke down crying. The ice was broken and the group started to come together. Later that day the group completed high and low ropes courses and team-building exercises. The barriers continued to fall. On the final day of the retreat, we started to think collectively about how an expanded learning day could be a platform for improving the school—and improving communication. Parents and teachers were each a little more able to see things from the other's perspective.

I recently read through feedback surveys completed by 353 classroom teachers working in our ELT schools. There were helpful points of critique pointing to areas for improvement. Several teachers, for instance, said they loved the apprenticeships but wanted to see standards raised for the academic lessons led by teaching fellows. Others had complaints about the furniture being rearranged in their rooms, or about students being tired from the long day. But the overwhelming sentiment of the comments was gratitude. Teachers in the schools we partner with feel like they have allies—new crews of professional colleagues who respect them and help them motivate, support, and teach their students.

Of all 353 teachers responding to the anonymous survey, 94 percent said that Citizen Schools staff responded to their needs, and 93 percent said they had been responsive to Citizen Schools; 96 percent said they interact with Citizen Schools staff as professional colleagues; 88 percent of teachers said that Citizen Schools staff had initiated a conversation about student academic progress in the last semester, and a majority said this happened at least weekly.

Looking at these numbers, I couldn't help but recall our start as a summer and after-school program at Dever School in Boston almost twenty years earlier. I remembered a painful incident at the end of our second year at Dever, when teachers we hardly knew were furious that students on our watch had damaged several blackboards in their classrooms. Ned and I went directly to the local hardware store and bought chalkboard paint and then spent the better part of a day re-painting large green classroom chalkboards and leaving behind new packets of white and colored chalk. Today we still have the occasional chalkboard incident. That's going to happen any time space is being shared. But now there is a foundation of trust built on a track record of results and appreciation.

In many ways American education overall is also headed in a positive direction. Despite the challenges this book has discussed, average college graduation and high school graduation rates are going up, math scores are improving, and we now have hundreds—maybe even thousands—of schools delivering excellent results for low-income students. More outstanding college graduates are choosing to teach. We are moving toward a voluntarily adopted national Common Core curriculum that focuses more on higher-order thinking skills rather than regurgitation of memorized facts. And tests are about to become better, assessing writing and scientific thinking, not just the ability to guess correct answers on a fill-in-the-bubble test. The challenge for America is that while our schools are improving, schools around the world are improving faster. And the challenge for low-income American students is that while they are learning more—and their parents and their teachers are working harder—they are falling relatively further behind, left in the wake of a tsunami of privatized extra learning opportunities that benefit their upper-middle-class peers.

When I started Citizen Schools I was not yet a parent, and I was just becoming a new type of teacher. The parents and teachers we worked with were role models for me, and I remember them vividly. I remember parents with six kids in tow traveling an hour on public transportation after a full day's work to attend a WOW!, eyes gleaming and smiles wide as they saw their child operate a robot she had built or argue a case in front of a federal judge. "It's all she talks about at home," I would hear. "She says she wants to be a lawyer now." I remember Hetty Mitchell, one of the parents in our first summer program, who worked at the Stop & Shop in Dorchester's Lower Mills section where I used to go for groceries. As I paid for my groceries, Hetty and I would talk about her daughter, Andrea, exchanging stories of accomplishments and challenges. I felt an important kinship.

I also felt kinship with Margie Tkacik, the fifth-grade teacher in Dever's Room 202 who let me work with ten of her students for a few hours a week to launch Citizen Schools. Margie was such an enthusiastic teacher that at times she seemed to almost bubble over as she described her plans and visions for her students. She reminded me a little of my mother. When I started Citizen Schools, I had a recurring conversation with people who loved the model but thought I should embed the program in the existing six- or seven-hour school day. But this was maddening to me. What I learned from Margie was *not* that her students needed me *instead* of Margie. They needed as much time as possible with Margie *and* some extra learning time with me.

As I look today over a troubled public education landscape—a landscape where innovation and personalized learning is growing rapidly, but so is inequality—I yearn for the chance to rebuild our national sense of shared public purpose. Public schools were intended to knit together a new country, giving children of immigrants and of business owners the same chance at an excellent education. Today public schools and their teachers feel under siege. Some of that is deserved, a consequence of resistance to fair-minded change and higher standards. But surely much of the acrimony is undeserved, driven in part by the lack of connection and therefore lack of empathy between upper- and lower-income parents, between business leaders and teachers, and between all of us as American citizens.

Gandhi said that we must *be* the change we want to see in the world. If we want better public schools, we can't wait for some new curriculum or management plan or market mechanism. We need to roll up our sleeves and make them better. We need to step into schools with minimal judgment and as much curiosity and energy as we can muster. That's how to change the opportunity equation.

LINDY SMALT, AMERICORPS TEACHING FELLOW

The backbone of the Citizen Schools second shift are teaching fellows, recent college graduates supported by the national AmeriCorps program. AmeriCorps members make Expanded Learning Time possible and support teachers and volunteers and parents, as described in the previous chapter. I believe dramatic expansion of AmeriCorps, as described in the final section of the book, is perhaps the most cost-effective and powerful investment we could make in equalizing opportunity in America. The following story is from AmeriCorps member Lindy Smalt, who served with Citizen Schools in Revere, Massachusetts, from 2010 to 2012.

> *Two years ago, I was a Wheaton College senior. I was undoubtedly one of the coolest kids on campus. I was a theater major, automatically mysterious and deep. Lindy was my name, and self-assurance was my game.*
>
> *And yet there was that constant, dreadful feeling in the back of my mind—What was I going to do after May? What if the rest of the world wasn't caught up on how cool I was? What was I going to do without my immense sense of purpose and popularity?*

■ ■ ■

I got very, very lucky—I stumbled upon a job in education.

Now, let me be clear: When I faxed back the signed offer letter to Citizen Schools, I thought the teaching fellowship was going to be a two-year break for me to figure out what my "real job" would be.

That couldn't have been less true. I might have been a rock star at Wheaton, but nothing, not even my twenty-five-credit semester, could have prepared me for the incredibly demanding work of teaching in one of our nation's low-income communities.

Once obsessed with political philosophizing, I was shocked to find that teaching in a public school was the first time I wasn't just ranting about politics—I was living them. A single forty-minute lesson at Garfield Middle School reflected so many of our nation's struggles, from the prison system, to immigration, to the drug war. In two years, I taught an Iraqi refugee, the daughter of a murderer, a boy who saw his parents murdered, a boy who got expelled for drug possession, a girl who spoke an unheard-of African dialect—and these people were eleven. Through their lives, their sometimes absent parents, their complete apathy toward school, I saw—for the first time—the necessity of my work and of my life, and the true depth of our nation's struggles.

■ ■ ■

"When we are very old," said one of my student's mothers to me this year, in half Arabic and broken English, as she placed her hand on mine, "we will always think of Ms. Smalt. We will say, 'Ms. Smalt is the one who changed everything. She was the start of a new life.'" She and her son, Abdellah, do not have a computer or a car; they walk to the local library to use the Internet. Yet with her support, Abdellah's unparalleled perseverance, and my resources in the community, we were able to secure a spot for her son in the high-performing charter high school in the next town, as well as garner a $2,500 grant for him to attend summer camp for the first time.

Students like Abdellah have all of the skills to succeed in college and beyond, but often there is no one to show them the way. He is small and gets swallowed in large classes of screaming, sassy preteens. But he is diligent, positive, and extremely kind, and he deserves a chance. And there are millions more like him.

SECTION THREE

NEXT STEPS FOR AMERICA AND FOR YOU

CHAPTER THIRTEEN

A CIVIC MARSHALL PLAN FOR EQUAL OPPORTUNITY

What will it take to bring Citizen Schools and similar ideas to scale—to truly reimagine and expand the learning day while narrowing class-based disparities in opportunity and achievement? Can we do it? Or as a nation have we lost our mojo, lost our heart, and lost our belief that big change is possible?

I believe America is still the place where Adam Barriga, the grandson of a Peruvian immigrant who polishes the State House floor, can become, like David Mantus, a chemist, or rocket scientist, or anything he wants. We can still be the place where Miguel wants to take a young immigrant from Central America out for ice cream, and where that immigrant, Francisco, has the opportunity to give something back. We can be the place where Earline has a chance to pass along her life's passion for sewing, and where Linda finally gets to take off her heavy wool coat. We can be the place where a lousy school no longer drags down its neighborhood, but instead leads a renaissance in learning, like the Edwards did, transforming itself from worst to first and serving as a beacon of hope and pride for an entire city. We can do all of these things, but only if in our hearts and actions we truly embrace opportunity for the many, not just the few.

This book starts with a problem—a well-documented and fast-growing achievement gap between the academic and career advancement of wealthier and poorer students—and then discusses the causes and potential solutions. Some of the achievement gap (20 to 30 percent) is caused by inequality between schools in wealthier and poorer neighborhoods. That inequality needs to change. But most of the gap comes from unequal access to learning opportunities offered after school or in the summers, at home or in a growing constellation of tutoring centers, skill-building camps, and paid enrichment and internship programs. Upper-income kids get many thousands of dollars invested in these types of extra learning opportunities, and as a result they hone their basic academic skills; they build new skills such as the ability to innovate and create and work on teams, and they build increasingly important social networks and social skills. This inequality needs to change too.

This book describes how Citizen Schools and similar programs deploy citizen power and an expanded learning day to provide children in lower-income communities many of the same learning opportunities that are routine in wealthier communities. Citizen Schools and others are using this playbook today to narrow and even eliminate achievement gaps. But while existing programs help hundreds of thousands of low-income children beat the odds stacked against them, we aren't fundamentally changing the odds. Unless we do something much bolder, the gap between upper-income and lower-income families will continue to get bigger, overall economic growth will stagnate, and the number of Horatio Alger success stories will continue to dwindle.

On July 4, 1861, four months after taking office and with the first major battle of the Civil War looming, President Abraham Lincoln wrote to Congress with a single message. The leading purpose of government, he stated, is "to elevate the conditions of men—to lift artificial weights from all shoulders—to clear the paths of laudable pursuit for all—to afford all an unfettered start, and a fair chance in the race of life." Each of us as individuals can take action to provide fellow citizens with that fair chance in the race of life. But government, as Lincoln said, must do its part too.

Following are six specific steps that government can take at the national, state, and/or local level to increase opportunity and strengthen the nation.

1. Fully fund the bipartisan Edward M. Kennedy Serve America Act and get at least 250,000 Americans into full-time service, with a majority deployed to schools. AmeriCorps members, including members of a new School Turnaround Corps run in partnership with the Department of Education, can be the heart of a massively scaled "second shift" in education and can in turn recruit, train, and support citizen change makers like those described in this book. Fully funding AmeriCorps would cost $2 billion, which would pay for itself many times over in the form of higher educational attainment and higher wages for the millions who would benefit. A recent study indicated that each dollar invested in national service ultimately returns four dollars to the Treasury through higher wages (which lead to higher tax receipts) and lower social service costs.[1]

2. Initiate a national marketing campaign for mentors and volunteer teachers on the scale of the Rosie the Riveter campaign during World War II or the designated-driver campaign in the 1980s, inspired by Mothers Against Drunk Driving. David Mantus and Alan Su and Earline Shearer and Deb Daccord are the early adopters. Now we need to use their stories to promote mentoring and volunteer teaching as a personally rewarding way to strengthen our communities and country. We should use the bully pulpit of the US president and First Lady (and of mayors and governors and other political leaders across the country) to call for more citizen teachers, mentors, and tutors, and to recognize and reward volunteers and the companies that sponsor them.

3. Pass the national Time for Innovation Matters in Education (TIME) Act. Introduced in 2008 by the late Senator Kennedy and reintroduced in 2011, the TIME Act would create an ELT fund allowing the federal government to offer matching grants to qualified schools. To ensure systemic shifts in funding priorities,

the TIME Act should provide annual funding of $750 or more per student, with winning schools and districts needing to free up an additional $750 per student from their own budgets and commit to adding at least three hundred extra hours of high-quality learning time. As the economy and tax revenues rebound from the recent recession, states should dedicate 10 percent or more of increased revenues to state versions of the TIME Act that support high-quality Expanded Learning Time programs. As with the federal act, states could make five-year renewable grants of $750 or more per student per year with a one-to-one match required from recipient schools and communities. This would ensure that a combination of new and repurposed funding streams support and sustain the type of high-quality extended-day programs and workplace internships that can narrow or eliminate opportunity and achievement gaps.

4. Revise the federal tax code so that contributors to local education foundations and private schools do not receive a tax break if they support schools that are already well funded and serve few low-income students. Donors would maintain their tax break if the school or district they are supporting is publicly funded at a lower than average level and serves a high percentage of low-income students. This idea aligns with a recent suggestion by Stanford professor of political science Rob Reich, who wrote a September 2013 *New York Times* column describing how the Schools Foundation in wealthy Hillsborough, California, received $2,300 per student in tax-deductible donations while, across San Francisco Bay, students in low-income Oakland benefit from less than $100 per student in private donations. "Private giving to public schools widens the gap between rich and poor," wrote Reich. "It exacerbates inequalities in financing. It is philanthropy in the service of conferring advantage on the already well-off."[2] Upper-income parents like me should absolutely contribute to the schools our children attend, whether public or private, but we shouldn't simultaneously withdraw funds from the public purse by deducting those contributions from our taxable income. Additional revenue

that would flow to the IRS by making this change should be earmarked to pay for other proposals discussed in this chapter.

5. Reauthorize the Elementary and Secondary Education Act (commonly known as No Child Left Behind), the principal federal policy governing education. Ensure that its various programs move toward allowing more flexibility in how federal funds can be used but also require reasonable accountability for results. Specifically, Congress should make the following changes relative to the themes of this book:

   a. Reserve 5 percent of Title I funding (this set-aside would equal about $750 million at current budget levels) for investments in partnerships between high-poverty districts and educational support organizations that have strong evidence of positively impacting student learning. Too much Title I funding is spent on what it was spent on last year without regard to effectiveness.

   b. Revise the 21st Century Community Learning Centers program ($1.2 billion) to explicitly authorize use of the funds for Expanded Learning Time models that serve all students in a school (in addition to optional after-school programs that extend the learning day for some students) and to explicitly require that funded programs involve a partnership between one or more schools and one or more community-based organizations and take a balanced educational approach that includes enrichment, as well as core academics.

   c. Revise the School Improvement Grants program ($500 million) to allow grants from states directly to nonprofit partners with proven school-turnaround models.

6. Organize a new round of Race to the Top funding focused on hands-on learning in science, technology, engineering, and math (STEM). A relatively modest one-time federal investment in hands-on STEM learning could stimulate lasting changes in local school policy, stimulate new partnerships with private industry, and scale up programs such as US2020, which match STEM professionals with teachers and students.

Offering Citizen Schools or similar programs to every middle school child in a majority-low-income school in America (about 4 million students) would cost about $6 billion, less than 1 percent of total US K–12 education spending. At least half this money could come from reallocations of current budgets and the AmeriCorps expansion described above. While some funds for ELT can come from stretching current dollars further and spending them more wisely, some new investment is also needed. This can come from modest changes to the tax code (reducing deductions for gifts to private schools and public schools that serve mostly upper-income children) as described above, or through allocation of a portion of additional revenues as the economy grows.

While there is much that government can do, there is a lot that we the people can do that won't require waiting for government. To narrow achievement gaps and broaden opportunity, citizens like you and me can:

1. Volunteer as a citizen teacher (www.citizenschools.org), a mentor (mentor.org or us2020.org for scientists and engineers and others in the STEM disciplines), or a tutor in a high-need school near your home or office.
2. Serve as a full-time AmeriCorps or VISTA member (www .americorps.gov) or a member of other full- and part-time service corps.
3. Invest. If you are an upper-middle-class or wealthy parent, calculate what you spend on extra enrichment and tutoring for your own children and consider making a tax-deductible contribution of this amount or an amount you can afford to one of the many effective organizations trying to close the opportunity gap. Our kids deserve everything we are giving them, but so do other kids.
4. Advocate for public schools, for extended-day programs, and for appropriate reforms to fully fund and reform public schools in your community.
5. If you work for or run a business, a government agency, or a nonprofit, host a summer intern from a low- to moderate-income

background. Try to pay them a stipend. But even if all you can cover is a few free lunches, provide a meaningful work experience that gives your intern a first step on her career ladder. If you work near an innovative high school that places students in for-credit internships (NAF, MET, High Tech High),[3] sign up to host a student extern so they can earn credit while getting exposure to the world of work.

6. If you are a social entrepreneur or want to become one, create a new program that lifts up opportunity for lower-income children. Evaluate it. Improve it. We need more examples of successful programs that are well evaluated, well documented, and marketed broadly. If you already run a promising or proven program addressing achievement and opportunity gaps, then grow it, tell your story, and share your methods.

America's success has never been about just government, or business, or individuals. At our best, our national character mixes rugged individualism with communitarian ideals. We celebrate the Horatio Alger story but also community barn raisings and volunteer fire departments and the neighborhood public school. In recent years, however, we have often lost sight of our community values. We've been distracted by our differences and have allowed a globalized economy to expand gaps of wealth and achievement. Equality of opportunity is a founding ideal of the nation, but we now have less of it than ever before.

Despite this lament, the students, volunteers, and staff of Citizen Schools show us that the American capacity for generosity, compassion, and love of neighbor runs deep. Our participants are narrowing achievement gaps, broadening opportunity, and strengthening America. Let us hope these actions will inspire more to stand up—together— to make the opportunity equation work for the many, not just the few.

AGOSTINHA DEPINA, STUDENT

Every spring, Citizen Schools hosts a fund-raising benefit in Boston. As with many benefits, there is chicken for dinner, some wine, a few brief speeches by staff and board members, and sometimes a video. But at these benefits the keynote speaker is always a student or a former student, someone who has lived the Citizen Schools program and who has the final word. The following speech was shared by alumnus Agostinha DePina on April 4, 2012.

> *Let me take you to my homeland.*
> *Bare feet feeling the hot sand,*
> *Chasing chickens, riding horses.*
> *These are my roots.*

My name is Agostinha DePina, and I am a senior at John D. O'Bry-ant High School in Boston. I spent the first eight years of my life on the island of Fogo in Cape Verde, where my parents grew up, and only my mom went to high school. We were really poor. I remember sleeping on the floor, hungry some nights with one dress and no shoes. But I also remember feeling free and happy.

I immigrated to the US when I was nine years of age. My parents brought me here for the opportunity. But I was terrified. I remember my first day of elementary school, being in the big yellow bus in the middle of strangers, without knowing a word of English, and entering a classroom where I did not know what to do or what to say. So I placed myself in a comfort corner.

I might have gotten lost right away if it weren't for my second-grade teacher, Ms. Gomes. With her charismatic and intellectual teaching, she taught me English and helped me see what was possible in my new country. In the Cape Verdean culture, women are taught that their dreams of success are their husband's dreams, that they don't need a voice because the man has a voice. But in the United States, I saw things I had never seen before: girls of all ages going to school, mothers being independent and working, and women striving to be a part of something. Ms. Gomes showed me that women can become queens without a king. But I was still shy—a quiet girl with a lot to say, but with no voice.

For several years I was a passionate student, always eager to go to school. My mom and my dad were always supportive of me. I could see how hard they worked for my six siblings and me—my mom is a housekeeper at the Westin Boston Waterfront Hotel and my dad is a cleaner at UMass Boston. They told me every day that I am responsible for my future and my success.

However, as classes became more rigorous and the material was harder to understand, my parents' motivational speeches were not enough. In sixth and seventh grade, I couldn't keep my grades up, and I began to lose my drive for school.

In eighth grade, though, I was lucky. I got a support network that kept me from going off track. A group of people believed in my potential and gave me the knowledge and skills that have gotten me where I am today. These were the people of Citizen Schools.

My team leader, Julianne, would always come over and talk with me. Every time I had a test or quiz at school, Julianne would help me *study. Then professionals from Putnam Investments came and taught us interview skills. Two volunteers from the law firm Choate, Hall, & Stewart—Eleanor and Cara—worked with me on writing essays that would be published in a magazine. They became my mentors.*

And every Tuesday and Thursday, I took apprenticeships. I measured my school's carbon footprint one semester, and I tried creative writing. We created stories by observing regular day people during their daily activities. My citizen teacher Jennifer made me read my poem to my peers, where I overcame my shyness.

Julianne and the teaching fellows took us to visit eight different colleges. I loved visiting Brown and Trinity. A panel of Trinity students talked to us about their experience. Initially, I wasn't sure I wanted to go to college. But I remember one student talked about how Trinity College really made it possible for her to attend college and persevere. I knew that if she could do it, I could overcome any obstacle I face.

I am proud to say that I've just been admitted to Clark University, where I will major in communications. But I would not have made it into Clark, or even be graduating from the great high school I attend, without Citizen Schools. I wouldn't have discovered my passion for writing. And most importantly, the people I saw coming to my school and giving back made me realize that my aspiration in life is to give back. I am currently writing and performing with Teen Voices *magazine, where I use writing to empower other teen girls. My dream is to start a nonprofit for girls, to help them find the confidence that others have helped me find, and give other girls the opportunities that many women never receive.*

All these people—Jennifer, Eleanor, Cara—they saw my talents and potential at the right time in my life, and they helped me reveal it. I'm especially grateful to my team leader, Julianne, who came over and sat next to that shy girl. I'm excited to say that Julianne is here tonight.

Thank you all. All of you in this room tonight are making it possible for teens to stay on track. You who volunteer, or send your employees to volunteer, are changing kids' lives. Your donations bring Citizen Schools to more schools and help students discover the drive to go to college. *You realize that there is nothing more important than education, and you know that you have a role to play in helping teens learn what they want to become in life.*

> *The girl who walked barefoot on the heat of the Cape Verdean sand*
> *With one dress to wear, no money in her hands*
> *Is the same girl who is now making her dreams come true*
> *Now it's my turn to give back so that everyone can see*
> *How this Cape Verdean girl who was a slave to poverty*
> *Is now the master of her destiny.*

EXPANDED LEARNING TIME SCHEDULE
WITH CITIZEN SCHOOLS

MONDAY	TUESDAY	WEDNESDAY	THURSDAY	FRIDAY
Homeroom	Homeroom	Homeroom	Homeroom	Homeroom
Literacy & ELA	Literacy & ELA	Literacy & ELA	Literacy & ELA	Literacy & ELA
Math	Math	Math	Math	Math
Lunch	Lunch	Lunch	Lunch	Lunch
Science/ Social Studies	Science/ Social Studies	Science/ Social Studies	Science/ Social Studies	Science/ Social Studies
Elective	Elective	Elective	Elective	Elective
Transition around 3pm				
Snack and Circle	Snack	Snack	Snack	Joint Professional Development
Academic Support 90 min.	Academic Support 60 min.	Academic Support 90 min.	Academic Support 60 min.	
	Apprenticeship #1 90 min.		Apprenticeship #1 90 min.	
College to Career Connections 60 min.		Explore! 60 min.		
	Dismissal around 6pm			SATURDAY
				8th Grade Academy College to Career Connections

ACKNOWLEDGMENTS

Writing this book brought together my family story, the Citizen Schools story, and a journalistic story about the growing opportunity divide between lower- and upper-income children and what we can do about it. Telling the story was a privilege. But the book would not have been possible without the contributions of many others.

My parents, Fritz Schwarz and Marian Cross, and my sister, Eliza Schwarz, gracefully accepted that in a book about childhood and opportunity I wanted to talk about my own childhood, which meant talking about them too. Thank you for believing in me when it wasn't easy to and for each being great role models in many ways.

My children, Ronan and Orla, grew up around Citizen Schools, hanging out in our offices, and at apprenticeships, and WOW! celebrations. I remember when Citizen Schools apprentices held them as babies. Now Ronan, a high schooler, is alumni age, and Orla, if she were in one of our schools, would only have a year remaining before her Citizen Schools graduation. Thank you, Ronan and Orla, for putting up with Dad heading up to the "man cave" to work on this book so many evenings and so many weekends. And thank you for allowing me to tell an uncensored version of my childhood story. I feel confident talking about my wayward ways because I am so confident in both of you.

My wife, Maureen, is an artist and the most amazing storyteller I know. She has been the most important critic and supporter of this book, catching me when I lost my voice or went off track and helping make words and paragraphs and the entire story better. Thank you, Maureen, for being such a loving and passionate mother, and wife, and friend.

I've worked on this book for two years, starting with an initial proposal and outline, gradually adding a few draft chapters, and then, after Beacon Press agreed to publish the book, writing most of the chapters in 2013 at a series of brief writing retreats and on a lot of weekend mornings. Along the way I have benefited from great encouragement and editorial advice worthy of William Strunk and E. B. White, from Susan Heath, Martha Eddison, David Stolow, Joel Horwich, Laura Pappano, Ted Fiske, Mike Kubiak, Melissa Ludtke, Sherif Nada, Diana Smith, Colin Stokes, Emily Bryan, David Shapiro, AnnMaura Connolly, Alexandra Bernadotte, and Jocelyn Glatzer. Each of you helped to make the book better. Thank you. Thanks as well to Ambassador Swanee Hunt and the Hunt Alternatives Fund for supporting the book and a writing retreat at the Columbine Ranch. Thanks as well to the great team at Beacon Press and to my editor, Alexis Rizzuto. Alex, I knew I was going to like you when I learned that Phil Rizzuto was your grand-uncle, and you've never disappointed. It goes without saying that any errors or oversights are my responsibility.

Important early research assistance came from Nina Barker and Renee Reid. Colin Lacy was my partner over the last year in tracking down footnotes, checking facts, and suggesting improvements to the storyline. And a number of Citizen Schools current or former staff helped me fact-check or track down stories. Thank you to Kelly Bernard, Allyson Crawford, Elle Ward, Rebecca Brown, Ruth Summers, Alana Siegner, Jessica Lander, and Holly Trippitt.

A special thank-you goes to the core team that helped bring Citizen Schools to life and lead its growth. You have made this story possible. Ned Rimer has been a great friend since college and was a tremendous copilot for the first dozen years of Citizen Schools. He joins John Werner, Anita Price, Stephanie Davolos, and Tulaine Montgomery as the fantastic founding team that brought Citizen Schools from idea to reality. So many have made major contributions since then, but I want to particularly call out from the past and current executive staff Anuradha Desai, Adrian Haugabrook, Kate Carpenter Bernier, Lisa Ulrich, Kate Mehr, George Chu, Lori Stevens, Priscilla Cohen, Nell Kisiel, Pat Kirby, Claudia Alfaro, Kait Rogers, and the amazing Emily McCann, now our president, who has been a great partner for the last decade. Five powerful leaders have served as chair or cochair of the Citizen Schools board of directors: Marsha Feinberg and Shashi Rajpal, then Sherif Nada, then Andrew Balson, and most recently Larry Summers. I appreciate each of you and all the board members past and present who have shaped and supported Citizen Schools.

Finally, I would like to thank the amazing volunteer citizen teachers and front-line staff of Citizen Schools who have made the work and the learning fun, and the young apprentices whose big dreams motivate us every day. Helping a child discover and achieve his or her dreams is the noblest job I can imagine, and it has been my great privilege to do it for the last twenty years.

NOTES

FOREWORD

1. Tom Mortenson, "Bachelor's Degree Attainment by Age 24 by Family Income Quartiles, 1970 to 2012," *Postsecondary Education Opportunity*, 2013.

2. National Center for Education Statistics, "Enrollment Rates of 18- to 24-Year-Olds in Degree-Granting Institutions, by Level of Institution and Sex and Race/Ethnicity of Student: 1967 Through 2010," table 213, August 2011, http://nces.ed.gov/programs/digest/d11/tables/dt11_213.asp

3. Aparna Mathur, Hao Fu, and Peter Hansen, "The Mysterious and Alarming Rise of Single Parenthood in America," *Atlantic*, September 2013, http://www.theatlantic.com/business/archive/2013/09/the-mysterious -and-alarming-rise-of-single-parenthood-in-america/279203/.

4. "The 6,000-Hour Learning Gap," The After-School Corporation, 2013, http://www.expandedschools.org/policy-documents/6000-hour-learning -gap#sthash.QsffhGWW.dpbs. Multiple original sources cited.

INTRODUCTION

1. "Distribution of Bachelor's Degrees Awarded by Age 24 by Family Income Quartiles 1970 to 2012," *Postsecondary Education Opportunity*, no. 256 (October 2013), www.postsecondary.org.

2. Greg J. Duncan and Richard J. Murnane, eds., *Whither Opportunity? Rising Inequality, Schools, and Children's Life Chances* (New York: Russell Sage Foundation, 2011), 98–99.

3. Joseph P. Ferrie, "History Lessons: The End Of American Exceptionalism? Mobility in the United States Since 1850," *Journal of Economic Perspectives* 19, no. 3 (2005), 199–215.

4. McKinsey & Company, Social Sector Office, *The Economic Impact of the Achievement Gap in America's Schools* (April 2009), http://mckinseyonsociety .com.

5. Duncan and Murnane, *Whither Opportunity?*

6. Horace Mann, Twelfth Annual Report to the Massachusetts State Board of Education, 1848.

7. Erickson Arcaira, Juliet D. Vile, and Elizabeth R. Reisner, *Achieving High School Graduation: Citizen Schools' Youth Outcomes in Boston* (Washington, DC: Policy Studies Associates, 2010), www.policystudies.com; *Citizen Schools ELT Evaluation: Preliminary Findings* (Cambridge, MA: Abt Associates, 2013), www.abtassociates.com.

8. Organisation for Economic Co-operation and Development (OECD), *Education at a Glance 2011: OECD Indicators*, http://www.oecd.org.

9. Organisation for Economic Co-operation and Development (OECD), *PISA 2012 Results*, www.oecd.org/pisa/.

10. National Science Board, *Science and Engineering Indicators 2012* (Arlington, VA: National Science Foundation, 2012), http://www.nsf.gov/statistics/.

11. Duncan and Murnane, *Whither Opportunity?*

12. "Distribution of Bachelor's Degrees Awarded by Age 24 by Family Income Quartiles 1970 to 2012," *Postsecondary Education Opportunity*, no. 256 (October 2013), www.postsecondary.org.

13. Joshua Wyner, John Bridgeland, and John Dilulio, *Achievement Trap: How America Is Failing Millions of High-Achieving Students from Lower-Income Families* (Washington, DC: Jack Kent Cooke Foundation, 2007).

14. Duncan and Murnane, *Whither Opportunity?*, 11.

15. Robert D. Putnam, Carl B. Frederick, and Kaisa Snellman, *Growing Class Gaps in Social Connectedness Among American Youth* (Cambridge, MA: Harvard Kennedy School of Government, 2012), 13.

16. College Board, *Education Pays: Update*, 2005, http://www.collegeboard .com. In 1972, the median earnings for males with a bachelor's degree were 22 percent higher than for males with a high school degree.

17. Anthony P. Carnevale, Stephen J. Rose, and Ban Cheah, *The College Payoff: Education, Occupations, Lifetime Earnings* (Washington, DC: Georgetown University Center on Education and the Workforce, 2011), http://cew .georgetown.edu.

18. Duncan and Murnane, *Whither Opportunity?*, 339–58.

CHAPTER ONE

1. Lauren Resnick, "Learning in School and Out," *Educational Researcher* 16, no. 9 (1987): 13–20.

2. In the race for the 1984 Democratic nomination, Gary Hart actually won more votes across the primary and caucus season than Walter Mondale, but Mondale secured the votes of most party superdelegates and cruised to a first-ballot win at the convention in San Francisco before being crushed in the general election by President Reagan. Hart was the odds-on favorite for the 1988 Democratic primary until being forced to drop out of the race when the *Miami Herald* photographed him and a woman who was not his wife aboard a yacht in the Gulf of Mexico.

3. Bruce Feiler, *The Secrets of Happy Families: Improve Your Mornings, Rethink Family Dinner, Fight Smarter, Go Out and Play, and Much More* (New York: William Morrow, 2013).

4. Organisation for Economic Co-operation and Development (OECD), *Economic Policy Reforms: Going for Growth 2010*, 185, http://www.oecd.org/. Similar data has been found by researchers with the Equality of Opportunity Project, http://www.equality-of-opportunity.org/.

5. Raj Chetty, Nathaniel Hendren, Patrick Kline, and Emmanuel Saez, Equality of Opportunity Project, 2013, http://www.equality-of-opportunity .org.

CHAPTER TWO

1. Teresa L. Morisi, "The Early 2000s: A Period of Declining Teen Summer Employment Rates," *Monthly Labor Review* 133, no. 5 (May 2010): 23–35.

CHAPTER THREE

1. Urban Institute, National Center for Charitable Statistics, Core Files (Public Charities, 2010). From Amy S. Blackwood, Katie L. Roeger, and Sarah L. Pettijohn, *The Nonprofit Sector in Brief: Public Charities, Giving, and Volunteering, 2012* (Washington, DC: Urban Institute, 2012), http:// www.urban.org/UploadedPDF/412674-The-Nonprofit-Sector-in -Brief.pdf.

2. Peter Kim and Jeffrey Bradach, "Why More Nonprofits Are Getting Bigger," *Stanford Social Innovation Review* (Spring 2012), http://www.ssireview .org/.

CHAPTER FOUR

1. National Commission on Excellence in Education, *A Nation at Risk: The Imperative for Educational Reform* (April 1983), available at the website of

the US Department of Education, http://www.ed.gov.datacenter.spps.org
/uploads/sotw_a_nation_at_risk_1983.pdf.

2. Massachusetts Education Reform Act of 1993, 215.

3. Jennifer McMurrer, *NCLB Year 5: Instructional Time in Elementary Schools:
A Closer Look at Changes for Specific Subjects* (Washington, DC: Center on
Education Policy, 2008), www.cep-dc.org.

CHAPTER FIVE

1. Erikson Arcaira, Juliet D. Vile, and Elizabeth R. Reisner, *Citizen Schools:
Achieving High School Graduation; Citizen Schools Youth Outcomes in Boston* (Washington, DC: Policy Studies Associates, 2010); Shaun Kellogg,
Brandy Parker, Cheryl Loiselle, and Michael Kubiak, *Achieving High
School Success: The Impact of Citizen Schools North Carolina* (Boston: Citizen
Schools Research & Evaluation, 2013).

2. Eric Schwarz and Ken Kay, eds., *The Case for Twenty-First Century Learning*, issue 110, New Directions for Youth Development (San Francisco:
Jossey-Bass/Wiley, 2006).

3. Jim Collins, *Good to Great: Why Some Companies Make the Leap—and Others
Don't* (New York: HarperBusiness, 2001), 85.

CHAPTER SIX

1. Quoted in Kate Carpenter Bernier, *Expanding Learning Time: How the Edwards Middle School in Boston Partnered with Citizen Schools to Transform the
Learning Day* (Boston: Citizen Schools, April 2008), 4.

2. In Worcester, Massachusetts, for instance, teachers at the Jacob Hiatt
elementary school proposed teaming up with artists from the Worcester Art Museum and historians from the Paul Revere House. But these
community-based educators would play an adjunct, not a leading, role.

3. Carpenter Bernier, *Expanding Learning Time*, 10.

4. Ibid., 13.

5. Randi Weingarten, "Evidence Matters," *New York Times*, April 23, 2011,
available at the website of the American Federation of Teachers, http://
www.aft.org/newspubs/press/columnsblogs.cfm.

6. Replicating the Edwards's success at five thousand schools would reach
approximately one million sixth graders—or about 25 percent of the
sixth-grade cohort and most low-income sixth graders. If these students,
on average, closed achievement gaps with their upper-income peers, as
happened at the Edwards, our national proficiency rate on international
exams like PISA would go up about six percentage points.

7. At Orchard Gardens, from 2010 to 2013, the eighth-grade math proficiency rate as measured by the statewide MCAS exams went from

8 percent to 63 percent. During this same time period, math proficiency rates within Boston Public Schools went up by three points (34 to 37) and in the state of Massachusetts they went up by four points (from 51 to 55). At Orchard Gardens, from 2010 to 2013, the eighth-grade English proficiency rate on the statewide MCAS exams went from 36 percent to 74 percent. During this same time, proficiency rates within Boston Public Schools and the state of Massachusetts remained flat, staying at 58 percent and 78 percent respectively.

CHAPTER SEVEN

1. On its website the Ashoka Foundation defines *social entrepreneurs* as "individuals with innovative solutions to society's most pressing social problems. They are ambitious and persistent, tackling major social issues and offering new ideas for wide-scale change. Rather than leaving societal needs to the government or business sectors, social entrepreneurs find what is not working and solve the problem by changing the system, spreading the solution, and persuading entire societies to move in different directions" (www.ashoka.org). The *Wikipedia* entry on social entrepreneurship (citing "The Meaning of Social Entrepreneurship" by the late J. Gregory Dees) gives this definition: "Social entrepreneurship is the process of pursuing suitable solutions to social problems. More specifically, social entrepreneurs adopt a mission to create and sustain social value. They pursue opportunities to serve this mission, while continuously adapting and learning. They draw upon appropriate thinking in both the business and nonprofit worlds and operate in all kinds of organizations: large and small; new and old; religious and secular; nonprofit, for-profit, and hybrid." Peter Drucker's observation on entrepreneurs is that they rearrange resources toward higher and better uses; social entrepreneurs seek to do the same toward addressing social challenges.

2. Blackbaud, Inc., "Index of National Fundraising Performance," 2013, http://www.blackbaud.com/files/resources/downloads/Target_Index _Results_Summary_Q1_2013.pdf.

3. Eric Schwarz, "Realizing the American Dream: Historical Scorecard, Current Challenges, Future Opportunities," working paper, A Gathering of Leaders: Social Entrepreneurs and Scale in the 21st Century, February 15–18, 2005.

4. Greg Parks, "The High/Scope Perry Preschool Project," *Juvenile Justice Bulletin* (October 2000): 3, available from the website of the National Criminal Justice Reference Service, https://www.ncjrs.gov/pdffiles1/ojjdp /181725.pdf.

5. FT 500, 2013, *Financial Times*, www.ft.com/intl/indepth/ft500.

6. "The 200 Largest US Charities," *Forbes* (2005), http://www.forbes.com /2005/11/18/largest-charities-ratings_05charities_land.html. In 2005, Habitat for Humanity was the only organization founded in the last forty years based on cash revenues. When in-kind contributions are included, there were two other organizations that had been founded in the last forty years, Gift In Kind International and AmeriCares.

7. Habitat for Humanity, "About Us," http://www.habitat.org/how/about _us.aspx.

8. Lawrence Mishel, Jared Bernstein, and Heather Boushey, *The State of Working America 2002/2003* (Ithaca, NY: ILR Press, 2003), 37–49. From 1973 to 2001, the percentage of American families in the lowest economic quartile who owned their homes declined from 51 percent to 49 percent. During this same period, Habitat built tens of thousands of homes for poor families across the country.

9. America Forward, *America Forward: Invent, Invest, Involve* (Boston: New Profit, 2007), www.newprofit.com. This booklet was shared with Obama, McCain, and other candidates. It impacted thinking on reforms, including the Social Innovation Fund, an effort to have the federal government team up with philanthropy to scale proven and promising organizations.

10. Barack Obama's first inaugural address, 2009, http://www.whitehouse.gov /blog/inaugural-address.

11. White House Office of Science and Technology Policy, http://www .whitehouse.gov/administration/eop/ostp.

12. US Department of Education, "Race to the Top Executive Summary," 2009, http://www2.ed.gov/programs/racetothetop/executive-summary .pdf. In 2009, $4.35 billion was appropriated for the Race to the Top Fund in the American Recovery and Reinvestment Act (ARRA). The program includes $4 billion for statewide reform grants and $350 million to support states working together to improve the quality of their assessments.

13. New America Foundation, Federal Education Budget Project, "American Recovery and Reinvestment Act: Background and Analysis," 2012, http:// febp.newamerica.net/background-analysis/american-recovery-and -reinvestment-act. Race to the Top funds were later included by Congress in regular appropriations, including nearly $700 million in fiscal year 2011 and almost $550 million in fiscal year 2012 for further rounds of the state competition and an Early Learning Challenge. The bill included language that would allow the department to create a district-level competition and continue the investment in the Early Learning Challenge.

14. US Department of Education, "Investing in Innovation Fund (i3): Funding Status," http://www2.ed.gov/programs/innovation/funding.html. $650 million was included in the 2009 ARRA for the Investing in Innovation

Fund. Almost all of that ($645,978,395) was spent in FY 10. The i3 competition is entering its third year, having been appropriated about $150 million each in fiscal years 2011 and 2012. In FY 2013, there is currently $134 million in estimated available funds.

CHAPTER EIGHT

1. Charles T. Clotfelter, "Patterns of Enrollment and Completion," in *Economic Challenges in Higher Education*, edited by Charles T. Clotfelter et al. (Chicago: University of Chicago Press, 1991), 31, available from the website of the National Bureau of Economic Research, http://www.nber.org /chapters/c6079.pdf. See also Richard Pérez-Peña, "US Bachelor Degree Rate Passes Milestone," *New York Times*, February, 23, 2012, http://www .nytimes.com; Amy K. Glasmeier, *An Atlas of Poverty in America: One Nation, Pulling Apart, 1960–2003* (New York: Routledge, 2006), "Introduction: The Paradox of Poverty in America" available at the MIT Poverty in America Project website, http://povertyinamerica.mit.edu;/download /atlas_of_poverty_in_america_p1.pdf, and US Census Bureau, "Income, Poverty and Health Insurance Coverage in the United States: 2011," press release, September 12, 2012, http://www.census.gov/newsroom/releases /archives/income_wealth/cb12–172.html.

2. Lawrence A. Cremin, *American Education: The National Experience, 1783–1876* (New York: Harper and Row, 1980).

3. James J. Kemple, *Career Academies: Long-Term Impacts on Labor Market Outcomes, Educational Attainment, and Transitions to Adulthood* (New York: MDRC, 2008), http://www.mdrc.org/publication/career-academies-long -term-impacts-work-education-and-transitions-adulthood.

4. High Tech High, "Results," http://www.hightechhigh.org.

5. FIRST, www.usfirst.org; iMentor, www.imentor.org; City Year, www .cityyear.org.

6. Transcript of Lester Strong video interview, from Shar McBee, "Why Volunteer with Children? Here's Why," *Huffington Post*, March 26, 2013, http://www.huffingtonpost.com./shar-mcbee/why-volunteer-with-childr _b_2950039.html. For more on Experience Corps: http://www.aarp.org /experience-corps/.

7. Nancy Morrow-Howell et al., *Evaluation of Experience Corps: Student Reading Outcomes*, publication no. 09-01 (St. Louis: Center for Social Development, Washington University in St. Louis, 2009), http://csd.wustl.edu.

8. Lester Strong, speaking on a panel at the Center for American Progress, "The American Way to Change, How National Service and Volunteers Are Transforming America," April 21, 2010, event video at http://www .americanprogress.org.

9. Ibid.

10. Rachel Schachter, "Ambition Musician: Showing Students Real Possibilities," Citizen Schools, *InspirED* (blog), 2012, http://www.citizenschools .org/blog/musician-ambition-showing-students-real-possibilities/.

11. David Jones, *The Citizen Teacher Experience Study: A Report of Research Results* (Burlington: University of Vermont, 2012).

CHAPTER NINE

1. Greg J. Duncan and Richard J. Murnane, eds., *Whither Opportunity? Rising Inequality, Schools, and Children's Life Chances* (New York: Russell Sage Foundation, 2011), 339–58.

2. Arne Duncan, "Making the Middle Schools Matter," Remarks at the National Forum's Annual Schools to Watch Conference, June 23, 2011, http:// www.ed.gov/news/speeches/making-middle-grades-matter.

3. National Institute of Mental Health, "Imaging Study Shows Brain Maturing," press release, May 17, 2014, http://www.nimh.nih.gov/news /science-news/2004/imaging-study-shows-brain-maturing.shtml. "The brain's center of reasoning and problem solving is among the last to mature. The decade-long magnetic resonance imaging (MRI) study of normal brain development, from ages four to twenty-one, by researchers at NIH's National Institute of Mental Health (NIMH) and University of California Los Angeles (UCLA) shows that such 'higher-order' brain centers, such as the prefrontal cortex, don't fully develop until young adulthood. . . . In the late 1990s, NIMH's Dr. Jay Giedd, a coauthor of the current study, and colleagues discovered a second wave of overproduction of gray matter just prior to puberty, followed by a second bout of "use-it-or-lose-it" pruning during the teen years. . . . Areas with more advanced functions—integrating information from the senses, reasoning, and other 'executive' functions (prefrontal cortex)—mature last."

4. Common Core State Standards Initiative, http://www.corestandards.org.

5. Rolf K. Blank, *What Is the Impact of Decline in Science Instructional Time in Elementary School?*, prepared for the Noyce Foundation, 2012, available at the website of the Council of State Science Supervisors, http://www.csss -science.org./downloads/NAEPElemScienceData.pdf.

6. Valerie Strauss, "Survey: Teachers Work 53 Hours Per Week on Average," *Answer Sheet* (blog), *Washington Post*, March 16, 2012, http://www .washingtonpost.com/blogs/answer-sheet/.

7. Jessica Edwards, *Mapping the Field: A Report on Expanded-Time Schools in America* (Boston: National Center on Time and Learning, 2012), http:// www.timeandlearning.org/mapping.

8. Thomas Kuhn, *The Structure of Scientific Revolutions* (Chicago: University of Chicago Press, 1962).

9. Malcolm Gladwell, *Outliers: The Story of Success* (New York: Little, Brown, 2008).

10. Ibid., 2.

11. Ibid., 23.

CHAPTER TEN

1. Organization for Economic Co-operation and Development (OECD), "Programme for International Student Assessment (PISA) Results from PISA 2012: United States," http://www.oecd.org/pisa/. See also Kyung Hee Kim, "The Creativity Crisis: The Decrease in Creative Thinking Scores on the Torrance Tests of Creative Thinking," *Creativity Research Journal* 23, no. 4 (2001): 285–95.

2. Blank, *What Is the Impact of Decline in Science Instructional Time in Elementary School?*, 8.

3. Robert Tai, Christine Qi Liu, Adam Maltese, and Xitao Fan, "Planning Early for Careers in Science," *Science* 312 (May 2006).

4. Lemelson-MIT Program, "2010 Lemelson-MIT Invention Index Reveals Ways to Enhance Teens' Interest in Science, Technology, Engineering and Mathematics in the Classroom and Beyond," press release, January 28, 2010, http://web.mit.edu/invent/n-pressreleases/n-press-10index.html.

5. US Congress Joint Economic Committee, *STEM Education: Preparing for the Jobs of the Future*, 2012, http://www.jec.senate.gov/.

6. National Action Council for Minorities in Engineering, "African Americans in Engineering," *NACME Research & Policy Brief* 1, no. 4 (February 2012), http://www.nacme.org/user/docs/AAEFINAL.pdf.

7. Richard J. Murnane and Frank Levy, *Teaching the New Basic Skills: Principles for Educating Children to Thrive in a Changing Economy* (New York: Free Press, 1996).

8. Richard Murnane, presentation at Reimagining After-School: A Symposium on Learning and Leading in the 21st Century, April 29, 2004, Cambridge, MA.

9. IBM, "IBM 2010 Global CEO Study: Creativity Selected as Most Crucial Factor for Future Success," press release, May 18, 2010, http://www-03.ibm.com/press/us/en/pressrelease/31670.wss.

10. Kyung Hee Kim, "The Creativity Crisis: The Decrease in Creative Thinking Scores on the Torrance Tests of Creative Thinking," *Creativity Research Journal* 23, no. 4 (2011), 285–95.

11. Peter Gray, "As Children's Freedom Has Declined, So Has Their Creativity," *Freedom to Learn* (blog), *Psychology Today*, September 17, 2012, http://www.psychologytoday.com/blog/freedom-learn/201209/children-s-freedom-has-declined-so-has-their-creativity.

12. 100Kin10, http://www.100kin10.org.

13. White House, "New Details: President Obama to Host White House Science Fair," press release, April 22, 2013, http://www.whitehouse.gov/the-press-office/2013/04/22/new-details-president-obama-host-white-house-science-fair. See also "Remarks by the President at the White House Science Fair," April 22, 2013, http://www.whitehouse.gov/the-press-office/2013/04/22/remarks-president-2013-white-house-science-fair.

14. Walter Isaacson, *Steve Jobs* (New York: Simon & Schuster, 2011).

15. Richard Florida, *The Rise of the Creative Class and How It's Transforming Work, Leisure, Community, and Everyday Life*, rev. ed. (New York: Basic Books, 2012).

CHAPTER ELEVEN

1. Robert D. Putnam, Carl B. Frederick, and Kaisa Snellman, "Growing Class Gaps in Social Connectedness Among American Youth," paper presented at the Saguaro Seminar: Civic Engagement in America, Cambridge, MA, Harvard Kennedy School of Government, August 8, 2012, p. 19, available at www.hks.harvard.edu.

2. Ibid.

3. Author's notes from interviews of those attending the Aspen Ideas Festival, 2012.

4. Putnam, Frederick, and Snellman, "Growing Class Gaps," 11. "Participation in chess clubs, debate teams, school bands, and student councils bolster self-esteem and feelings of self-worth, boost high school grade point average, shape educational aspirations and attainment, as well as wages and occupational choice (Lamborn et al., 1992; Newmann et al., 1992; Eccles and Barber, 1999; Borghans et al., 2011)."

5. Ibid., 11–17.

6. Greg J. Duncan and Richard J. Murnane, eds., *Whither Opportunity? Rising Inequality, Schools, and Children's Life Chances* (New York: Russell Sage Foundation, 2011).

7. James S. Coleman, "Social Capital in the Creation of Human Capital," *American Journal of Sociology* 94 (1988): 95–120.

8. Sean F. Reardon, "The Widening Academic Achievement Gap Between the Rich and the Poor: New Evidence and Possible Explanations," in *Whither*

Opportunity?, eds. Duncan and Murnane, http://cepa.stanford.edu/sites /default/files/reardon%20whither%20opportunity%20-%20chapter%205.pdf.

9. Richard Florida, "Where the Skills Are," *Atlantic*, October 2011.

10. Ibid.

11. Robert D. Putnam, *Bowling Alone: The Collapse and Revival of American Community* (New York: Simon & Schuster, 2000), 405.

12. Tom Wolfe, *The Bonfire of the Vanities* (New York: Farrar, Straus and Giroux, 1987).

13. Jennifer Engle and Vincent Tinto, *Moving Beyond Access: College Success for Low-Income, First-Generation Students* (Washington, DC: Pell Institute for the Study of Opportunity in Higher Education, 2008), http://inpathways .net/COE_MovingBeyondReport_Final.pdf.

14. Nancy DiTomaso, "How Social Networks Drive Black Unemployment," *New York Times*, May 5, 2012, *Opinionator* (blog), http://opinionator.blogs .nytimes.com/2013/05/05/how-social-networks-drive-black-unemployment/.

15. Paul Tough, *How Children Succeed: Grit, Curiosity, and the Hidden Power of Character* (Boston: Houghton Mifflin Harcourt, 2012).

CHAPTER TWELVE

1. Randi Weingarten, "Evidence Matters," *New York Times*, April 23, 2011, available at the website of the American Federation of Teachers, http:// www.aft.org/newspubs/press/columnsblogs.cfm.

2. Boston Teachers Union, *e-Bulletin* 22, December 13, 2011, http://www.btu .org/btu-publications/ebulletin/.

3. Matthew Ronfeldt, Susanna Loeb, and James Wyckoff, "How Teacher Turnover Harms Student Achievement," *American Educational Research Journal* 50, no. 1 (2013): 4–36.

4. Agency for Healthcare Research and Quality, "The Number of Practicing Primary Care Physicians in the United States," 2010, http://www.ahrq .gov/research/findings/factsheets/primary/pcwork1/index.html.

5. Frederick M. Hess, *The Same Thing Over and Over: How School Reformers Get Stuck in Yesterday's Ideas* (Cambridge, MA: Harvard University Press, 2010).

6. Benjamin Scafidi, *The School Staffing Surge: Decades of Employment Growth in America's Public Schools* (Indianapolis: Friedman Foundation for Educational Choice, 2012), http://www.edchoice.org/. Note: Data from US Department of Education, National Center for Education Statistics, 1990 *Digest of Education Statistics*, table 76, and the 2011 *Digest of Education Statistics*, table 69.

7. Catherine Rampell, "The Lawyer Surplus, State by State," *Economix* (blog), *New York Times*, June 27, 2011, http://economix.blogs.nytimes.com/2011 /06/27/the-lawyer-surplus-state-by-state/?_r=0.
8. Frederick Hess, "How to Get the Teachers We Want," *Education Next* 9, no. 3 (2009): 34–39, http://educationnext.org/.how-to-get-the-teachers -we-want/.
9. For more information on these types of programs, see EnCorps, http:// www.encorpsteachers.com, and Encore Fellowships, http://www.encore .org/fellowships.
10. These programs include partnership with Relay GSE, Reach, the University of Massachusetts Graduate School of Education, and the Drexel Universtity Graduate School of Eduction alternative certification and master's programs.
11. Afterschool Alliance, "Afterschool Essentials: Research and Polling," 2012, http://www.afterschoolalliance.org/.

CHAPTER THIRTEEN

1. Clive Belfield, *The Economic Value of National Service* (New York: Center for Benefit-Cost Studies of Education, Teachers College Columbia University, 2013), http://cbcse.org.
2. Rob Reich, "Not Very Giving," *New York Times*, September 4, 2013, http:// www.nytimes.com.
3. National Academies Foundation, www.naf.org; Met, www.metcenter.org; High Tech High, www.hightechhigh.org.

INDEX

Abecedarian Project, 108
academic disengagement, 21
academic skills, 12, 63, 66, 68, 89, 152
accountability, 86, 88
achievement gap, 63, 195; class-based, 4–5, 12–15; closing of, 68, 92, 101–2; debate over cause of, 14–15; early-childhood education and, 108; income-based, 3–5, 9–10; race-based, xi, xiii; school-related factors in, 14–15
adolescents, 23–24, 41, 50
affiliate model of nonprofits. *See* franchise model of nonprofits
African Americans: achievement gap and, xi; college completion rate for, 125; STEM careers and, 152
The After-School Corporation (TASC), 73–75, 142–43

after-school programs, 50, 86, 137–38, 143, 155–57, 185; After-School Corporation (TASC), 73–75; for English-language learners, 143; Massachusetts 2020, 77. *See also* Expanded Learning Time (ELT) program; out-of-school experiences
AIM (Aspire, Invest, Make the grade), 68
Altonji, Joseph, 14
Amateur Athletic Union (AAU), 137
American Federation of Teachers (AFT), 176
AmeriCorps, 78, 89, 110, 112, 199; funding of, 196; teaching fellows, 67, 89, 97, 142, 178, 190–92
analytical skills, 166–67
Apple Computer, 103–4, 159

apprenticeships, 6–9, 23, 41–43, 78–79; carpentry, 58–59; cognitive, 23; fading, 23; modeling success, 23; scaffolding, 23; format for, 68; power of, 127–32
art, 63, 139–40
assessment data, 181
at-risk students, 68

Bain Capital, 71, 105, 114
Baiz, David, 180
Balson, Andrew, 71
Barnsley, Roger, 149
Barrett, Michael, 42
Barriga, Adam, 1–2, 97, 194
Barriga, Eduardo, 3, 94
basic skills, priority on, 152–54
Beasley, Caroline, 90
behavior management, 60
Bennett, Joel, 10–11, 58–59
Bogy, Tyeisha, 156
bonding social capital, 167–68
Boston City Singers, 137
Boston Teachers Union, 176
Bowling Alone (Putnam), 164–65, 167
Bradach, Jeff, 73
branding, 76–77
Bridgespan, 70
bridging social capital, 168
Brookline, Massachusetts, 14–15
Brown, Michael, 103, 115
Bryan, Emily, 91–92, 94–97
Burke, Gil, 23
Bushkin, Kathy, 26
Business Planning Council, 78–79

Campbell, Karen Webb, 132
campus directors, 67
capitalism, 12

career success: education and, 13; social capital and, 166–67
Carnegie Corporation, 157
carpentry apprenticeship, 58–59
Carter, Jimmy, 110
The Case for Twenty-First Century Learning (Schwarz and Kay), 78
Castillo, Yoelinson, 83
Chambers, Ray, 55
charter schools, 62, 95, 113, 143, 177, 185
China, college graduation rates in, 11
church attendance and social networks, 165, 166
citizen power, 124–34, 142, 195
Citizen Schools: accomplishments of, 9–10; after-school programs, 52–53, 66; approach of, xii–xiii; beginnings of, 5–9; benefits of, 64–65; challenges for, 48–49, 60, 63–64, 78–81; curriculum changes in, 66; ELT program and, 142; evaluation of, 68–69; founding staff of, 47–48, 54–55; fund-raising for, 56–57, 70–72, 78; growth of, 9–10, 58–61, 69, 72–81, 105, 116–17; i3 grant and, 114–17; idea for, 41–44; launch of, 40–57; national expansion of, 75–81; organizational infrastructure of, 66–81; protocols for, 60–61; Race to the Top and, 113; scaling, 114–15; staffing model of, 67; teacher support and, 176–85; Teaching Fellow program, 67, 78, 88–89, 97, 142, 178–85, 190–92; transformation of, 101–2; volunteers, 46, 48, 60, 64, 67–68, 97–101, 120–23, 131–34; WOW!

events, 1–3, 49–52, 54, 61, 126. *See also* Clarence Edwards Middle School; Expanded Learning Time (ELT) program

citizen teachers, 7–9, 43, 48, 104, 184, 199; experiences of, 120–23; impact of, 97–101, 127–34; training of, 67–68. *See also* volunteers/volunteering

City Year, 8, 45, 54, 73, 115; author's employment with, 40–41, 81, 103; as example of citizen power, 127; as model for Citizen Schools, 105

Clarence Edwards Middle School (Boston): ELT program at, 82, 85–102; problems at, 82–84, 89–90; reforms at, 84–87; teacher buy-in at, 88; teachers at, 94–97; tensions at, 90–91; transformation at, 92–101

class divide, xiii, 4–5, 12–15, 165

coaching, 23

Coffey, Maureen, 46, 52, 168

cognitive apprenticeships, 23

Cognizant, 133

Cohen, Ed, 45

Cohen, Priscilla, 69

Coleman, James S., 165–66

college completion rate, xi, 11–12, 125, 172, 188

college enrollment, 69, 102, 127

college graduates, 11–12; earnings of, 13; first-generation, 170–72; skills of, 13

Collegiate School (New York City), 19–20

Collins, Jim, 81

Common Core curriculum, 140, 188

communication skills, 153

company-owned store approach, 73, 79

competitive drive, 27–28

computer science classes, 152

confidence, role in success, 22, 31, 65, 173–74

co-teaching, 179

creative class, 160

creativity, 10, 118, 139, 151–63

crime, 185

Cromer, Mary, 24–25

Cross, Marian Lapsley, 27

crowdsourcing, 112

cultural reform, 106, 110

curriculum development, 67–68

Daccord, Deb, 10, 169–70, 173

DARPA (Defense Advanced Research Projects Agency), 160

Davolos, Stephanie, 54–58

Dees, Greg, 73

DeLatte, Marcus, 128–29, 152

democracy, 12

Department of Education, 113, 115, 116

Department of Energy, 112

Depina, Agostinha, 201–4

Desai, Anuradha, 70–71

Dever (MA) Community News, 8–9, 43–44

Dever Elementary School (Boston), 7, 43, 52, 59, 63, 88, 187–88

DiTomaso, Nancy, 173

Dougherty, Dale, 160

dropout rates, 63, 93

Drucker, Peter, 117

Du Bois, W. E. B., xiii

Dukeshire, Erin, 177–78

Duncan, Arne, 113, 139

Duncan, Greg, 12

early-childhood education, 107–9
early-stage professionals, 133
Echoing Green, 45
economies of scale, 108
economy, influence of social capital on, 166–67
Edmeade, Stephanie, 84, 94
Edna McConnell Clark Foundation, 71
education: career success and, 13; early-childhood, 107–9; as equalizer, 5–6; funding, 62; K–12, 104; STEM, 113, 151–52, 157–59, 198; system, 182–83; systemic change in, 103–10, 113
education reform, 61–64, 84, 104–5, 124; Investing in Innovation (i3), 114–17; plan for, 194–200; Race to the Top initiative, 112–14
Edward M. Kennedy Serve America Act, 112, 196
8th Grade Academy, 66, 170
Einstein Fellowship, 159
Elementary and Secondary Education Act, 198
Emerson, Ralph Waldo, 44
employment inequality, 173
employment opportunities, 39
Engels, Kendra, 180–81
engineers, 11, 152
English language arts (ELA), 140–41
English language learners (ELLs), 1, 143, 181
enrichment experiences, 3, 5, 12–14, 63, 94–95, 136–39. See also apprenticeships; extracurricular activities; out-of-school experiences
entry-level jobs, skills needed for, 153–54

Environmental Protection Agency (EPA), 112
equal opportunity: ideal of, x, 164; steps to improve, 194–200; in Europe, xi; in US, xi
Erikson, Erik, 24
Escalante, Jaime, 174–75
escape velocity, 32
Expanded Learning Time (ELT) program, 2, 82, 104–5, 142; at the Clarence Edwards Middle School , 85–102; expansion of, 101–2, 196–97; funding of, 198, 199; grant for, 86–87, 114–17; reasons for lack of broad adoption of, 146–49; results from, 101–2; stresses and challenges of, 143–46; teacher support and, 176–82; time schedule for, 205
Experience Corps, 129–31
extended-day learning, 135–49, 177–78, 185. See also Expanded Learning Time (ELT) program
external focus in organizations, 80–81
extracurricular activities, 136–39, 166. See also enrichment experiences

FAO Schwarz, 29–30
Feiler, Bruce, 30
Feinberg, Marsha, 55
financial aid, xi
FIRST, 127
first-generation college students, 170–72
Flanagan, Leo, 93–95
Florida, Richard, 160, 165, 166–67
foreign language, 140
4-H, 127

franchise model for nonprofits, 72–78, 110
Frank Friday assessments, 60–61
Friedman, Lucy, 74
Fuller, Millard, 110
fund-raising, 56–57, 70–72, 78

Gabrieli, Chris, 77–78. *See also* Massachusetts 2020
Garfield School (Brighton, MA), 60, 61
Gates, Bill, 148
General Aptitude Test Battery (GATB), 154
Genera, Luis, 90
Generation Schools, 185
genetics, 147
Gergen, David, 106–7, 108
gift giving, 59
Girl Scouts, 127
Gladwell, Malcolm, 147–49
Global Network Navigator (GNN), 160
Gordon, Robert, 112
government: actions by, to improve equal opportunity, 196–200; funding, 108–10, 112, 113, 196, 198; role of, in nonprofit sector, 111–12
Greenlaw, Mark, 133
growth models for nonprofits, 72–78

Habitat for Humanity, 109–10
hands-on projects, 1, 2–3, 6, 19, 51, 63, 88–89, 151, 198. *See also* apprenticeships; learning-by-doing approach
Harbor Point housing community (Boston), 7
Harrington, Barry, 105
Hart, Gary, 24–27, 42, 70, 168

Head Start, 107–9
Helies, Tony, 85–86, 97–101
Hess, Rick, 183
higher-order thinking skills, 152–54, 188
high school graduation rates, 68, 102, 106, 127, 188
high school sports, 166
high-stakes testing, 62–64, 151, 181
High Tech High, 126–27
high-wage jobs, 13
hiring process, 153–54
Hirsch, E. D., 152
hockey players, 148–49
Holdren, John, 158
homework, 21, 32, 68, 178
Hudy, Joey, 161
Hughes, Brendan, 47
human service businesses, 105
Hunt, Jim, 135–36

i3. *See* Investing in Innovation (i3)
IBM, 103–4, 154
iMentor, 127
immigrant identity, 37
income inequality, 3–4, 12
inequality: in education, 195; employment, 173; income, 3–4, 12; increase in, xi; of opportunity, 164, 305
innovation, 10, 118, 151, 157, 159–63
intergenerational self, 31
internal focus in organizations, 80–81
internships, 6, 23, 24, 32, 39, 126, 158, 200
Investing in Innovation (i3), 113, 114–17
Isaac Newton Expanded Learning Time Middle School, 184–85

Jobs, Steve, 103, 104, 159
John F. Kennedy School of Govern-
  ment, 45
Jones, David, 133–34
JumpStart, 105
junior teachers, 185

K–12 education, 104
Kamen, Dean, 127
Kanter, Rosabeth Moss, 155
Kennedy, John, Jr., 20
Kenney, Jack, 22
Khan Academy, 184
Khazei, Alan, 103
Kikuko, 48
Kim, Kyung Hee, 155
KIPP (Knowledge Is Power Pro-
  gram), 115
Kirby, Pat, 145
Kirsch, Vanessa, 45
knowledge-based economy, 12
Kopp, Wendy, 45
Kuhn, Thomas, 146–47
Kumon, 138

labor market, 166–67
leadership opportunities, for teachers, 181–82
learning by doing approach, 54,
  56, 60; See also apprenticeships;
  hands-on projects
learning experiences, positive, 21–23,
  32
learning opportunities: extra, 3,
  5, 13–14, 63, 94–95, 136–39,
  166; unequal access to, 136–37,
  195
learning time, 42, 104, 124, 135–49;
  expanded, 9, 10, 77–78, 86–87,
  118, 195; importance of, 147–49;

insufficient, 139–41, 151; staffing
  extra, 142–43; unequal access to,
  136–37. See also Expanded Learning Time (ELT) program
Lesley University, 67
lesson plans, 60
Levy, Frank, 153–54
Lieberman, Aaron, 45
life skills, sharing, 6–7
Light, Sarah, 47
Lincoln, Abraham, 195
low-income students, 1; academic
  skills of, 12; building blocks of
  success for, 117–18; childhood
  experiences for, 31–33, 35, 36–39,
  165–66; college completion rate
  of, 12; disadvantages for, 4, 32–33,
  165–66, 195; expectations of, 14,
  147; opportunities for, 13–14;
  work experiences for, 39
low-skilled jobs, 13

MAKE magazine, 160
Maker Corps, 160–61
Maker Education Initiative (Maker
  Ed), 160–61
maker movement, 159–63; Maker
  Faires, 161–63
Mann, Horace, 6
Mansfield, Richard, 14
Mantus, David, 2–3, 10, 94, 97–99,
  152, 159, 194
MAP (Middle School Apprentice-
  ship Program), 76
Mascoll, Keith, 47
Massachusetts Comprehensive
  Assessment System (MCAS),
  62–63, 83, 92
Massachusetts Department of Edu-
  cation, 86–87

Massachusetts Education Reform Act (1993), 62
Massachusetts 2020, 77–78, 86–87
MATCH charter school (Boston), 143
Match Corps, 143
math instruction, 11, 140, 143
McAfee, Chuck, 83
McCann, Emily, 69–70
McCormack Middle School (Boston), 52–53
McKeen, Cindy, 82–83, 94
McKinney, David, 178
medical system in US, as compared to US education system, 182
Mendez, Nydia, 7, 43, 63, 88
mentors/mentoring, 10, 31, 118, 127–34, 169; advertising campaign for, 196; teachers as, 180–81
meritocracy, 149
merit pay, 113
Mersereau, Bob, 132–33
Met School (Providence, RI), 126–27
middle school, 139–41; middle school students, 74–75
Miran, Seth, 184
Mitchell, Hetty, 188
moderate-income students, 4
Montessori, Maria, 19
Montessori schools, 19
Montgomery, Tulaine, 54–57, 60–61
Morgan, Dan, 28
mothers, shared experiences of, 50–51. See also parents
Murnane, Richard, 12, 153–54
music, 63, 139–40

Nada, Sherif, 77
National Academies Foundation (NAF), 126
A Nation at Risk (report), 61–62

nature vs. nurture debate, 147–48
Nelson, Lisa, 184
New Profit Inc., 106
New York Maker Faire, 161–63. See also maker movement
No Child Left Behind Act, 198
nonacademic skills, 175
nonprofit organizations: building blocks of, 46; funding and growth of, 44–45, 108–9, 112, 114–17; Obama election and, 111; scale and spread of, 105, 109–10

Obama, Barack, 110–13, 158, 159
Obama, Michelle, 111
100Kin10, 157
online learning, 184
opportunity: building blocks of, 10–11; employment, 39; equal, x, xi, 164; gap, wealth-based, 3–5; steps to improve equal, 194–200; for upper-income students, 12–13, 14, 136–39; wealth and, 31
opportunity equation, 3, 12–13, 33, 59
optimism vs. skepticism in nonprofit organizations, 80–81
Orchard Gardens school (Boston), 177–78
organizational reform, 106
out-of-school experiences, 3, 5, 12–14, 20–23, 39, 42. See also enrichment experiences; extracurricular activities

parents, 188; concerns of, 50–51; as models of success, 14, 23, 27–29; relationships between teachers and, 186–87; support for, 10, 185–87; support of, 22–23, 27, 32, 118; time spent with, 13, 166

Perry Preschool Project, 107, 108
perseverance, 157
philanthropy, 71–72, 112, 197–98
Picciolini, Britton, 132
Pinsky, Biz, 47–48
Pinsky, Robert, 48
political reform, 106, 110
poor children. *See* low-income students
poverty, 14, 117; escaping from, 31–33; increase in, 106; and consequences of making mistakes, 32–33
Power Learning Out of School apprenticeship, 156–57
practice time, 147–49
Price, Anita, 46, 47, 55, 80
private schools, 19–23
problem-solving skills, 151, 156
professionalization, 80
Proskauer, Tim, 48
public schools, 117, 189; criticism of, 4, 176; funding of, 113; private donations to, 197–98, 199. *See also* schools
Putnam, Robert, 164–65, 167–68

race-based achievement gap, xi, xiii
Race to the Top initiative, 112–14, 198
racial equality, xi–xii
real-world experiences, 127–28, 158, 180. *See also* apprenticeships; hands-on projects
recruitment, 89
Reich, Rob, 197
Reimagining After-School symposium series, 78, 155–57
ReServe, 130
Resnick, Lauren, 23

Retired and Senior Volunteer Program, 130
retired volunteers, 129–31
Reville, Paul, 5, 87
Riley, Jeff, 85, 93
Rimer, Ned, 46, 53, 55–56, 69, 171, 172, 173
Robin Hood financing scheme, 62
Robinson, Steve, 158–59
Rodgers, Charles, 75
Rodgers, Fran, 75
Rodriguez, Anthony, 161–62
role models, 27–31, 51, 127–28, 152, 169
Romaine, McCalvin, 150–51
Rorie, Denis, 48, 186
Rothschild, Katie Brown, 179–80

Sabin, Mike, 85–86, 87, 88, 92, 93
Saintil, Emmanuel, 90
scale, of nonprofits, 105, 108–10, 114, 194
Schachter, Rachel, 132
school day: in Boston, –84; ELT grant, 87; length of, 10, 42, 74, 78, 104, 118, 135–49, 151; and Massachusetts 2020, 77, 86; typical schedule for, 139–41. *See also* learning time
School Improvement Grants, 198
school-reform movement, 61–64
schools: accountability for, 86; changing climate of, 62–63; charter, 62, 95, 113, 143, 177, 185; disengagement from, 21; funding of, 62, 113; leadership opportunities in, 181–82; private, 19–23; private donations to, 197–98, 199; role of, in achievement gap, 14–15

schools of education, 62
school year, length of, 42
Schwarz, Frederick, 29
Schwarz, Fritz (author's grandfather), 27, 29, 30
Schwarz, Henry (author's great-grandfather), 30
science in schools, 11, 63, 141, 143, 151–52, 157
science, technology, engineering, and math (STEM) education, 113, 151–52, 157–59, 198
scientific thinking, 151
Selby, Moriska, 90, 97
senior citizen volunteers, 129–31
Serve America Act, 112, 196
Shaheen, Jeanne, 26
Shea, Barbara, 15
Shearer, Earline, 11
Sheckel, Sara, 178–79, 182
Sherman, Robert, 56–57
Shore, Bill, 26
Singer, Henry, 41
skepticism vs. optimism in nonprofit organizations, 80–81
Skloot, Ed, 56
Skoll, Jeff, 111
Skoll World Forum, 111
Smalt, Lindy, 190–92
social capital, 125, 139, 164–75; effect on world economy, 166–67
social change, 106–10
social entrepreneurs, 45, 106, 111, 199–200
Social Innovation Fund, 112
social media, 165
social mobility, xi, 31–32, 33
social networks, 10, 102, 118, 139, 165–66, 173–75, 195

social skills, 4, 10, 102, 118, 139, 165, 167, 195
social studies, 63, 141, 143
Soros, George, 74
special-education students, 143–46
special-education teachers, 183
sports, 139–40, 166
spread, of nonprofits, 105, 108–9
staffing model, 67, 75
Stand and Deliver (film), 174–75
standardized testing, 62–64, 151, 181, 188
STEM (science, technology, engineering, and math) education, 113, 151–52, 157–59, 198; professionals, 157–58, 159, 198
Stockdale, James, 81; Stockdale Paradox, 81
Strong, Lester, 129–31
student engagement, 101, 102
Student Leadership Council, 90–91
student motivation, 180
student outcomes, 68–69, 101–2
Students for Hart, 26
study hall, 140
Sturz, Herb, 74
Su, Alan, 10–11, 97–98, 133, 159
suburban teachers, 177
success: building blocks of, 117–18; factors in, 147–49; models of, 14, 23, 27–31, 43
Sullivan, Kerry, 115
summer camps, xii, 12, 22–23, 39, 41–42
summer programs, 67
supplemental learning, 136–39
Surdna Foundation, 56

Tai, Robert, 151
Tamarack Tennis Camp, 22, 41

TASC (The After-School Corporation), 73–75, 142–43
tax breaks, 197
Taylor, Jeff, 156
teacher conferences, 21
teachers, 189; attitudes of, toward Citizen Schools, 176, 187–88; blame of, 117; buy-in from, 88; collaboration between, 179; evaluation of, 113; junior, 185; levels of, 183–84; licensure standards for, 62; as mentors, 180–81; merit pay for, 113; number of, 182–83; pathways to leadership for, 181–82; quality of, 14, 136; recruitment of, 89, 183; relationships between parents and, 186–87; role of, 182–85; science and math, 157, 158–59; special-education, 183; suburban, 177; support for, 10, 176–85; supportive, 37, 118; turnover rates, 177; work day for, 142. *See also* citizen teachers
teachers' unions, 117, 176
Teach For America, 67, 105, 115
Teaching the New Basic Skills (Murnane and Levy), 153–54
teamwork, 152, 153, 157
TechBoston High School, 170
technology skills, 153
television, 185
test scores, 62, 92, 94, 113, 177, 181
Therapeutic Learning Community (TLC), 144
Thomas, Joyce King, 120–23
Time for Innovation Matters in Education (TIME) Act, 93, 196–97
Timilty School (Roxbury, MA), 60, 61
Title I funding, 198
Tkacik, Margie, 7, 43, 189

Tocqueville, Alexis de, 125
training, 67–68, 89
Tucker, Jake, 48
tutors/tutoring, 137, 138, 143, 166
21st Century Community Learning Centers program, 198
twenty-first-century skills, 152–57

United States: class divide in, xiii, 4–5, 12–15, 165; college graduation rate in, xi, 11–12, 125, 172, 188; decline of creativity in, 155; equal opportunity in, x–xi; social mobility in, 31–32, 33
University of Vermont, 170–72
upper-income students: advantages of, 3–5, 12–15, 136–37, 165–66, 195; childhood experiences for, 18–23, 27–31, 165–66; college completion rate of, 12; expectations of, 14; opportunities for, 12–13, 14, 136–39
Upward Bound, 170
urban schools, 82, 86–87, 93, 94–95
US2020, 158, 161, 199

video games, 185
violence, 89–90; in schools, 82–83, 86
vision, 80, 147
VISTA, 199
volunteers/volunteering, 11, 46, 48, 60, 64, 97–101, 120–23, 196, 199; benefits for, 131–34; impact of, 127–34; senior citizens, 129–31; training of, 67–68

Wandenchaft (wanderlust) period, importance for adolescents, 24
Webby v. Dukakis, 62

Weikart, David, 107
Weingarten, Randi, 93, 176
Werner, John, 46, 47, 55, 60
West Side Montessori School (New York City), 19
WFD, 75–77
WGBH-TV, 114
Wiatrowski, Lynn, 115
William H. Lincoln School (Brookline, MA), 14–15, 136
Wolfe, Tom, 168
Woodrow Wilson School (Dorchester, MA), 58–59

workers, educated, 12
work experiences, 24–27, 37–39
Work/Family Directions (WFD), 75–77
work skills, 153–55, 166–67
WOW! events, 1–3, 49–52, 54, 61, 126
Wozniak, Steve, 159

Yarde, Jadine, 173–74
Year-Up, 105

Zigler, Edward, 107